Let Them Be Not FORGOTTEN

EULOGIES WRITTEN IN A COUNTRY CHURCHYARD

MICHAEL SMATHERS

LET THEM BE NOT FORGOTTEN
Eulogies Written In A Country Churchyard

Copyright © 2024   Michael Smathers

Library of Congress Control Number: 2023950709
                    Paperback: 978-1-961119-54-3
                    eBook: 978-1-961119-55-0

Printed in the United States of America

Contents

MEDITATIONS AND REMARKS

PREFACE

HILLCREST CEMETERY, BIG LICK, TENNESSEE, MAY 20, 2015: I am standing in Hillcrest, the Big Lick cemetery, the "Old" Section. For over one hundred years, Big Lick families have been burying their dead at this place. That there is a cemetery here at all is a historical accident. An early settler dug a grave farther down the hillside to bury one of his children. That grave was filled with water. They moved up to the crest of the hill where they found it was not only dry, but the soil was deeper, an anomaly around here. Rather than the usual three feet or less to bed rock it was four to five feet at this place. Not yet "Hillcrest," but this spot of earth had become the Big Lick burying place. The oldest inscribed tombstone here indicates that the person who rests there died in 1912. However, there are 22 graves marked with simple un-inscribed stones, some of which are undoubtedly older than 1912.

This place is familiar to me. I grew up among and around many of the stones here. Of the 578 remains that rest here, my father and I combined, as preachers, pall bearers, or mourners, have helped to bury over 200 of them. Most of the more than one hundred funerals I have participated in over the past forty years have ended here. The names on many of the stones are familiar to me. I know the stories behind the unique stones that mark many graves here. I ran by here almost every day in my teenage years. It is my home territory.

The cemetery overlooks Hinch and Bear Den mountains along Walden's Ridge and always brings to my mind the 121 Psalm. Though nominally attached to the Presbyterian church that sits 200 yards west of here, this plot of earth is not really deeded to anyone. It is a community institution. It is, in fact, the last true community institution left in this rural neighborhood. The last communal place that gets the attention of and draws participation from virtually every family in the community.

Most of what I know about Christian funerals is in one way or another centered upon this space. I have been conducting or helping to conduct funerals that have ended here since 1960, when I first served as a pall bearer to this place. I expect my remains to be buried here. To some degree it is to preserve the continuity of this place and the memory of some who are buried here that I have assembled this Collection.

This Collection represents in part a personal journey – a continuation of a quest and odyssey which began in 1974. That personal quest and odyssey are one of the reasons for producing this book. It helps me understand what I was doing and why I was doing it that way. But the primary motivation for this Collection has been the requests from many whose loved ones I have helped bury. This book is for them. It is my hope that they, their children, and their children's children will find some help here in their own journey from the cradle to the grave. If it proves of any benefit beyond that, it will be a bonus.

It was barely eight months after I returned home in 1974, after some years of absence, that a family asked me to conduct the funeral service for their husband and father. I had previously done a total of one funeral service. I was not their pastor. I was not at the time professionally attached to any church.

The family was estranged from the local church, and the request to "preach Ralph's funeral" did not come unexpectedly. I had been close to this man in my youth, and he remained one of my mother's closest friends. His sons and I were childhood playmates. Thus began a personal quest and odyssey to better understand and more meaningfully conduct a Christian funeral.

ACKNOWLEDGMENTS

First of all, I must acknowledge and thank those families who have permitted me to participate in the funerals of their loved ones. Secondly, I want to kindly thank all those who have granted me permission to include material from some of those funerals in this Collection. Thirdly, I must acknowledge the dozens of people who shared insights, information, and anecdotes with me about the deceased whom I have helped bury. Without these, many of my funeral eulogies/messages/remarks would have been much poorer and not as meaningful. Finally, I must acknowledge my wife who has constantly encouraged me in this project and has proofread some of this material correcting many of my typos and grammatical errors. If errors of fact, spelling, grammar, or style remain herein they should be charged to my account.

Most Biblical quotations used herein are taken from the Revised Standard Version of the Bible. Acknowledgment has been made above for the generous permission of the Division of Christian Education of the National Council of Churches of Christ in the U. S. A. for use of these passages.

Any other Biblical quotations are either translations of the author himself or are taken from the King James Version (KJV), which is in the public domain.

FOREWORD

THE CHRISTIAN FUNERAL A PERSONAL ODYSSEY

BIG LICK, TENNESSEE, MAY 20, 2015: I knew that "You Can't Go Home Again,"[1] but I tried. I returned to the place of my birth in Southern Appalachia in 1974 at the age of thirty-three. Indeed, it was not and is not the same isolated rural community in which I grew up. It is now more a rural neighborhood of the nearby town. But some things never change. *"In the midst of life there is death."*[2] And in Southern Appalachia this is doubly true.

A lot has changed in Southern Appalachia since the minions of the War on Poverty spread bureaucracy over the region like green on a gecko. Death is not one of them. The region's mortality rate and life expectancy have remained virtually unchanged since the late 1960's. This means the region has more funerals per capita than any other region in the United States. I have spent virtually all of my life and all of my ministry in the Southern Appalachians. The communities I have lived in and the churches I have served have all been small and had higher rates of elderly people and higher mortality rates than the average community or congregation. This means higher rates of funerals per capita. In forty-eight years of ministry, I have conducted or participated in over one-hundred funerals.

Moreover, if books on the contemporary funeral[3] are accurate, the funeral plays a more important role in the life of Southern Appalachia than it may in other places. The funerals I have done over the past forty years have not been substantially different than those my father did in the prior forty years. The only real difference is that now most (but not all) funerals are held in the chapel of funeral homes rather than in churches. Although funeral homes attempt to make these "chapels" as church-like as possible, they are frequently a windowless, stark, dimly lighted room in a house for the dead. It detracts from rather than adding to the worshipful sense of a funeral.

New ways of doing things are sneaking in with new second-home and retiree in-migrants. We now have more cremations and "Celebration of Life" parties than was once the case. However, the incidence of traditional funerals is more frequent here than elsewhere for several reasons. It is due in part to the higher rates of persons over 65 and the higher mortality rates for people of all ages. But it also has economic, cultural, and religious roots. Higher rates of poverty and hard living, more tightly woven kinship ties, and a higher percentage of other-worldly expressions of the Gospel make funerals an integral part of the Southern Appalachian way-of-life.

The yin and yang of Southern Appalachian funerals may be expressed in two traditional songs. On the one hand, is the traditional dying dirge, *"O Death:"*

> *"O death, won't you spare me over til another ye'r*
> *Well what is this that I can't see?*
> *With ice cold hands takin' hold of me . . .*
>
> *. . .*
> *Please don't take me at this stage; My wealth is all at your command If you will move your icy hand . . .*
>
> *. . .*
> *O Death,*
> *Won't you spare me over til another ye'r?"*

On the other hand, is the spirited gospel song, *"I'll fly away:"*

> *"Some glad morning when this life is o'er. I'll fly away. . .*
>
> *. . .*
> *When I die, Hallelujah, by and by . . .*
>
> *. . .*
> *Just a few more weary days and then I'll fly away*
> *To a land where joy shall never end . . ."[4]*

I choose the terms yin and yang deliberately because they express the opposite yet complimentary and equal forces that exert counterbalancing influence on the life of an individual or a community. At Southern Appalachian funerals, both the yin and the yang are present. The minister's job becomes to pay equal attention to both. A usual custom here is that mourners file past the open casket after the service is ended. The family goes last and often spends several minutes mourning over the deceased before they are ushered out of the room. Whatever the minister does must at least balance the yin (dark) impact of this last pass by the deceased's coffin.

It is my contention that in order to balance the yin and the yang a Christian funeral must accomplish at least five tasks. It must:

1. Pay attention to sorrow;
2. Take account of change (the reality and finality of death);
3. Honor the person who has died, and thank God for his/her life;
4. Celebrate a homecoming and reassure people that death is not the end – hope and victory remain in the Resurrection of Jesus Christ from the dead;
5. Begin the healing process.

"Death is, for most people, the most acute type of deprivation they will encounter."[5] Deaths leave wounds. Wounds can heal, but they may remain raw for a long time. Moreover, they are subject to flare-ups that can reproduce the pain and suffering of the initial wound. There is no more important task for the minister than to try to begin the healing process. I have found that, for me at least, the best way to accomplish these things is by way of a Christian Eulogy.

It's called an Obituary here, and it is an obligatory part of every funeral. It may consist of no more than reading a few notes prepared by the funeral director consisting of the dates of birth and death, occupation, religious affiliation, precedents in death and survivors of the deceased. There may be a few remarks about the deceased. But I have made it more than that. I believe it is part of the Christian emphasis on the importance of the individual. It is the only real way to honor the deceased as well as the most effective way to begin the healing process.

My grandfather was a tobacco farmer, a year-round occupation. When tobacco was sold in the fall, a whole year's labor and a person's worth as a farmer and as a human being was passed over and given a cash value in a few fleeting seconds. A person should not be treated that way in death. A person's whole life should not be ignored nor summed up too quickly. I have discovered that if an Obituary/Eulogy is done correctly, it is able to evoke the essence of the deceased - what about he/she made him/her the unique person that he/she was. In addition to noting a person's accomplishments, it may also note exceptional character traits such as integrity, dependability, humility, neighborliness, helpfulness, and faithfulness. It was immeasurably helpful to me in this process that I had a lifelong (or at least an extended and in depth) acquaintance and friendship with most of those I helped bury.

I have attended several funerals or memorial services (and hopefully, I have conducted a few myself) when such an obituary/eulogy was done in a way that made it unnecessary for the deceased body to be present because his/her essence was present. At some of these services, the body was present in an open casket, at some, it was present in a closed casket, in some only the deceased ashes were present and at several there was no physical evidence of the deceased body present at all. It is the essence of the deceased, not the body, which must be in evidence at a funeral.[6] This may be more difficult in the absence of a body, but it is not impossible. My aim in my obituary/eulogies is always to evoke the essence of the deceased.

The motivation that moved me to assemble this collection came primarily from the families of those for whom I have conducted funerals. I assume those families are primarily interested in the Obituary/Eulogies. Therefore, I have divided this collection into two sections. The first section contains the Obituary/Eulogies I have done at about one-half of the funerals I have helped conduct. These obituaries/eulogies are arranged in chronological order according to the date of the funeral, except for that of Mrs. Stacy Roy. Mrs. Roy's is placed first because it contains an explanation and defense of my use of eulogies.

The second section contains Meditations I have done for certain services. The numbers of the Meditations correspond to the numbers of the Obituary/Eulogies. For inclusion, I have selected those services whose families still remain in the community, those that I think would be of most interest to the broadest number of people, and those in which the deceased was especially important to the life of the local church and/or community.

Charles Schulz (late author of the "Peanuts" cartoons) said: "A cartoonist is someone who has to draw the same thing day after day without repeating himself." Much the same can be said of funeral preachers except not with the same frequency. Because of the lower frequency, funeral preachers get away with repeating themselves fairly often. There is no great mystery as to why this is so. If a minister finds material that is effective and useful at one funeral, it makes sense to use the same material again.

You will find much repetition in this collection. This repetition is mitigated by the limitation on quotations (hymns, poems, and so forth). Copyright restrictions limit an author to using no more than eight lines of another person's work without special permission (very hard to get). Therefore, all the quotes from poems, hymns, and other sources are limited to eight lines or less in this Collection. I have provided an **Appendix A** which will give you some more information about some of the quotations, but no more than eight lines of text from them.

In a deeper sense, no two funeral services are exactly alike. "No man can step into the same river twice, for it's not the same river, and he's not the same man." 7 No two funeral services are the same, even if the same words and metaphors are used. The deceased is different, the mourners are different, the preacher is different because he is "not the same man" who delivered the previous service.

None of my seminary classes dealt meaningfully with funerals. In none of the books I read in Seminary on the Christian funeral and certainly not in the Presbyterian _Worshipbook_ did I ever find anything about a eulogy. In fact, such was discouraged, and there was very little said at all about how to treat the deceased. I paid these instructions little attention because I had learned from a master, my father, who, though he thought himself a poor preacher, was renowned for the manner in which he conducted funerals.

I have always split a funeral service into two parts: An Obituary/Eulogy and a Meditation of Hope and Healing: A Witness to the Resurrection. However, you will find that I often leaned heavily on the Obituary/Eulogy. Moreover, in exceptional cases, the entire funeral message takes the form of a eulogy. In other cases, the eulogy spills over into the meditation so that it is hard to distinguish between them. In many services, I did only the Obituary/Eulogy, and another minister delivered the meditation of hope and witness to the resurrection.

Emotions with religious overtones fill a funeral parlor: grief, sadness, anger (at God and perhaps at the deceased), hope, hopelessness, happiness, guilt, animosity (toward God; toward siblings; toward the deceased), defeat, crushed, cursed, relief, regret, brokenness, emptiness, isolation ("I alone am left"), darkness, loss, inability to cope, fearfulness of one's own mortality, blame, recriminations, bewilderment, thankfulness, stress, feeling burdened, depression, love, faithlessness, false faith, and genuine faithfulness. A minister can be sure that many, if not all, of these emotions are lurking somewhere in the conscious or subconscious of the broken hearts and minds that are present at a funeral.

Still, the funeral preacher will succeed to the degree that he/she accomplishes the six items enumerated above. At times I have accomplished them; at other times, I have failed to do so. You will find some of the enumerated tasks uncovered in some of the material contained herein. At other times I have come up short. To the degree that I, and those who shared the service with me, have failed to accomplish all these tasks, I/we failed in my/our responsibility as a funeral preacher.

People usually think that they do not like funerals. They want them over, yet at the same time they may never want them to end. I have often been asked prior to a service to "Keep it short." Equally often, I have not done so, primarily because of the length of the eulogy. I have seldom been criticized at the end of a service for it being too long. That, too, can be attributed to the obituary/eulogy.

Whatever else it is, funerals and internment service are part of the worship life of the church and part of its ministry to the world. It would be ideal if they could be conducted in a church. Frequently, this is not the case here in the Southern Mountains. Churches are often too small and/or out-of-the-way to accommodate all the people who wish to attend a service. Instead, as noted above, they are often held in what passes for a chapel in a funeral home.

Nevertheless, every funeral conducted by a minister of the Gospel is a Christian funeral. This is so because it is the only kind of funeral that a minister of the Gospel can perform with integrity. It is so because every person deserves no less than a minister's best. It is so regardless of the religious status of the deceased because many of the mourners at whom the funeral message is directed are Christian. It is so because the God who makes "the sun rise on the evil and the good and sends rain on the just and unjust" demands that we do no less. It is so because it is part of the Church's ministry to both those inside and those outside its membership. ("He came and preached peace to [both] those far off and those who were near." Ephesians 2: 17)

This is so whether the deceased was a devout Christian or a complete reprobate. If for a devout Christian, the funeral is part of the fellowship and worship life of the church and part of the way it demonstrates its love for one another to the world, in order that the world too may believe. If for a reprobate, it is part of the church's service to the world and part of its evangelistic outreach. For these reasons, I have never refused on theological or ecclesiastical grounds to conduct or help conduct a funeral, even if it violated some jot or title of ecclesiastical policy.

I quickly learned one of the great assets of including a eulogy in a funeral service was that it forced me to talk with the family of the deceased in some depth. On my pre-funeral visitations, we do not just sit and look at each other, we talk about the deceased. And I have a feeling that these visitations are as much responsible for the positive feedback I get to my funerals as the funeral itself. This is especially helpful in those cases where I do not know the deceased very well. This pre-funeral visitation opens up creative ways to deal with all the emotions that attend the death of a loved one, both during the visitation itself and at the funeral.

Another asset was, as I lengthened the "obituary/eulogy" part of the funeral, I was forced to shorten and sharpen the other parts of the service. These did not become less moving or meaningful. In fact, they got more focused and memorable, but they also got shorter in duration.

This Collection may not resonate as well with those who read it as the services did with those who first heard them spoken. Funeral services are composed to be spoken. Mine have often been composed from notes scribbled on 3 X 5 cards or on a tablet. They lose some of their import and impact when isolated from the inflections and emotions of the spoken word and from the immediacy and emotions that surround them at a funeral service.

NOTES:
1. Thomas Wolfe.
2. Edgar N. Jackson, _The Christian Funeral_, Channel Press, 1966, p.3.
3. Thomas G. Long, _Accompany Them with Singing_, Westminster John Knox Press, 2013; Thomas G. Long and Thomas Lynch, _The Good Funeral_, Westminster John Knox Press, 2013; Caitlin Doughty, _Smoke Gets in Your Eyes_, W. W. Norton & Company, 2014.
4. Albert E. Brumley, _Wonderful Message_, Hartford Music Company, 1932.
5. Jackson, Op Cit., p. 21.
6. For contrary opinions see Long, Lynch, Doughty, Op. Cit.
7. Heraclitus (Greek Philosopher). A similar aphorism is credited to some unknown Native Americans.

OBITUARIES/
EULOGIES

STACY DELLA MYERS ROY OBITUARY/ EULOGY/REMARKS

MARCH 6, 1985

I did this whole service, but I am including it all together and at the beginning of this Collection because it contains my best explanation of why I use eulogies. Prior to the pre-funeral visitation, I barely knew this woman, though I knew her family.

[At the beginning, I read some of the Scripture passages listed in
Appendix B.*]*

We are here today to give thanks for the life of Stacy Della Myers Roy, who was born May 19, 1888, in the Vandever Community of Cumberland County, Tennessee. As a young woman, she attended Grandview Academy. Later she moved to the Creston Community to work in her brother's store and post office, which also served as the train depot. No doubt a goodly number of people passed through that depot. One of them though made a greater impression on Stacy Myers than all the rest. He rode the rails hobo style into Creston one day in 1907 or 1908. He had undoubtedly been to many places before and probably intended to ride the rails to many more. He was John Roy, and after he met Stacy Myers, he never went anywhere else without her. They were married on March 22, 1908, and lived together as loving husband and wife over 69 years until his death in May 1971. To their union, seven children were born.

Their travel together took them to many places, most notably to Arkansas in a covered wagon. But on January 1, 1918, they returned to Vandever to the place where they lived until Mr. Roy's death and where Mrs. Roy remained until eleven months ago when her failing health required her to move to the Life Care Center.

In 1919, Mrs. Roy opened a store, which, second only to her family, became her life's occupation and preoccupation. She ran it for 54 years until she was forced to retire at age 85. Her greatest joy, however, came from her children, their children, and their children's children. She lavished her affection on them all. No one remembers how far back it began, but it continued until her failing strength made it impossible for her to continue. Every evening they came – all of them – children, grandchildren, great-grandchildren – to soak up Mrs. Roy's love and to eat her cakes and pies lovingly baked fresh every day, seven days a week, 52 weeks and 365 days a year – and on leap year 366.

It is a remarkable testimony to the compelling magnetic love, the emotional force field that emanated from Mrs. Roy. Her strong sense of family and how she held her family together is one of the things that sticks indelibly in the memory of those who knew her best

In the Middle Ages builders discovered that they could build stronger and taller buildings by using a rounded arch. These early arches were constructed of stone, and in the middle, at the top of everyone was a wedge-shaped stone which supported the whole arch. It is called the keystone because it is the key to the arch's strength. Mrs. Roy was the keystone – the one that held it all together – the one who gave it strength.

I hesitate to use this term for fear that some might misunderstand and be offended, but Mrs. Roy was a truly liberated woman - prior to the invention of that term – wife, mother, homemaker, businesswoman. She was her own person – independent of mind and action – yet she gave her strength to others through her family and her business.

She was a woman of enormous energy and strength. In addition, to running the store – not 9-5 but daylight to dark; in winter daylight until after dark; six days a week, fifty-two weeks a year. And her store was her business – she ran it, and she not only did the bookkeeping for it but also for her husband's and later her son's sawmill business. She did it without ever making a mistake although she never used a calculator or any help except an old adding machine. She loved to garden and did not appreciate others messing around in her garden. She made many of her children's clothing and later some of her grandchildren's; cooked and backed every day; taught Sunday School and played the organ and piano at Hale's chapel church; worked crossword puzzles and cuddled and rocked her grandchildren and great-grandchildren in the evenings.

She was seldom sick, never seriously, depending for medicine on home remedies, a patent liniment and her own blackberry "cordial." In addition to her attention to her family, the one thing that lingers most in the memories of those who knew her best is her strength and energy. It wears me out just to hear people recite all that Mrs. Roy did. It is no wonder that she is remembered as always busy, never idle, and as one who never walked but always went at a trot.

Yet, at the end of her life, this woman of constant motion and inexhaustible energy expressed a calm serenity and patience – never complaining to her family or to those who cared for her. At the end, two months and two weeks before her ninety-seventh birthday, when her strength finally gave out, she seemed at peace with herself and her God.

Mrs. Roy died on March 6, 1985. She was preceded in death by her husband and four of her seven children. She is survived by: [I read a list of survivors.]

How great your rejoicing must be today to have had the high privilege of being loved by Mrs. Roy. How much poorer your lives might have been without her. Praise to God who gave her life and gave her to us!

[I led an interim prayer, a song was played, and I continued.]

Mrs. Roy will be remembered for her strength and her energy – like unto the strength of God. When you remember her strength and energy, remember God's strength and energy as well as God's patience, for it is infinitely greater. And remember what the Scriptures have to say about such strength:

> *"Have you not known? Have you not heard? The Lord is the everlasting God, the Creator of the earth and all that is in it. God does not faint or grow weary . . . God gives power to the faint, and to him who has no might God increases strength. Even the young shall fall exhausted; but they who wait for the Lord shall renew their strength; they shall mount up with wings likes eagles; they shall run and not become weary; they shall walk and not grow faint."*
>
> (Isaiah 40: 28-31; MFS translation]

Mrs. Roy will be remembered for the quality of her love. Her love compelled a devotion that drew her family to her the way a magnet draws metal shavings. It was a love which those who experienced it could not escape and cannot forget. For those who were the objects of her love, nothing that they might do could destroy that love. They could stop loving themselves or think that they were unlovable at times, but she never stopped loving them.

It was like the love of God. That is the message of Good Friday and Easter. Good Friday comes along and says: "wrong, evil, hate always kills." Then Easter comes with a yes, but message: "Yes wrong, evil, hate always kills, but love never dies. Remember that God's love is greater still. God loves each and every one of us in the way that Mrs. Roy loved her children, grandchildren, and great-grandchildren – God is waiting for us to respond.

A word about eulogies: Some people believe that it is inadvisable to say much about the deceased person at a Christian funeral. They have a good reason for their belief – namely, that the focus of a Christian funeral should be neither on death nor on the loved one now departed. It should be, rather, about the promises of God and the Resurrection.

There is a danger in eulogizing the dead. It is, that they, rather than God, may become the object of our worship – we may make them an idol; an object of veneration and we forget that whatever they were, whoever they are, they owe to God – God who gave them life and gave them to us. God who loves unconditionally and who sent his only Son to express his love for us are the only ones whom we should honor and worship at a Christian funeral.

However, if you have paid attention up to this point, you know that I do not fully subscribe to the view that it is inappropriate to eulogize a dead loved one at a funeral. I do it with a warning; however, a warning against using it sinfully.

If it is, as I believe, appropriate and acceptable to speak extensively about the characteristics of the dead loved one, then it can only be so for two reasons. First, it helps those of us left behind to begin working through our grief in a healthy manner. By being reminded of those things which made the deceased so beloved, we can and should be reminded that a funeral and the season of grief is not a time to feel sorry for ourselves because of our loss. But rather a time to rejoice and give thanks for the life of the one who has died and to the Grace of God who gave them life and gave them to us. It is God's grace that made possible all those lovely characteristics we so fondly remember.

Secondly, I believe that God would instruct us through the life of the one now deceased. It is God's intention to use our grief to make us stronger – more loving – more humble – more gracious persons. And one of the primary tools God has for doing that is the example of our loved one, now dead. If there are things in that person's life worth remembering and immolating (and there are some good qualities worthy of remembrance in most people), it is for our instruction that God would have us remember. Not so we can make an idol or false god of the deceased person, but that we may be instructed through the better qualities of the life of the deceased.

If what I said earlier – which was merely a reflection of the thoughts and feelings already in your hearts and minds – served only to concentrate your minds on Mrs. Roy, they were a vanity and of no-good purpose. But if in recalling the characteristics and virtues of Mrs. Roy, your hearts and minds are relieved of some of their pain and bitterness – if the words I spoke made these moments and the moments ahead a time of rejoicing as well as a time for grief, then they have served a part of their purpose. Finally, is they help you to stretch your soul's eye to see beyond the present and truly worship the God who alone gave Mrs. Roy life and gave her to us. If we are enabled to see that the God who gave her life has now received her back into God's bosom enfolded in everlasting arms; if we allow her and her life to become a window through which we view the eternal more clearly, then it was faithful, effective, and true.

RALPH HAMILTON
DECEMBER 20, 1974 OBITUARY/ EULOGY

I did this entire service by myself. It was the first Funeral I did after returning to Tennessee in 1974, and the second funeral I had ever done.

[The service was opened with the playing of The Old Rugged Cross.]

OPENING

Let us worship God, for we do not grieve as those who have no hope.

OBITUARY/EULOGY

Ralph Hamilton was a good man with no more shortcomings than most and more strengths than many. He loved his family, all his children, the animals he raised, and all other living things. His industriousness was exceeded only by his impatience to get things done. His good humor overcame the more exasperating characteristics of his personality. He lived a full life and leaves behind a legacy of fond memories with his family and friends.

He was one of a fast-disappearing generation of men and women whose doggedness – perhaps more exactly – bullheadedness matched by strength and determination helped to carve homes out of near wilderness. His death diminishes the richness of life for each and all of us.

We remember: The enthusiasm with which he loved life;
The intensity of his seemingly boundless energy;
His boisterous good humor and characteristic laugh;

His dogged perseverance;
His diligent care of the earth;
The warmth of his love, and
The joy he brought to us as husband, father, brother,
grandfather, neighbor, and friend.

And we know what a privilege it has been to have known him, loved him, and been loved by him. We know that our lives will be poorer now without him, but we rejoice in the fact that we had him with us so long. We praise your name, O God, for giving life to him and for giving him to us.

Ralph died suddenly of an apparent heart attack on December 17, 1974, twelve days before his 64th birthday. He is survived by:

[I read a list of survivors.]

A good man is dead and we will miss him, but life goes on, and God's love remains from everlasting to everlasting.

Let us pray: *[I offered an interim prayer, and a hymn was played.]*
                  [I finished with a Meditation.]

JOHN HARRISON TOLLETT OBITUARY
NOVEMBER 17, 1975

The second funeral I did after returning home. I did the whole service. I was still young then and new to the practice of funerals.

Amidst the seemingly endless list of names in the Fifth Chapter of Genesis each with the dreary refrain so and so lived so long and then he died, there is one notable exception. Of Enoch it is written "He walked with God, and he was not, for God took him." The writers of that passage knew that Enoch's life led not to the grave but to God.

The words written of Enoch come to my mind today because John Harrison Tollett walked with God and then he was not, for God took him. It is our belief that Mr. Tollett's life leads not to a grave but to God.

OBITUARY

John Harrison Tollett (named probably for President Benjamin Harrison) was the son of James and Martha Selby Tollett, born in the Sequatchie Valley on November 6, 1886. As a young man, he married Gracie Belle Hale with whom he moved to Big Lick where they had a good life together until her death in 1939. Mr. Tollett continued to live on their home place until his death.

From their marriage came six children, five of whom survived Mr. Tollett.

> *[I inserted a list of surviving children.]*

Mr. Tollett is also survived by:
> *[I inserted a list of surviving brothers, sisters, half-brothers and half-sisters.]*

He is also survived by 17 Grandchildren, 41 Great-Grandchildren, and 3 Great-Great-Grandchildren, and by a host of neighbors and friends.

Mr. Tollett died in an auto accident on November 14, 1975, eight days beyond his 89th birthday.

It is sobering to me in thinking of my personal recollections of Mr. Tollett, that he was fifty-five years old when I was born. By the time I was old enough to remember him, he was by standard reckoning an old man. Yet somehow, I never thought of Mr. Tollett as old. His infectious smile, his firm handshake, his warm humanity conveyed a spirit of life and vigor and youth.

He was a loving father, a helpful neighbor, a conscientious carpenter, a faithful churchman, a warm, courteous human being. He was a Charter member of Calvary Presbyterian Church of Big Lick where he served as an Elder for many years and as a Trustee of the Calvary Church Homestead project.

When the church was built, the men worked a total of 147 days. Harrison worked on 114 of those days, the most of any individual. We who still worship at that church have come to take for granted many marks of his craftsmanship.

Truly Mr. Tollett was one of God's good men.

In remembrance, we ask "What sort of man was he?" What more can be said than what was said of Enoch. "He walked with God." Micah asks, *"What does the Lord require of you except that you do justice, love kindness, and walk humbly with your God?"* What more can one say of Mr. Tollett than that "He did."

Mixed with every happiness is the certainty of sorrow. Our sorrow comes from remembering the warmth, the love, the care, the joy that Mr. Tollett brought into our lives as father, brother, grand-father, great-grandfather, neighbor or friend. And we would not trade those things for any amount of good feelings today. Our sorrow is but the flip side of that joy.

Remember, it was our privilege to have known, loved and been loved by John Harrison Tollett. Our lives are poorer now without him, but how much poorer they would have been had he never been a part of them. So let us rejoice in the fact that we had him with us for so long. Let us praise God for giving him life and for giving him to us.

I stood yesterday at the head of the grave where we will soon lay Mr. Tollett to his final rest. I could see his house from there. So, I went to his house. It was lonely, but it bore his marks.

Some of Mr. Tollett's greatest joys and satisfaction came from his garden

- he loved life and all growing things. He already had his garden plowed ready for the winter and the spring to come. But by God's wisdom, he was not to plant that garden again. Instead, like trees in the fall, he has taken on the cloak of death so that he may find a new and resurrected life in the springtime of God's Garden.[1]

Let Us Pray.

NOTES:

1. Portions adapted from a Funeral Message for T.V. Hale by Eugene Smathers, 1932-1968.

FANNY RECTOR HALE OBITUARY/EULOGY
JANUARY 22, 1979

[I did the complete service]

OPENING SCRIPTURES

[read some of the Scripture passages listed in Appendix B.]

OBITUARY/EULOGY

Let me begin with a history lesson. Come back with me to the year 1889.

- Benjamin Harrison took the oath of office as President in March, although he had lost the popular vote to Grover Cleveland (but won the Electoral vote) —one of only two times that has happened in U.S. history.[1]
-Henry ford was 26 and 7 years away from his first "horseless carriage."
-Orville Wright was only 18 and started a newspaper with a homemade press. He and Brother Wilbur were
  *4 years away from opening their first bicycle shop;
  *10 years away from their first experiments with gliders, and
  *14 years away from their first powered flight.
-Last of the official Indian territories disappeared with the opening of western Oklahoma to white settlement.
-Jane Adams opened Hull House in Chicago beginning a new occupation called Social Work.
-Tennessee was not yet the "Volunteer State."
-In Big Lick the "new" Oak Grove School was five years old.

And on Halloween of that year, on what is still known as "the old Rector place," a baby girl was born to Samuel and Katherine Brown Rector.

Of all these events historians have chosen to ignore only the last one, but those of us who came to know that little girl as Frances Rector, Fanny Hale, or Aunt Fanny should know better. Because of all these events surely her birth has had the greatest impact on our lives.

Among other things, funerals are for remembering, and they should serve to remind us that what really matters in life are individual persons and what happens to others through the life of those individuals. It is a time to be reminded that, in the final analysis, the real substance of life is not defined by technological advances nor political conquests but by the content of the character and the strength of the soul of those persons whom we count as loved ones and friends.

Frances (Fanny) Rector Hale was born to Simuel and Katherine Brown Rector on October 31, 1889. In 1917 she married T. Virgil Hale and in 1919, they moved to the farm near the church where they had a good life together for 45 years until Mr. Hale's death in 1962. They helped to raise Mrs. Hale's nephew, James Tinch.

Having accepted Christ at an early age, she was a Charter Member of Calvary Church of Big Lick, Presbyterian. She took an active role in the life of the church until her health slowed her down.

> *She is survived by: [I read a list of survivors including "a host of neighbors and friends."]*

I had some good professors in seminary, and they tried their best to teach me how to preach a funeral sermon. But when I got back among the kind of folks with whom I was reared, I found out that there are some people for whom no one can adequately preach at a funeral. That is because, as I was frequently reminded, some folks have already preached their own funeral in the life they have lived.

Well, there is little that my frail words can add to the sermon that Mrs. Hale preached. What a sermon it has been - powerful, but filled with humility, faithfulness, generosity, neighborliness, and humor. We laugh too little – take ourselves too seriously, but who can forget her smile and her laugh.

Let us pay heed to some of the wisdom from that sermon.

There is an old hymn that was composed by a group known as the Shakers. The shakers stressed simplicity, humility, kindliness, and generosity, and they expressed these attributes in the way they lived and the way they sang. The lyrics of the first verse and the chorus (the only words I know) go like this:

Tis the gift to be simple, tis the gift to be free, Tis the gift to come down where we ought to be;
And when we find ourselves in the place just right, It will be in the valley of love and delight.

When true simplicity is gained
To bow and to bend we will not be ashamed To turn and to turn will be our delight
Till by turning, turning we come round right.

[In Public Domain. See Appendix A for explanation.]

Mrs. Hale had the gift of simplicity. Like the God she served since she was a girl, her life was a miracle of simple grace, dignity, and humility. She was "turned round right." How much better off the world and each of us would be if more of us had the gift of simplicity. No more "rat race;" no more greediness; fewer heart attacks; fewer ulcers; fewer divorces; more time for family; less wastefulness; less envy; more inner peace. How glorious it would be if more of us, like Mrs. Hale, had the gift of simplicity and kept turning, turning til we came round right.

The other day, I came across a record book for the Big Lick Ladies Aid Society. Founded in 1919, until it disbanded around 1970 it was the longest standing organization in Big Lick. The book I found covered the years 1922 - 1925. November was the anniversary month and every November, the book records that they met at Fanny Hale's, and the first entry in the minutes for each of those meetings was "[We] had a good dinner" or "[We] enjoyed a nice dinner." The meetings at Mrs. Hale's seemed to be special.

But there is something else more revealing in that book. For 1922-23 there is a list of members, forty-seven in all. It reads like a who's who of the early years of the Big Lick church - Nora Kerley, Amy Burgess, Verdie Hall, Carrie Murphy, Elzada Hyder, Lizzie Selby, Ollie Burgess, and others. The church was founded in 1921, and the Ladies Aid Society was its primary mission outreach. Among all the names, one name stands out. It is the name of the only woman who was present at every meeting. That name is Fanny Hale. It was the kind of person she was - faithful, dependable, persevering.

She taught us all a lot about caring for others. And about being self- sufficient, careful, watchful, and conserving. The Tinches have told me how many times in the middle of the night - 10 – 11 12 PM - during the coldest time of bitter cold spells, they saw Mrs. Hale, flashlight in hand, leave her trailer and go to the can house to make sure the door was shut so the potatoes wouldn't freeze. If our leaders and the oil company executives took the responsibilities we have entrusted to their hands as seriously as Mrs. Hale took the responsibilities God had entrusted to her – what a different world it would be.

And what about generosity. She was always making something to give away - quilts and baby outfits and leaving buckets of apples on her porch to be "discovered" and stolen - or so we thought – by Halloween Goblins.

When her sister and infant son needed a home, Mrs. Hale was there, becoming like a mother to both James and Mandy. In the days before Public Assistance, she walked over the whole community, how often God only knows, delivering food from her storehouse and quilts from her frame to many who otherwise would have gone hungry and cold. When the pastor and his wife used to visit (before they lived in the community) the Hales took them in. When a Displaced Person's family came after World War II, the Hales found a place for them on their farm.

Had the Apostle Paul known her, he could easily have had her in mind when he wrote to the Galatians, "the fruit of the Spirit is love, joy, peace, patience, kindness, goodness, faithfulness, gentleness, and self-control." [Galatians 5: 22-23] And the writer of Proverbs surely knew someone like her when he wrote:

> "A true lady is hard to find;
> She is far more precious than jewels...
> She delights to work with her hands... And goes to work with a will...
> She opens her hands to the unfortunate, And stretches out her arms to the poor.
> She does not fear for her family when it snows,
> For they are all more than adequately clothed...
> She makes her own bedcovers...
> Her clothing is of good quality and dignified; She has no worry about tomorrow.
> When she opens her mouth she speaks wisely, And kindly instruction is on her tongue...

Her children rise up to pronounce blessings on her; Her husband, too, sings her praises:
'Many women have proved their worth, But you have surpassed them all.'
Charm is deceitful and beauty is fleeting,
But the intelligent woman who fears the Lord is to be praised.
Give her the reward of her labor,
And let the gates ring with praise of her deeds."

[Proverbs 31: 10-21; 25-31 MFS translation]

"More precious than jewels."
"Reaches out her hand to the needy."
"Strength and dignity are her clothing."
"Speaks wisdom and teaches kindness."
"Called 'blessed' by those who love her."
"She is to be praised!"

So, we are gathered here to praise Mrs. Hale, not to mourn her, but to thank God for the fine sermon of her life. Not to mourn her death as much as to rejoice in her life.

BILL OSCAR REED
MAY 5, 1979

I did not know Bill Oscar Reed. I had never met him. I had known his mother and part of his family, but he had lived in Ohio all the time I knew them. He was brought to Big Lick for burial because that is where most of his family was buried, and it was considered home. What I know of him I learned in the pre- funeral visitation with his family. At his funeral I spoke from notes scribbled on a 3 x 5 card during this visitation. Mr. Reed died young in a motorcycle accident.

OPENING SCRIPTURE

[Here I read some of the Scripture passages noted in Appendix B.]

OBITUARY/EULOGY

I never knew Bill Oscar Reed. It seems odd since I knew the rest of his family. But I have gotten to know something of him over the last few days. It's a long journey from the side of Bear Den Mountain to owning your own business in Dayton, Ohio. Bill/Oscar had made that journey with dignity, distinction and class. Some are remembered for their accomplishments, some for a long life, but too few because they have achieved something special for the people whom they touch.

Bill/Oscar was glad to be alive, and he made others glad to be alive. He had a zest for life, a gusto about him. For him, life was for living not just for making a living. He loved camping, cave exploring, canoeing, working with the Jaycees, traveling, but perhaps best of all coming home to plant a garden.

But I sense there was a restlessness in him, a certain frustration with the restrictions of body, time, and space. It was a restlessness expressed in his love of flying, piloting a plane, in his love of motorcycling or simply lying on his back looking at the sky. In a way he died as he lived – squeezing some of the sweet juice out of life.

His spirit is free now, in God's care, free to travel worlds uncharted by human hands, free to explore worlds beyond our imagining. He can sing in the words of the old spiritual, "Free at last, free at last, great God almighty, I am free at last."

Bill/Oscar died suddenly in a motorcycle accident on May 3, 1979. He is survived by:

[I read the list of survivors.]

[I led an interim prayer, a hymn was played, and I finished with a Meditation.]

JAMES FINLEY
03/03/1980
OPENING and OBITUARY

I conducted this service entirely by myself. It is one of the few funerals I have conducted in a church (as opposed to a "chapel" in a funeral home).

"... There is... a time for every matter under heaven: A time to be born, and a time to die; a time to plant, and a time to [harvest] what is planted; a time to kill, and a time to heal; a time to break down, and a time to build up; a time to weep, and a time to laugh; a time to mourn, and a time to dance; a time to throw stones away, and a time to gather stones together; a time to embrace, and a time to keep your distance; a time to seek, and a time to lose; a time to keep, and a time to throw away; a time to tear, and a time to sew; a time to remain silent, and a time to speak; a time to love, and a time to hate; a time for war, and a time for peace." (Ecclesiastes 3: 1-8)

A funeral is a time for many things.

It is, first of all, a time for sorrow. We are brought together by loss. It is our sense of sadness, of emptiness, of indescribable loss that brings us here today. Except for funerals and times like these, we get caught up in the struggle, the making of a living, entangled with material things, enamored by visions of rapture, we tend to forget that sorrow is one of the signs that life has beauty and meaning.

Sorrow is a mark of our humanity and a sign of our fellowship with Jesus Christ, who was called "a man of sorrows, acquainted with grief." Anyone who lives and loves will eventually and inevitably experience the sadness of loss.

There is no shame in our tears of sorrow, for they are a mark of our common humanity. To be without sorrow would mean to do without friendship and love, the kind of affection that binds us together and makes life bearable and living meaningful. The only shame (if there is any) is our failure to allow our sorrow to knit our hearts together with all our brothers and sisters. What a different world this would be if more were humanized by suffering rather than suffering by inhumanity.

OBITUARY/EULOGY

Wordsworth, in one of his poems, speaks of "Lucy, a girl who dwelt among the untrodden ways,

> *"A violet by a mossy stone, half hidden from the eye.*
> *She lived unknown, and few could know when Lucy ceased to*
> *be. But she is in her grave, and, oh, the difference to me."*

"And, oh the difference to me." That is the real sadness. Not for Jim who has passed beyond the pain and suffering, the cares and burdens of this life. But for us who remain, when the voice of the one we love is no longer heard among us. That brings on the emptiness that cannot be filled and which will not go away. Indeed, it is a time for sorrow.

But it doesn't end there because funerals are also a time for gladness. The sorrow and loss we experience today must be mingled with the gratitude and joy of victory, for we gather to pay our tribute of affection and respect for one of God's good men. A man that God will not let go. A man who lived s quiet, simple life, close to the family and friends he loved. A plain, humble man never accounted great or important, as the world measures such things but great in those qualities of character that truly endure. Never the possessor of a multitude of goods, he lived a good life always faithful to the family and place and work to which God had called him.

These words of the Psalmist fit the life and character of Jim Finley;

> *"Blessed is the man who walks not in the counsel of the wicked,*
> *nor walks in the way of sinners, not sits in the seat of slanderers;*

but his delight is in the way of the Lord, and on His way, he meditates and night. He is like a tree planted by streams of water, that yields its fruit in its season, and its leaf does not wither."

On the banks of Daddy's Creek not far from where I live, there stands a giant tree that towers above those around it. Known to most of us simply as the "Big Pine," it was, according to foresters, a seedling when the Pilgrims landed at Plymouth Rock. Somehow it has withstood or avoided the storms of nature and the woodman's ax for all this time - each year dropping its seeds to start new trees.[1]

Jim Finley reminds me of that old pine - straight, tall, beautiful, productive, unique. Like the Big Pine he had roots planted deep in the soil of dedication, and he was watered by living streams of faith. He stood amid the storms of life with quietness, strength, unpretentious, always giving of himself. Frugality, morality, faith, integrity – old-fashioned values came alive in Jim. In a time when many stand for nothing and fall for anything, it was refreshing to find in Jim a person who stood for something.

He found richness and the joy of life in simple, elemental things - family, friends, faith, work. Closest to his heart and deepest among his concerns were his family. He found in their life together and in the growth of his children his richest satisfaction and most bountiful joy - and sometimes his most relentless frustration.

He will be remembered as diligent, dedicated, determined, demanding, but even more for his rich and unique sense of humor. Jim is the only person I can remember hearing laugh out loud during one of my sermons. Perhaps he saw humor in the same thing I did, or perhaps he recognized humor which I had missed.

We will remember him for the quality and character of his mind which seemed at times to wander but was never lost or bewildered. Some people are said to have a mind like a steel trap. Jim's reminded me more of an alarm clock – suddenly and unexpectedly going off and awaking one to a new thought.

Never one for small talk or idle chatter, Jim loved to explore issues in depth. No one talked to him long without being presented with some new insight or some fresh interpretation of an old thought. He did it to me at least three times in a two-hour conversation shortly before he died. He quoted a familiar but long piece of poetry filled with new meaning and he explored fresh interpretations of scripture during our time together.

Let us Pray: *[I led an interim prayer.]*

[A hymn was played.]

[I finished with a Meditation.]

IDA RHEA PARHAM
OCTOBER 3, 1980

[The service began with the reading of a selection of Bible Passages from among those listed in Appendix B]

OBITUARY/EULOGY

Ida Rhea Parham was born in a little cabin on the banks of Lick Creek in the Big Lick Community on October 15, 1911, the tenth and youngest child of John Wesley and Florence Fryar Rhea. As a young woman, she married Leonard "Jack" Parham who preceded her through death's door.

She was a plain and uncomplicated woman who was never accounted great or important as the world measures such things. Ida's greatness lay in those qualities of character and strength of soul that endure long after mold and rust have destroyed the treasures of this world.

Never the possessor of a multitude of goods, she lived a good life, content with the things she had. She will be remembered for her quiet and simple life, for her selflessness, for her slightly stubborn streak, for the warmth of her hospitality, for her love of children, and for the skill of her hands. She was one of the very few left who could take raw wool and turn it into something useful and beautiful with nothing but a few simple tools and the skill of her hands.

Ida died peacefully in her sleep, exactly the way she would have chosen if such choices were ours to make. She died quietly, privately, peacefully, without any fuss and without bothering anyone else. Ida had lived, as too few of us do, in accordance with the words of the Lord Jesus:

"Do not lay-up treasures on earth where moth, rust, and worm consume and where thieves break in and steal, but lay up for yourselves treasures in heaven. . . For where your treasure is, there will your heart be also." (Matthew 6: 19-21)

We think that treasures follow where our heart is, but not so says Jesus, heart follows treasures.

Ida is survived by: *[I inserted a list of survivors.]*

There is a small and dwindling group of Christians known as "Shakers" for the shaking movements they made during their worship services. Some of you may recognize the name from the style of furniture they bequeathed to us. It is plain, sturdy, handsome but not ornate, serviceable in its beauty and beautiful in its serviceability. The furniture expresses the Shakers profound belief in humility and simplicity.

The other thing they bequeathed to us are some beautiful hymns. They are meant to be sung without any musical accompaniment, and when they are, many of them have a compelling, almost haunting power. One of them is entitled "Simple Gifts," and part of it goes:

SIMPLE GIFTS
A Shaker Hymn
By Elder Joseph Brackett, Jr.

"Tis the gift to be simple, tis the gift to be free Tis the gift to come down where we ought to be. And when we find ourselves in the place just right It will be in the valley of love and delight.

When true simplicity is gained
To bow and to bend, we will not be ashamed To turn and to turn will be our delight
Til by turning, turning we come round right."

Ida would have liked Shaker furniture, and they would have liked Ida. She was their kind of folks because Ida had the gift of simplicity. At the visitation yesterday, someone said to me: "You and I are still seeking for things, but Ida was satisfied long ago." I can't help but think that perhaps she was the one "turned round right;" the one who had discovered the key to the "valley of love and delight."

What a different world this would be if more of us accepted the gifts of humility and simplicity. There would be less envy and greed and jealousy that turns brother against brother, husband against wife, Iranian against Iraqi, white against black, nation against nation. How glorious it would be if more of us would allow ourselves to be "turned, turned til we came round right."

[I led an interim prayer and a hymn was played.]

[I finished with a Meditation on Hope and Healing: A Witness to the Resurrection.]

ALBERT H. HALL FUNERAL EULOGY/ MEDITATION MAY 26, 1981

At the beginning of this service I read the following scripture: Psalms 90: 1-6, 10, 12-17; Isaiah 40: 28-31; II Corinthians 4:13 - 5:9; John 14: 1-6; I

The Eulogy is also the Meditation for this service, for Mr. Hall had indeed "Preached his own funeral" as is sometimes said here in Southern Appalachia. The medium was the message. This was a long service, but my spoken part was broken at least twice, by prayers and hymns.

Funerals are historic occasions because for most of us, they mark the passing of time and the progression through the ages more definitively than any other events. ("I remember that, that was the year aunt so and so died.") More than most this is such an occasion. The man for whom we praise God today was with us so long and was of such great influence in many of our personal histories.

Come with me in your mind's eye back to the year 1888:

> Western Oklahoma was still Indian Territory - There were only 38 states; The Apache campaigns had just ended with the surrender of Geronimo;
> The open range and long cattle drives of the west were coming to an end, victims of barbed wire, windmills, steel plows, and combines.

Benjamin Harrison lost the popular vote to Grover Cleveland, but won the presidency in the electoral college, one of only two times that has ever happened.1 In Big Lick three boys were named after President Harrison, John Harrison Tollett, John Harrison Bradley, and Albert Harrison Hall.

Rudolf Hertz produced the first electric waves that would make radio possible; and gave us the name by which such waves are still known.

Bell Telephone and Standard Oil Trust were in the process of being organized; it would be a year before they were in full operation.

And on December 2 of that year a son was born to James Thomas Hall and his wife, the former Florence Minerva Lowe.

This boy would be seven when radio was first introduced and x-rays were discovered - eight when the first gasoline powered carriage was successfully tested in the U. S., and a young man of twenty when the first Model T rolled out of Henry Ford's shop in Detroit, Michigan. He was ten when Tennessee became "The Volunteer State;" fifteen when the Wright brothers finally got an airplane in the air off Kill Devil Hill in Kitty Hawk, NC; 30 when the U.S. entered World War I; and fifty-three when penicillin was first introduced.

It is somewhat sobering for me to realize that by the time I was old enough to have memories of Mr. Hall, he was already an old man of sixty.

Yet of all these events, historians have ignored only one. But we will not make that mistake today, for this funeral serves to remind us that the genuine substance of life is not defined by technological advances, political conquests, or social innovations, but by the content of the character and the strength of the soul of those whom we count as loved ones and friends.

And it is the content of Mr. Hall's character and the strength of his soul, not merely the magnitude of his years, which makes this such a special occasion for thanksgiving to God. The sorrow and loss which we experience today must be mingled with gratitude and the joy of victory.

We gather here to pay our tribute of affection and respect for one of God's good men. A plain, humble man never accounted great or important as the world measures things, but great in those qualities of character which truly endure. Never the possessor of a multitude of goods, he lived a good life, faithful to the place and work to which God had called him.

Albert Hall was a good businessman who ran his store as the cupboard of the community - a cupboard from which no one was ever turned away hungry for lack of money to pay. He provided work and income to some who otherwise would have had neither.

He was a devoted husband, father, and grandfather who shared with his wife, children, in-laws, grandchildren, and their children a bounteous love. He was a committed Christian and a consummate churchman. A charter member of Calvary Church of Big Lick, Presbyterian, he was one of the first three Elders elected at the organizational meeting in 1921. He attended his last official Session (Board) meeting fifty years later at the age of eighty-two. He has served the longest tenure of any Elder to date. He served with distinction in other offices of the church — Sunday school teacher, Sunday School Superintendent, and Trustee. Until prevented by the infirmity of age, he seldom missed a Sunday service.

Many of us can remember when much of the social and civic life of this community revolved around Mr. Hall. He was storekeeper, postmaster, package wrapper, welfare clerk, telephone operator, taxi driver, and horse doctor. If you needed a doctor, or groceries on credit, or a coffin made, or a letter mailed, or if your horse or mule was lame, you went to Mr. Hall. . . Or if you had a useless dog or worthless mule to trade, you went to Mr. Hall... - his notoriety for generosity sometimes made him a sucker for a bad trade.

No one could have been more totally involved in the life and times of his community. . . He did everything he could to make the world a place where it is a little bit easier to be good by making his community a place where it was a little bit easier to live well. Those who wish to honor Mr. Hall's memory could find no better way than to carry on his tradition of community service without which no community can endure and no democracy survive.

But still, I talk of surface things, of outward appearances, when we must speak of inward graces if we would understand what God is saying to us through the life and memory of Mr. Hall.

When someone like Mr. Hall dies, we may wonder not so much "Why did he die?" as "Why did he live so long?" What was it in his character and soul that kept him alive so long?

Perhaps it was partially his curiosity. Curiosity may have killed the cat, but it helped keep Mr. Hall alive. He always wanted to know what was going on and what was new in the life of those who visited him. As age began playing tricks on his memory, he was known to ask a visitor about their new car or truck - even if they had owned it for years. It looked new to him, and he was curious to know about it. His last day - a good day for him by all accounts - was characteristic of this curiosity. Would we all are so fortunate to spend our last day doing something that gives us satisfaction and then die quickly and painlessly.

Or perhaps it was his frugality. He couldn't bear wastefulness of any kind. He rescued items from the dumpsters which he "knew" would someday have a good use. Perhaps his frugality applied equally to his reservoir of health and energy so that he did not exhaust it as quickly as most of us do. In any case, what a different world this might be if more of us conserved resources more frugally and were less indifferent to wastefulness as was Mr. Hall.

Or maybe it was the love he shared with the young girl he followed to Kansas and returned with to live as loving husband and wife for over 70 years. The statistics on divorce, child abuse, and unhappiness in marriage would be far different if more of us learned to love like that.

Or perhaps it was that special blend of fire and steel that lay at the center of his soul. Though he was small of stature, it is almost impossible to think of Mr. Hall as a small man. There was nothing about him - not anything important anyway - which made one think "small."

In 1946, 20 years before the civil rights movement, a small group of Christian young people from all over the South came to visit Big Lick and spend six weeks working with the community on various projects. Among these visitors was one young black man, a ministerial student. They were forced to leave after three weeks because of the threats, intimidation, and near mob violence perpetrated by a gang of local young toughs. Mr. Hall was there the night the mob tried to attack the group. The next week he wrote a letter to the Chronicle [the local paper] entitled "Is this Free America?"

In this letter he briefly described the events at Big Lick on the night of the raid, and then he wrote:

> "...On this occasion these visitors, along with the pastor of the church, were insulted and threatened in a manner sufficient to shock the imagination of any loyal American citizen...I sometimes wonder where we are headed. For the last four years our boys have fought and died by the thousands for what we call 'liberty.'

Let me ask: 'Is this it? . . . 'Is this free America?'...NO, not as long as American citizens are treated as this Negro boy was treated in our county or any other place in the U. S. A Are we to turn our county over to persons of prejudice and hatred? The group of Christian young people mentioned above came for a six-weeks stay...They were here less than three weeks. Let us pray for those who did this evil deed. Let us pray the prayer the Master prayed while hanging on the Cross, hanging there because of prejudice and hatred, 'Father forgive them, for they know not what they do.'" [1]

Strong and risky words for Cumberland County in 1946, but they are only a sample of the unique blend of fire and spirit, courage and conviction which marked Albert Hall as someone special.

Or again maybe it was his consummate compassion for others - the way he cared for others without counting the cost to himself. The example that stands out for me is the way he ran his business. That is usually where one's real values are tested. During the Depression when he did not have enough income to pay his own creditors, time and again, at his own expense, he went to town and hauled back Red Cross flour to be distributed free while his store was stocked with flour he could not sell.

I once ran across some old documents which showed that Mr. Hall had sold a horse and a Ford truck to pay a grocery wholesaler. No one will ever know how many families that horse and truck saw through some very difficult days. People traded whatever they had - a worthless dog, a starved mule - or nothing more than their word that they would pay when they could. He almost lost his store, yet he went on giving credit without counting the cost. He believed that only God got him through those times.

When he sold his store thirty years later some people still owed him money. He gathered up all of each family's credit tickets, stapled them together, wrote "cancelled" across them, and mailed them back to the families to which they belonged. It was like the Old Testament Jubilee which required that every fifty years all debts were cancelled, and everyone started over - except unlike the people of the O.T. - Albert Hall really made it happen.

He lived in a house by the side of the road. I have long known that a poem by Sam Walter Foss, inspired by a line from Homer, and entitled "The House by the Side of the Road" was meant to be read at Mr. Hall's funeral. Part of it goes:

"I see from my house by the side of the road, By the side of the highway of life:
The men who press with the ardor of hope; The men who are faint with the strife.
But I turn not away from their smiles nor their tears, Both part of an infinite plan –
Let me live in a house by the side of the road And be a friend to man." [2]

The psalmist asks: "O Lord, who shall sojourn in your house? Who shall dwell on your Holy Hill?" And he answers, "He who walks blamelessly, and does what is right, and speaks truth from his heart; who does not slander with his tongue, and does no evil to his friend, nor castes blame upon his neighbor; . . .who swears to the truth even when it hurts him; who does not collect interest, nor take a bribe against the innocent. He who does these things shall never be moved." (Psalms 15, RSV)

That psalmist was thinking of someone an awfully lot like Mr. Hall.

Hidden away among the list of inconsequential names in the 5th Chapter of Genesis, we find this remarkable and beautiful commentary on one of them: "Enoch walked with God, and then he was not, for God took him." A child explained this passage by saying: "Enoch and God used to take long walks together. And one day they walked further than usual, and God said, 'Enoch, you must be tired; come into my house and rest.'"

Because of the kind of man Enoch was his friends believed that death was not the end - because they knew that the direction of his life led not to a grave but to God. Albert Hall and God used to take long walks together, and - well, you know the rest of the story. . .

In the language of the church, we have a word far more fitting than "deceased" to explain this occasion. When a Christian moves from one church to another, we say that he or she has "transferred" his/her membership.

In 1921, Albert H. Hall transferred his membership to Calvary Presbyterian Church of Big Lick, and now, 60 years later, it is my responsibility and great privilege to announce the transfer of our beloved brother, Albert H. Hall, with the highest recommendation of his pastor, fellow Elders, and church members to that Church Triumphant and Eternal, "located in that city whose builder and maker is God."[3]

[This ended this funeral service.]

NOTES:

1. I own the rights to this quotation from A.H. Hall. It is part of the Eugene Smathers papers.
2. I read the whole poem at the service, but can only print this one verse here by law. For more information, see Appendix A at the end of this Collection.
3. This ending adapted from a funeral closing by Eugene Smathers 1932-1968.

CREED TOLLETT
JANUARY 24, 1982

[I opened this service by reading some of the Scripture passages listed in Appendix B.]

OBITUARY/EULOGY

Today is a day of thanksgiving for the life of Creed Tollett. Creed was a native of Cumberland County, born in the head of the Sequatchie Valley on June 15, 1909, the first son of George and Martha Wilson Tollett. For over thirty years, he was married to Louise Henry with whom he established a loving home and family.

Creed died at home on January 22, 1982 - dying as he had lived, with quiet dignity, peace and serenity. He is survived by:

[I read the list of survivors.]

Creed was a loving husband and father, and a good neighbor. He was a friendly and gregarious man who never met a stranger and who had a knack for making people feel welcome.

He was a veteran of World War II, during which he saw action all over Europe as a member of the 945th Field Artillery. His War service was a duty he accepted willingly and courageously, but one which he never enjoyed, relished or talked about. He was more a lover than a warrior, far more capable of compassion than of vengeance.

He was a concerned, well-informed, and farsighted citizen. He was active in politics, once serving as a member of the County Court.

He was a respected and valued member of Calvary Presbyterian Church of Big Lick. During his later years, one of his great joys lay in attending Sunday school and church. His avid storytelling and chortling laugh will long be remembered and sorely missed by those who shared his fellowship on Sunday morning.

His former partners and opponents will remember how he enjoyed rook - and how his expressions always gave away whether he held a strong or weak hand. Those who knew him well will remember how his able mind dove into crossword puzzles - wearing our two dictionaries in the process, and once even writing a dictionary of his own.

He enjoyed watching wrestling, but his real love in athletics was baseball and softball. He had a passion for the game and understood its intricacies and nuances far better than most. As a young man, he was a player with considerable skill and a lot of the intangible that athletes call "heart." One of his fondest memories from later years was of the time coached an inexperienced bunch of Big Lick teenagers to the county softball league championship their first year in it. He continued to help coach the Calvary Church league team as long as he was able. One of his former teammates related to me last night how, in the game that effectively ended his playing career, Creed had crawled home from third base after tearing a ligament in his leg.

My earliest personal memory of Creed is related. It happened one Sunday afternoon (in 1960 I think) when a bunch of us, teenagers and young men, had gathered in the old ball field behind the Big Lick School to play a pick-up game. After we finished, some of us stayed around to see how well and how far we could hit a ball. Creed was there watching, perhaps giving helpful hints, but never imposing himself. He was over fifty, an old man in my eyes then. After we all finished, some of the fellows invited Creed to take a turn with the bat.

We were playing with an old softball and wooden bats. I expected him to hit a little grounder or a soft fly ball. Instead, he hit a line drive that cracked as it left the bat and took off like it was shot from a cannon. It was still rising when it broke a limb out of a tree about 250 feet away. I had never seen a softball hit like that. I didn't know a softball could be hit like that. I have played that scene over repeatedly in my mind during the last few weeks because in so many ways that time at bat and that softball shot symbolizes Creed's life - quiet, humble, unassuming but clean, straight, surprisingly powerful.

Citizen, soldier, ballplayer, husband, father, neighbor, friend - all of these but much more, because Creed was one of God's gentle spirits. He was a plain, humble man never accounted great or important as the world measures things, but great in qualities of character which truly endure.

Creed's house sat near the side of the road. This poem by Sam Walter Foss, inspired by a line from Homer and entitled _The House by the Side of the Road_ seems appropriate:

> "I see from my house by the side of the road, By the side of the highway of life:
> The men who press with the ardor of hope; The men who are faint with the strife.
> But I turn not away from their smiles nor their tears, Both part of an infinite plan –
> Let me live in a house by the side of the road And be a friend to man." [1]

[I offered an interim prayer here, and a song was played or sung.]

[I completed the service with a Meditation.]

NOTES:
1. I read the whole poem at the service but can only print this one verse here by law. For more information, see Appendix A at the end of this Collection.

WALTER FRED HASSLER OBITUARY/EULOGY FEBRUARY 1, 1983

I did this entire service.

OPENING SCRIPTURE

Psalm 23; Psalm 90: 1-6; 13-17; Psalm 107: 1-9; John 14: 1-3; From the Apocrypha, Jesus Ben Sirach 38: 24-32.

OBITUARY/EULOGY

Walter Fred Hassler, the son of George and Martha Rhea Hassler was born in the head of the Sequatchie Valley in Cumberland County on January 21, 1890.

His first wife, Zenobia ("Zenobie") preceded him in death, dying in 1934. Together they had seven children, three of whom, Frances, Mark, and Jack also preceded their father in death.

In 1936 he married Stella Mae Hale, and they have been devoted husband and wife ever since, caring for each other through sickness and health, good times and bad times.

Fred died on January 30, 1983, nine days past his 93rd birthday after several years of failing health. He is survived by: *[I read a list of survivors.]*

Fred was the kind of man you count it an honor to know. How fortunate we are to have known, loved and been loved by him. How much richer we are today for the fact that God gave him life and gave him to us.

Fred was reared in a Christian home. His parents were charter members of Calvary Church of Big Lick, Presbyterian, and he was a devout believer. He accepted Christ, made a profession of faith, and united with the Big Lick church on August 25, 1926. Since that time, he has been a respected member of that congregation.

Fred was a sawyer by trade — one of those rare individuals who had mastered the multiple skills required to operate an old circular sawmill. He was a leader in the Big Lick Farmers' Association Cooperative Community Sawmill. He was a simple, humble, gracious man, satisfied with a simple existence. Never accounted mighty or wealthy as the world measures such things, but rich in those qualities of character which make communities stable and livable.

He was a devoted husband and father, an esteemed and respected member of his community who in his younger years served several terms on the County Commission (then the County Court). He was an informed and responsible citizen who kept abreast of public affairs. The day before he died, he asked me what Congress was doing about Social Security. He was a concerned and involved citizen to the end. The kind of citizen the Founding Fathers envisioned when they founded this nation.

My Daddy used to say that the responsible Christian citizen is a person who reads with equal attention both his Bible and his daily newspaper. When he said that, he had someone a lot like Fred in mind.

[After a prayer and hymn, I completed this service with a Meditation.]

AARON H. WOOD
08/02/1983

I did this entire service.

OBITUARY

Aaron H. Wood was born Feb 15, 1919, in Haywood County, NC, the youngest son of Bryson and Maude Raines Wood.

On September 12, 1942, he married Bernice Hubbard with whom he made a happy marriage for nearly 41 years, making their home in the same house on Lantana Road for 35 of those 41 years. To their union were born 3 daughters, Carol, Sue, and Denise.

On Nov. 27, 1941, Aaron was inducted into the army and for the next four years he saw action in North Africa, Sicily, the Normandy Invasion, in Northern France and Germany, ending up on the Elbe River which is still today the border between West and East Germany. He served as a member of the 2nd Battalion of the 67th Armored Regiment of the 3rd Army, serving under General George Patton – "old blood and guts" as he was called. He was twice wounded and was awarded the Purple Heart and the Silver Star for gallantry in action.

But Aaron never dwelt much on his wartime experience for he was more a lover than a warrior. He was a heavy equipment operator and worked for several years for the Cumberland County Road Department.

He was a quiet and gently man, remembered by those who knew him best for his ready smile and his appreciation of a good practical joke. Kindly and personable, he loved the outdoors, and enjoyed hunting and fishing, and working in his yard as long as his health permitted it. He was one of God's little people, the ones Jesus loved so much. Aaron died as he lived, quietly and peacefully, on July 31, 1983, at the age of 64 years and 5 months. He is survived by

[I read a list of survivors and precedents in death.]

[I led an interim prayer and a hymn was played.]

[I completed the service with a Meditation.]

GLADYS WOOD SELBY
SEPTEMBER 06, 1983

[This service was opened with the reading of some scripture from among those passages noted in Appendix B. I did the whole service.]

OBITUARY/EULOGY

Gladys Wood Selby was born on May 3, 1916, to Bryson and Maude Raines Wood in Haywood County, North Carolina. At age 15 she moved with her family to Cumberland County, Tennessee.

In 1937 she married James Leonard Selby, and to their union two sons and four daughters were born. Gladys was devoted to her children and her family - always giving them the best of herself. She gave them her time, her sense of humor, her strength of character, her sense of discipline, and her love.

Through some very hard times when her husband was away during WWII, and then after he died in 1957, she held her family together and provided for her children both materially and spiritually. The character of her children - the warmth with which they greet old friends and strangers, the ease with which they can laugh even in the face of death, the sincerity and confidence with which they share the strength of her faith and theirs - bear testimony to the kind of woman Gladys was.

She was a nurse; a profession she was first exposed to at the Warren H. Wilson House of Health in Big Lick. She loved her nursing work, a profession she pursued from 1954 until she retired in 1968. She spent her last days at the same hospital where she once worked - and where she had helped design the Emergency Room and spent her last working years as its supervisor.

She never wanted much for herself but like her Suffering Servant Lord spent herself in service to others. After her death, her children found, hidden among her personal belongings, several awards recognizing her voluntary service to others.

She enjoyed sewing, ceramics, and flowers, but above all else she loved walking in the woods. Gladys was a Christian who never let her children forget that she knew who her Lord was. When she called them to her bedside to pray with her shortly before her death, she passed on to them a calm serenity about her future and theirs. In witness to the Resurrection, she prayed for them to be given strength and peace in the days ahead.

Gladys died September 3, 1983, at the age of 67 years and 4 months.

She is survived by: *[I read a list of survivors including "A host of relatives, neighbors, and friends".]*

Jesus' parable of the separation of the nations is told in Matthew 25: 31-

40. You probably know it as the parable of the sheep and goats. In it he explains the basis he will use on the Day of Judgment to separate the nations as a shepherd separates the sheep from the goats. The basis will be the manner in which those being judged have treated "the least of these."

One of the fascinating points of this parable is that the righteous, the ones who have done right, do not know that they were doing anything unusual. They did what came naturally to them. They did it out of compassion without thought of return or reward. Doing the merciful thing, the loving thing came so naturally to them that they never considered the glory they were perfecting.

Gladys was a lot like that. Never concerned about herself, but always giving of herself for others. Have no fear about where Gladys is today. She is on the right hand of the King.

Last night Jay, Pat, Ted, and Nina, with whom I spent a goodly part of my first 12 years, reminded me of how I would often be on the receiving end of their Mother's firm discipline right along with them. I had forgotten that, but it took only a little reminder for me to recall the sting of the switch.

What stands out in my memory of Gladys is her crackling cornbread - cornbread laced with cracklings and onions. (If you don't know what cracklings are, ask some of us that are older.) Today when kids come home from school, they get a candy bar or some such treat. But Gladys did not have the money for candy bars. When her kids came in from school, they often got a piece of crackling cornbread. I know because I was often there with them.

I did not know then what I know now. That cornbread was a sign of hard times and resourcefulness. A mother with four children, a husband away at war, and a neighbor brat underfoot had a hard go of it. That cornbread was a sign of her ability to make do - to get by in hard times. I don't know why I remember it so clearly. I didn't even like cornbread that well, let alone cracklings and onions. But mixed together in Gladys' cornbread, I remember them as tasting good. It sticks to my memory the way it once stuck in my throat.

That cornbread hangs in my memory, reminding me of who Gladys was and what she was like – resourceful, warm, generous, neighborly, kind.

Let us Pray: *[I led an interim prayer and a hymn was played.]*

[I completed the service with a Meditation.]

VERDIE CROFT HALL NOVEMBER 29, 1983

This is one of the longer services I ever did. The family did not think it overly long, but were well pleased with it. I did the whole service.

[I opened this service by reading some of the scripture passages noted in Appendix B.]

OBITUARY/EULOGY

Funerals are historic occasions because for most of us they are one of the ways we mark the passage of time and the changes in our lives. For over 94 years God has marked and shaped and brightened little bits of His world – including every one of us here, through the life of Mary Verdie Pearl Croft Hall. As of November 27, 1983, that has changed; history passes on, only eternity remains unchanged.

Since this is a historic occasion let us begin with a history lesson. Think of the year 1889.

March 4 - Benjamin Harrison lost the popular vote but won the electoral vote and was inaugurated President - one of only two times that has ever happened.[1]
- Henry ford was 26 and 7 years away from his first "horseless carriage."
- Orville Wright was only 18 and he and his brother Wilbur were
- 4 years away from opening their first bicycle shop;
- 10 years away from their first experiments with gliders, and
- 14 years away from their first powered flight.

March 23 -Last of the official Indian territories disappeared with the opening of western Oklahoma to white settlement.

March 31- The Eiffel Tower was completed in Paris, France. May 31

- 5,000 die in disastrous Johnstown, PA flood.

- General George Crook ended a year of fruitless negotiations with Sitting Bull and other Indian chiefs in attempt to settle the last of the Indian wars. A year later Sitting Bull would be murdered, Big Foot's band massacred at Wounded Knee, and the Indian wars essentially ended forever.

And on April 13 of that year, a baby girl was born to Tom and Molly Fryer Croft. They gave her three names - Mary Verdie Pearl.

This girl would be

-6 when X-rays were first discovered and radio was first introduced;

-7 when the first car was successfully tested in the U. S.;

-9 when Tennessee became the "Volunteer State;"

-15 when the first airplane flew at Kill Devil Hill in Kitty Hawk, NC;

-19 when the first Model T rolled out of Henry Ford's shop in Detroit;

-52 when penicillin was first used to treat infection,

-56 on VE Day when World War II ended, and

-70 when man first walked on the moon.

Of all these events, historians have chosen to ignore only the birth of the Croft's daughter. But those of us who came to know her as Mary Verdie Pearl Croft, or as Mrs. Hall or Verdie or Aunt Verdie or mother or grandma or friend will not make that mistake. For of all these events, none has touched our lives more meaningfully than that birth.

Mary Verdie Pearl Croft Hall was born in Cumberland County on April 13, 1889, the fourth daughter and fifth child of Tom and Mollie Fryer Croft. On March 29, 1910, she married Albert Hall with whom she lived as loving husband and wife for 71 years until his death in 1981. To their union seven children – three daughters and four sons – were born, all of whom survived their parents. She was a Charter Member of Calvary Presbyterian Church of Big Lick and faithful to it to the very end. On November 27, 1983, she died as she had lived – in the same house that had been her home for over fifty years – with quiet dignity and serenity, less than five months short of her 95th birthday. She is survived by

[I read a list of survivors including "A host of neighbors and friends."]

Among other things, funerals are for remembering. And they should remind us that what really matters in life are individual persons and what happens to others through those individuals. The genuine substance of life is not defined by technological advances nor political or military conquests nor social innovations – but by the content of the character and the strength of the soul of those persons whom we count as loved ones, neighbors, and friends. And it is the content of Mrs. Hall's character and the strength of her soul, not merely the magnitude of her years, which makes this a time for rejoicing and marks today not as a low point in our life's journey but as a day of rare privilege.

Indeed, how fortunate we are to grieve today because our grief means that we had the rare privilege of knowing, loving, and being loved by one of God's good women. How gracious and generous God is to have shared her with us and for so many years.

Mrs. Hall was a plain and humble woman, never accounted great or important or mighty as the world measures such things, but great in those qualities of character which truly endure – those qualities which the Apostle Paul called "Fruit of the Spirit: love, joy, peace, patience, kindness, goodness, faithfulness, gentleness, self-control. . ." [Galatians 5: 22-23a]

In the 31st chapter of Proverbs, there is a passage which praises the characteristics of a worthy woman. Listen as I read and expand on portions of it.

> "A [true lady] is hard to find;
> She is far more precious than jewels...
> She delights to work with her hands... And goes to work with a will...
> She opens her hands to the unfortunate, And stretches out her arms to the poor.
> She does not fear for her family when it snows, For all of them are doubly clothed...
> She makes her own bedcovers...
> Her clothing is of good quality and dignified; She has no worry about tomorrow.
> When she opens her mouth she speaks wisely, And kindly instruction is on her tongue...
> Her children rise to pronounce blessings on her; Her husband, too, sings her praises:

'Many women have proved their worth But you have surpassed them all.'
Charm is deceitful and beauty is fleeting,
But the wise woman who fears the Lord is to be praised.
Give her the reward of her labor,
And let the gates ring with praise of her deeds."
[Proverbs 31: 10-31, Selected verses. MFS translation.]

"More precious than jewels" – how aptly named she was, though it was one of the names she never used – Pearl – The Pearl of great price.

"She rises before daylight to provide food for her family." How she excelled at feeding not only her own family but all who put their feet under her table, be they field hands, visiting preachers, neighbors over for a Sunday dinner, or strangers.

Among the things listed in the second chapter of Acts as the distinguishing actions of the early Christians is this: ". . . and breaking bread in their homes, they partook of food with glad and generous hearts . . ." They would have enjoyed having Mrs. Hall among them, for she always prepared and served food with a glad and generous heart. Her children and neighbors still marvel at how she could take a can of tuna or half a chicken and feed a multitude. No matter how many descended upon her at mealtime, expected or unexpected, it seemed that she could invariably come up with a delightful and satisfying meal.

How? I don't know, but I suspect that she had learned what so many of us forget – the lesson that the little boy with the five loaves and two fish - learned from Jesus. Namely, that our capacity to share our resources with others has more to do with our attitude and our faith than it does with the amount of resources we have. The ability to feed hungry people has more to do with what's in our heart than what is in our cupboard. How different this old world might be if more of us could develop that strength of soul which makes such miracles possible.

There was simply something extraordinary about the Croft girls - at least in the ones I have known - Annora, Maggie, and Verdie. It's not simply their devotion to the church though Mrs. Hall (and her sisters) had plenty of that - charter member, Sunday school teacher, as regular in attendance as it was possible to be. She loved her church. It's not simply in their devotion to their duties as homemakers, wives and mothers, though Mrs. Hall exhibited an abundance of that. It has to do more with their sense of family.

They seemed to understand better than most what Jesus meant when he said we all belong to one great family. It seems that no one ever entered Mrs. Hall's house without being as welcome as the dearest of her children and grandchildren. There was always room for more, and no stranger ever set foot under Mrs. Hall's table, although she did feed people whom she barely knew. When you sat in her house or at her table you became part of the family. Perhaps that's an example of what Jesus was talking about, and why it was so important to those early Christians that they ate at each other's tables as well as praying and studying scripture together.

Back to Proverbs, it is written there: "She opens her hand to the poor and reaches out her hands to the needy."

Generosity is a sign of God's grace in our lives and the breadth and depth of it a measure of our devotion to God.

Mrs. Hall was always available to her neighbors in times of need. She acted as kind of a community nurse in the days before a trained nurse or doctor was available to the people of Big Lick. She seemed to have a knack for binding up wounds and comforting people in pain. And her natural ingenuity and common sense made up for what she lacked in formal training. It is no accident that two of her daughters are nurses, and no surprise that two of her sons married nurses. Healing seems to run in the family.

Proverbs continues: "Strength and dignity are her clothing. She opens her mouth with wisdom and the teaching of kindness is on her tongue."

My earliest recollection of Mrs. Hall is as a Sunday school teacher. She awed me. In fact, I was a little scared of her – not in a bad sense – but in the sense that she gave you the feeling that you better not do anything wrong. And if you did, she would know about it. (There may be more fact than fantasy in that for the store was the center of all news and most of what happened was sooner or later reported to someone at the store.) It was not until later that I learned what I took for sternness and strictness was really a deep love for children and a desire that they grow true and straight.

It was even later in my life that I came to recognize and appreciate her keen wit and sharp (sometimes biting) sense of humor. Sometimes when I was too long between visits, she would greet me by saying: "Do you still live in the community?" Or "It's good to see you. I'd almost forgotten that you live in the community."

Only a short time ago when Judy and Susie stopped to see her, she noted Susie's growth by saying to Judy, "You're going to have to put a brick on her head or she's going to outgrow you." Her mind and her wit never betrayed her – except for brief spells – until the very last few days of her life.

The Proverbs passage continues: "Charm is deceitful and beauty is vain, but a woman who trusts the Lord is to be praised."

Charm she had, but it was not deceitful. And beauty, too; the fine features and clear complexion remained evident to the very end. But above all else she trusted the Lord. So, we are all gathered here not to mourn her but to praise her and to thank God for giving her life and sharing her with us.

[I led an interim prayer, a hymn was played, and I finished with a meditation.]

NOTES:

1. It happened a third time in the 2000 election, but this message was composed and delivered prior to that election.

EUCLE BURGESS
July 7, 1986
OPENING/
OBITUARY/EULOGY

I did this complete service by myself.

CALL TO WORSHIP, OPENING SCRIPTURE and REMARKS

Let us worship God - For we do not grieve as others do who have no hope.

This is a service of thanksgiving and joy. Thanksgiving for the life of Eucle Burgess and joy for the fact to which his life bore such eloquent testimony

- the power of the Resurrection: the victory of light over darkness; of love over hate; of forgiveness over sin; of grace over guilt; of life – Eternal Life - over death.

For in spite of our sorrow, this is not a day of defeat, but a day to celebrate a victory.

Hear and believe the Good News of the Gospel:

> *Jesus said: "I am the Resurrection and the life."*
> *"Come to me all who are burdened and I will give you rest."*
> *"Blessed are those who mourn, they shall be comforted."*

"Our help is in the name of the Lord who made heaven and earth."

OBITUARY/EULOGY

Eucle Burgess was born on April 28, 1916, the second son of Vance and Amy Seiver Burgess. They gave him an unusual name - a name for which the derivation cannot be found - a name no one had ever heard before and few have heard since. They named him Eucle. An unusual name for an unusual man.

In 1929 he united with Calvary Presbyterian Church of Big Lick on profession of faith, and he remained a model member all his life. He served 37 years as a Deacon or Elder, and never missed a service except for illness or absence from the community. When his grandson, Chad, was born, he said, "I'm going to see that he gets to Sunday school every Sunday."

In June 1938, he married Cora Wilbanks with whom he spent 48 years as loving husband and wife, and with whom he had three children - Sherry, Linda, and Butch.

His work often took him all over the state, but his heart remained in Big Lick. Wherever he went and whatever he did, he remained deep down a husband, father, farmer, foxhunter, and friend.

He was infectiously friendly with everyone he met.

He was a worrier who hated scarcity and went to great lengths to avoid it. His family used to joke that every year he planted potatoes as if he was preparing for another potato famine. And the way he put up hay, always stockpiling more than he would ever need, was a summer ritual in Big Lick. Had he been among the ten maidens in Jesus' parable in the 25th Chapter of Matthew, he definitely would have been among those who had planned ahead and had enough oil for their lamps.

He had an alert, inquisitive and agile mind, and a thirst for knowledge. As a young man he walked to the head of the valley to catch a bus to high school - three miles in the morning and three miles back at night. He was an active participant in Sunday school and discussion groups at church, and an avid listener to sermons. He made me a better preacher, I am sure, because with Eucle you could never relax in the pulpit. He always sat near the back, often in the back row, but he was always leaning forward, straining to hear every word. Whenever you looked at him, there he was, listening as if what you were saying was the most important thing in the world. And you knew that his mind was churning up, mulling over, and sorting out everything you had to say.

He loved baseball and softball, a most suitable sport for a man so intent on expending his individual talents on molding the common good. He was one of a group of individuals in Big Lick and Calvary Church who truly understood the nature of community: the necessity of the individual seeing and thinking beyond himself; the necessity of acting beyond one's own self-interest - conscious in all of his actions not only of what it meant for him and his family but what effect it would have on his neighbors and the whole community.

He will be missed.

Eucle died suddenly, but without extensive or prolonged pain or suffering on July 5, 1986.

He is survived by: *[I read a list of survivors.]*

Standing here I have memories. Many of you are deeper and richer than mine. But one that sticks indelibly in my mind is of a Sunday afternoon about thirty-five years ago in the back of Eucle's pick-up truck. We were heading for a ball game, and a bunch of boys were in the back. We had just rounded Dead Man's Curve (just beyond the Homestead intersection) at what we considered a thrilling if somewhat scary rate of speed. We fell into a discussion of the proper technique for negotiating a curve. Being 9-12 years olds we each had an expert opinion on the subject, each one of them different. Then one among us said, "Uncle Eucle says... " And whether reported correctly or not, and though it ran counter to most of the conventional wisdom we knew, Eucle's reported opinion silenced the debate - such was our respect for him.

This recollection stands out in my mind because it illustrates why today is a time for joy as well as for sorrow.

It was not just that Eucle was at the center of a community outing - giving his time and using his resources for the benefit of us all, as he so often did.

It was not merely that Eucle could successfully negotiate a dangerous curve in the road.

It was not just that Eucle had an opinion about the proper way to negotiate such curves - Eucle had opinions, if not on everything, at least on a lot of things, and he was not particularly shy about expressing them - it was part of what made him the unique and marvelous person he was.

It was not merely that Eucle's opinion went beyond conventional wisdom, though his ideas, insights and solutions often sparkled with originality.

It was not just that Eucle was held in such high regard and his opinion valued so highly, especially by the young.

Beyond all these, what makes this story special to me is that it illustrates Eucle's skill in negotiating the Dead Man's Curves of life - not in the mundane sense of driving around a crooked place in the road, but in the far more important transcendent sense of his ability to negotiate the Dead Man's Curves in the more important aspects of our lives – those bends and twists and turns in life that tempt and taunt and tantalize us into moral and spiritual danger. Life is filled with Dead Man's Curves, and to a large extent our effort to live faithfully before God is defined by how successfully we learn to negotiate these curves without sliding off the road or endangering someone else.

It was Eucle's skill in negotiating those curves that makes his life a testimony to the victory we celebrate today – the victory Christ won at Gethsemane, at Calvary, and in Joseph's Garden – the victory of powerless love over loveless power, of righteousness over sin, of brotherhood over divisiveness, of grace over guilt, of life over death. It is this which makes today a time to rejoice as well as a time to grieve. It is what makes today a victory celebration.

[I led an interim prayer and a hymn was played.]

[I completed the service with a Meditation.]

LARRY CARPENTER EULOGY
APRIL 4, 1986

[Opposite to my usual practice, I opened this service with a Meditation which is included in the Meditations section of this Collection.]

LARRY CARPENTER – A EULOGY

The first verse of the very first Psalm begins: "Blessed is the man who walks not in the counsel of the wicked, not stands in the way of sinners, nor sits in the seat of scoffers. He is like a tree planted by streams of water that yields its fruit in its season, and its leaf does not wither. . ."

On the banks of a small stream near where I live there is an ancient pine tree. We call it simply the "Big Pine." It is over four feet in diameter, over twelve feet in circumference and towers over the lesser trees which surround it. It is reputed to be the largest pine tree in the state of Tennessee. It was, according to foresters, a seedling when the Pilgrims landed at Plymouth Rock. Somehow through all these years, it alone has withstood the ravages of wind and wildfire and the woodman's ax, each year dropping its seeds to begin new life.

That verse and that tree remind me of Larry Carpenter – steadfast, straight, strong, abiding, productive, dependable. Like that Big Pine, Larry had roots firmly planted in the rich soil of traditional values, and nourished by streams of living faith, he stood amid the storms of life with quiet strength and dignity, with steadfastness of purpose, unpretentiously giving of himself, dropping seeds of kindness and good cheer, of quality workmanship and dependable service.

Had Jesus named Larry he might have called him Peter - the Rock. He was the one that could always be counted on to be there when he said he would - the one most constant in purpose and trustworthy in action.

Some would have called Larry predictable, in a perhaps condescending kind of way. He was not a particularly complex nor subtle person. You seldom had to guess what Larry thought or where he stood or whom he favored or where his values lay. His loyalty was unswerving - to his family, his friends, his community, the teams he supported, his clients and his partners.

But other words come to my mind when I think of Larry – frugality, fidelity, fealty, family, honor, integrity. He we completely lacking in pretentiousness and dedicated to excellence in all that he did. He was like a tree planted by streams of water.

The 15th Psalm asks:

> *O Lord, who shall you invite to your house? Who shall come to live on your Holy Hill?*
>
> *He who walks blamelessly; who does what is right; Who seeks truth with his heart; who will not lie; Whose word can be trusted. Who speaks no slander;*
> *And does no evil to a friend; nor repeats gossip against his neighbor; Who sticks by his word, even if it causes him harm;*
> *Who is dependable, trustworthy, and not two-faced;*
> *Who will not cheat nor harm the innocent for any amount of money.*
>
> [MFS Translation.]

Whomever wrote that Psalm would have liked Larry, would have liked him a lot.

Talk to anyone who knew him and one of the first things they will recall is Larry's absolute honesty and integrity. One of his closest friends said to me last night, "You cannot say this," he cautioned me, "but Larry was too honest to be a lawyer." [The congregation was filled with lawyers and there was an audible gasp when I said this.] The same thing, by the way, might also be said of preachers. I do not agree with what the Mann1 said, nor do many of you, I expect, share that low esteem for the barrister's trade. But I do understand what the Mann1 meant. The fact is that if more attorneys were like Larry

Carpenter, there would be fewer lawyer jokes around. Larry insisted upon abiding by the letter of a contract and with him his word was his bond.

Larry would have disagreed with his friend's assessment. For him honesty and integrity were the essence of being an attorney. He took pride in his craft. He served the law with gladness. He saw it as the way to insure decency, fairness, justice, goodness, and truth. And he served the whole community. The fact that some could not pay right away or that their case might not be very significant was not, in Larry's mind, sufficient reason to refuse them legal counsel. And every client received the same meticulous, thoughtful, thorough attention, regardless of their station in life, their status in the community, or their ability to pay.

He was successful in an adversarial business without ever becoming contentious. Frequently exposed to some of the worst in human nature, he steadfastly refused to denigrate anyone. He never discussed a client's case outside the proper context. He seldom spoke ill of anyone, even an adversary. He was scrupulously fair in all his dealings. He was unfailingly considerate of others. Though widely known and highly respected by many, he never sought personal gain out of a relationship. He never betrayed a friendship, not deserted a client.

Even last week when Dave and his closest friends visited him, what he talked about, what concerned him most, were his clients with whom he had been working before he got sick. He was the consummate professional to the very end. He suppressed the pain in his own body by sheer will power in order to make sure that those who depended on him – family, friends, clients – were cared for.

I read recently that crop duster pilots want to be known as Aerial Applicators. It seems that everyone wants a more prestigious title. But not Larry. He knew who and what he was. He was a small town, mid-western attorney, and he took pride in being the best that he could be at what he was. He was not, on the other hand, a handyman or backyard mechanic, and he never pretended to be. With Larry what you saw was what you got. There was nothing pretentious about him.

Larry's passions were: his family, his law practice, the city of Norwalk, and golf, not always in that order. He often thought with his heart. It was not that he did not have a quick and agile mind which he used ably, for he did - but the forces that shaped his life and motivated his actions flowed not from his head but from his heart. He was devoted to his family especially in the later years, finding great satisfaction in telling his friends about his children and grandchildren. Those of you who are here out of respect for Judy or Dave or Marcia should reflect on how it was they came to be the kind of persons they are. It did not just happen by accident. And in an age of serial monogamy and revolving door marriages, it is no accident that all the Carpenter children have created, with their spouses stable, happy, fulfilling marriages.

From breakfasts at Berry's to the Citizen's Bank to the "new" "Truckers"-"Flyers" field house to this church, Norwalk was Larry's town and Larry was Norwalk's citizen. Though I expect Larry will flinch at the comparison, he shared with John Mellencamp a visceral understanding of and appreciation for small town life and its values. He coveted no greater honor that to be counted a useful citizen of Norwalk and a friend to her people. Reticent to talk about himself, he was quick to brag about his town. Though his abilities might have afforded him a greater fortune or permitted him to have a larger impact on the world elsewhere, he chose to stay where God had placed him and invest his talents and energy in this relatively small place.

And then there was golf. Though he enjoyed games of cards and bowling, golf was the game that preoccupied his time and his mind (sometimes to the consternation of his wife and family). Some people play golf for recreation, some for the exercise, some for the comradery, some to get outdoors, some for business, some who are as good as Larry, play for the recognition. Though Larry may have played golf for all these reasons, he played primarily, I think, for the metaphysics of the game.

For Larry Golf was more a passion than a pastime. And to fully appreciate Larry Carpenter you must understand something of the metaphysics of golf. Though not a golfer, I believe it was his relationship to and his passion for golf that opens up the deepest insights into the content of his character and the strength of his soul.

Golf is a game of infinite challenge in which one competes not so much against an opponent as against one's own best past performance and future potential. In golf there is no defense. The mastery of golf requires the mastery of oneself. It is the triumph of learned technique over brute strength – of hard and consistent work and laborious practice over inherent skill. It is a game of such intricacy and such variety of variables that improvement is always possible. Successful golf requires infinite patience and self-control, ceaseless concentration, and conscious mastery of one's physical and emotional responses. Golf both demands and refines those very characteristics that so typified Larry – self-control, diligence, perseverance, hard word, a desire for excellence and self-improvement. Golf is a humbling game and well-suited for a humble man.

In life and in golf, Larry measured success not by how well he did against someone else but by how well he did in comparison with his own best past performance and the best of which he thought he was capable. In life and in golf Larry expected more of himself than he did of others. He played golf equally comfortably with pros and duffers. He was measuring himself not against them but against himself. In his work, he was extremely demanding of himself (almost a perfectionist), but patient with the mistakes of others.

Among other things Larry enjoyed was a good game of cards. He and Myra played frequently, even after Larry was hospitalized. Cards is a good metaphor for the way Larry lived out the last few months of his life. A cardinal rule of cards is that you play the hand you are dealt. And that's what Larry did at the end – played out the hand he was dealt so skillfully that few of us knew just how bad a hand it was. He played it out with the same mixture of grit and grace, patience and perseverance, self-denial and self-discipline that he played out the other hands he had been dealt in life. He faced death and he died as he had lived – with quiet serenity, dignity, and self-control.

Last Thanksgiving, I was struck by how much joy Larry found in taking walks with his youngest grandchild, Andrew – on the same street where he must have once walked with his own father. I was reminded of a passage from Genesis. In the midst of a lot of "begats" and "begones," there is this unique passage about a man named Enoch. "Enoch walked with God and he was not, for God took him." Enoch's friends knew that the direction of Enoch's life led not to the grave but to God. A child once explained that passage by saying, "Enoch used to take long walks with God. One day they walked further than usual, and God said, 'Enoch you must be tired, come into my house and rest.'" Perhaps we can say that Larry, too, used to take long walks with God, and, well, (in the words of Paul Harvey) you know the rest of the story.

Let Us Pray.   *[I led a closing prayer.]*

[Benediction and dismissal to place of burial for a committal service.]

NOTES:
1.   This is not a misprint. It is done deliberately because the person who told me that was an old railroad rat, one of Larry Carpenter's best friends, named Sam Mann. When he told me this, saying that I could not use it, I knew I had to use it in the service because it signified as well as anything could what Larry's non-attorney friends thought of him.

JAMES ALLEN TINCH
09/02/1987

I did this service by myself

OBITUARY/EULOGY

We are gathered to give thanks to Almighty God for the life of James A. Tinch and for all that in him was good and kind and beautiful.

James Allen Tinch was born in Overton, County, Tennessee, on December 18, 1927, the only son of Paul and Amanda Rector Tinch. He was reared in the home of his aunt and uncle, Fanny and Virgil Hale in the Big Lick community, Cumberland County, Tennessee. He became to them as a son and so they treated him and so he treated them.

As a young man of 16 he accepted Christ as his Lord and Savior and united with Calvary Presbyterian Church of Big Lick where he remained an active member until his death. He never wavered in his faithfulness to his church and in 1971 was elected an Elder in the church, a position he also held until his death.

He served in the U.S. Army at the end of World War II, being stationed with the occupation forces in Okinawa and the Philippines. He willingly served his duty for his country, but he neither liked nor talked about it much. He was more a lover than a warrior, more a man of peace than a man of war.

In 1950 he married Louise Webb with whom he lived for 37 years as a loving husband and father to the two sons born of their union, Ricky and Randy. In 1952 he and Louise moved to the place that remained their home for 35 years. During that time, they transformed what can fairly be described as a ramshackle shack on a bare piece of ground into a place of beauty and comfort, turning a forsaken piece of land into a garden. And they did this "the old-fashioned way" (as the commercial has it) - by hard word, sweat and tears, diligence, perseverance, and patience.

James loved his yard and enjoyed working in it. He appreciated the beauty of a well-kept lawn filled with flowering shrubs and well- maintained shade trees. He had worked hard to get it that way, and he worked hard to keep it that way.

A conscientious worker, James was employed for years at the Crossville Rubber plant. It was not the cleanest or most pleasant place to work, but in spite of poor health, James stuck with it for 22 years.

James was a homebody who loved nothing more than being home with family and friends. Although he was a quiet, shy, retiring person, he loved people and enjoyed company. During the last few weeks of his life, he rejoiced when the house was filled with people and despaired when it was empty. He would have enjoyed the good fellowship evident at his visitation last night.

As long as he was able James enjoyed reading, keeping up with events in the world through newspapers and magazines. James lived out the last few days of his life as he had lived all the rest of it, with quiet dignity, courage, serenity, humble forbearance, and more concern for the well- being of his family than for his own comfort.

He is survived by: *[I read a list of survivors, a hymn was played, and I completed the service with a Meditation. Dismissal to place of burial for a committal service.]*

GEORGE WILLIAM COOKE, JR. OBITUARY/ EULOGY JUNE 22, 1988

[The Service was opened with the playing of Amazing Grace.] [I opened with an Invocation.]

[I read a selection of Scripture passages from among those listed in Appendix B.]

[I led an opening prayer.]

[A Hymn, In the Garden, was played.]

OBITUARY/EULOGY

George William Cooke, Jr. was born in Englewood, New Jersey on August 8, 1937, the third son of George William and Nydia Anderson Cooke.

As a teenager he was active in scouting, attaining the rank of Life Scout.

On June 21, 1959, he was married to Ellen M. Conklin, with whom he had one son, Tedi, and with whom he lived together happily and joyously for 29 years until his death. On their honeymoon, George and Ellen drove through the Sequatchie Valley, through Nine Mile, and through Pikeville, on their way to Lookout Mountain and Rock City. Little did they know then how much this valley would come to mean to them.

It is sometimes said that if a couple wants to stay married, they should not try to build a house together. It is a mark of the quality and strength of their love for each other that George and Ellen built not one but two houses together -

and they did not have them built, but designed and built them together, doing much of their own labor. And having built them, they proceeded to turn them into happy and loving homes that were always open to family and friends.

George served in the National Guard and was called to active duty as a Staff Sergeant with the 101st Signal Battalion during the Berlin Crisis in 1661-62.

For the first 46 years of his life he lived in Blauvelt, New York, where he served as a member of the Volunteer Fire Department, the Rockland Masonic Lodge # 723, and a member and trustee of the Greenbush Presbyterian Church. In Blauvelt he was active in Scouting, serving as Scoutmaster and District Commissioner for over 16 years, during which time he twice received the highest honor awarded to volunteer Scout leaders.

After moving to the Valley, he worked on his house and farm, attended Calvary Presbyterian Church of Big Lick, and assisted in organizing the Nine Mile Fire Company where he served as Assistant Chief. He was instrumental in helping the Fire Company get a fire truck. It was the same truck that his father had previously helped get for the Blauvelt Fire Department.

He had been a businessman and was retired from the New York State Thruway Authority where he was a high-level bridge painter. He worked as one of the crew of sixteen that maintained the three-mile-long Tappan Zee Bridge, one of the longest bridges in the world. He was severely injured twice in this dangerous work, the last time by a hit-and-run driver who left him with permanent injuries which forced his early retirement. But New York State's loss is the Sequatchie Valley's gain.

That he overcame these potentially disabling injuries (both physically and emotionally) and turned an experience that might have left his crippled and embittered into and opportunity for a new life of blessing to his family and his new community is a mark of his character, strength, determination, and joyful spirit. That spirit may best be summed up by one of his new neighbors who told me last night that, "He was just more full of joy than anybody else I ever saw."

George was a dreamer, a doer, a learner, a lover; an energetic and visionary man who enjoyed people and loved to talk. He was a gregarious, outgoing, warm, friendly, open person who shared himself freely. He brought to his new community the same spirit he had shown in Blauvelt. What a different world this might be if more people were willing to extend themselves for others as George did.

He was a competent, careful, creative, skillful craftsman who believed that any job worth doing was worth doing well. When he did a job, it was done right. You did not need to know George to know this about him; all you need to do is look at some of his work.

George had an enthusiasm for living. He enjoyed life and all living things. He often walked on the edge of life, not so much because he was reckless (though that may have been true at times), but more because he loved life and desired to live it to its fullest – and to do that one must go to the very edge of life. That may be why those who like George are brim full of the vitality and energy of life sometimes skirt close to the edge of danger and death.

It seems strange that one whose like and work often took him into dangerous situations, should die so quietly, so peacefully - sitting in a rocking chair looking over the serene meadows in front of his Sequatchie Valley home. Yet, in a way, he died as he lived, calmly, confidently, without trace of regret or remorse, hastily without delay, with words of endearment on his lips. When things had to be done, George wanted them done right now! He could not stand being idle.

When it came time for him to die, it was as if God granted him his wishes. It was done quickly, without a long period of suffering, disability, or inactivity. If such choices were ours to make, he died the way he would have chosen – at the end of a week and weekend when he had been able to do those things and spend time with those people whom he most loved.

George died on June 19, 1988.

He is survived by *[I read a list of surviving relatives.]* Also, by his dogs Ace and Saint, by the crew of the Nine Mile Fire Company, and by numerous neighbors and friends in both Tennessee and New York.

Ellen and her family want to thank you for your prayers and support during this difficult time, and they invite all of you to come by her house after the service.

[I led an interim prayer and the hymn "Sweet Hour of Prayer" was played.]

[I closed the service with a Meditation.]

ANNA MARY EVERMAN BRADLEY OBITUARY/ EULOGY - June 30, 1989

I conducted this service by myself

OPENING SCRIPTURES

[I read some of the Scripture passages listed in Appendix B. I have no record of and do not remember which ones I used.]

OBITUARY/EULOGY

We are gathered to give thanks to God for the life of Anna Mary Everman Bradley.

Anna Mary Everman was born in Kentucky on February 28 sometime before 1920. (I know the year but am sworn to secrecy and Anna Mary would probably come back to haunt me if I revealed it.) As a young woman Anna Mary displayed the independence of mind, the strength of conviction, and the unconquerable, indomitable spirit that were to mark her as the remarkably unique woman that so enriched our lives. In opposition to her parents' wishes, she entered nursing school at Berea College. Her father felt that nursing was not a fit profession for a young lady. Her parents wanted her to stay closer to home, attend Morehead College and become a teacher. Anna Mary went to Berea where she graduated from the Nursing School in 1939. Had she not made that decision it is unlikely that most of us would ever have had the opportunity to know her.

From Berea she went to serve as a missionary nurse at Pitman Center in Sevier County, the home of Dolly Parton. Had Anna Mary stayed a little bit longer in Pitman Center she would have been the attending nurse/midwife at the birth of Dolly. As it was, she had to be satisfied with having helped deliver some of Dolly's older brothers and sisters.

Instead, in 1940 she followed the calling of the Lord to an even more remote outpost, a place called Big Lick where she became the resident nurse at the Warren H. Wilson House of Health, opened only two years previously.

Upon arriving in Big Lick, she shortly caught the eye of a young red- headed gentleman by the name of Elmo "Red" Bradley. They both loved folk and square dance at the Friday night Socials in Big Lick. They began "seeing each other," as it was said back then, and before long their relationship began to get serious, although it had its ups and downs. I remember one story of a certain Sunday in particular when Anna Mary, independent and spunky as she always was, showed up at church with another young man much to the chagrin of Elmo. (I know the name of that young man also, but in order to protect the innocent, I won't reveal it.)

But whatever differences they may have had, there were soon reconciled. And on October 2, 1942, Anna Mary Everman became Anna Mary Bradley and embarked on a remarkable career as nurse, wife, mother, grandmother, mother-in-law, community worker and neighbor for which most of us remember her. They were married by the Rev. Eugene Smathers who had recruited Anna Mary to come to Big Lick.

Anna Mary and "Red" immediately revealed the adventuresome spirit, determination, and quest for life and learning that would mark so much of their life together. In some defiance of the local draft board, they took off on a two months long honeymoon trip that took them through seven states – wherever they could find relatives or someone else to take them in and bootleg gasoline available.

For 46 years and 8 months, Anna Mary and Elmo made a marriage, built a life, and reared a family together. To their union five children were born, one of whom, John, preceded his mother in death.

Anna Mary loved her home, her family, her garden, her chickens, her flowers, her neighbors and her community. She was open, generous and kind. She enjoyed giving things away and would often caution the recipient of a plant or vegetable, "Don't thank me. If you do it may die or spoil."

Some people are said to have a "green thumb." Anna Mary must have had a green hand. Anyone who has seen her gardens can attest to that.

She was a good nurse - conscientious, caring, and gentle with patients. However, she never really liked the routine or constraints of hospital duty.

She preferred community nursing. She was too much of a free spirit to be comfortable under the thumb of doctors and hospital rules (though she understood their necessity.)

I can speak personally about the quality of Anna Mary's nursing skill. She spent many days and nights helping care for my father during his last illness and was present when he died. But it goes back further than that. Though some of you have known her longer than I have, none of you have known by her for a larger percentage of your years. She was one of the first two people to see me enter this world (a tale she loved to tell). A doctor was scheduled to be there but was late. Anna Mary as the attending nurse did the job of helping my mother deliver me. She saw me, touched me, and cared for me even before my mother.

Anna Mary loved music. She played the auto-harp and the piano and organ a little. She loved to sing with her grandchildren. Some of her grandchildren's fondest memories are of grandmother singing to them. However, she could also be gruff and blunt – almost shockingly so sometimes. She had an independent streak, a quick mind, and firm opinions. She could be set in her ways as if in concrete. On the other hand, especially with children, she could be patient, gentle, loving, and forgiving. She knew how to forgive, and she could tolerate an unworldly amount of commotion.

She was supportive of her children, grandchildren, and children-in-laws. Though the bodily organ we call a heart may have failed he, the spiritual center of our being which we also refer to as heart never wavered or weakened. As weak as her physical heart was, her spiritual heart remained strong to the end.

Anna Mary died after an extended period of declining health on June 27, 1989, some years past the three score and ten allotted to us by Scripture. She is survived by:

[I read a list of survivors.]

[I led an interim prayer and a hymn was played.]

[To get the full impact of this Eulogy you must also read the Meditation contained in the Second Section of this Collection. That Meditation is part Eulogy.]

BELLE BLAYLOCK KERLEY BITUARY/ EULOGY – AUGUST 17, 1989

Funerals are historic occasions. For most of us they are one of the ways we mark the passing of time and the changes in our lives. For 86 years, God has blessed and brightened little bits of His world, including every one of us here, through the life of Belle Blaylock Kerley. As of August 15, 1989, that has changed. History passes on; only eternity remains unchanged.

We are gathered to bear witness to our faith in the Resurrection through Jesus Christ and to give thanks to Almighty God for the life of Belle Blaylock Kerley. Praise be to God for giving her life, for endowing her with such fine qualities of character, and for sharing her with us.

[I led an opening prayer here and a hymn was played.] OBITUARY/EULOGY

Yes, let us give thanks to God for the life of Belle Blaylock Kerley. In the third year that Theodore Roosevelt was President; in the year that Orville and Wilbur Wright first achieved flight on a sandy dune below Kill Devil Hill in Kitty Hawk, North Carolina; five years before the first Model T rolled out of Henry Ford's Piquette Plant in Detroit, on January 27 of that year, 1903, in the south end of Cumberland County a new baby girl was born to Edward and Zenia Burgess Blaylock. They named her Anora Belle. She never liked that first name, though it was also the name of her best neighbor, so we came to know and love her simply as Belle.

Of all those events, historians have failed to note only that birth. But we will not make that mistake today, because none of these events has touched our lives as meaningfully as that birth. Among other things, funerals are for remembering, and they should remind us that the real substance of our lives is not defined by political conquests, technological advances, or mechanical innovations, but by the content of the character and the strength of the spirit of those persons whom we count as loved ones, neighbors, and friends.

It is the content of Belle's character and the strength of her spirit which makes this a time for rejoicing; which makes today not so much a low point in our own journey from the cradle to the grave as it is a day of rare privilege. Indeed, how fortunate we are to grieve today, because our grief means we had the rare privilege of knowing, loving and being loved by Belle Blaylock Kerley.

On May 1, 1921, she married Alvin Kerley with whom she lived as loving and devoted wife until his death in 1968. They were together 47 years, the last 29 of which Alvin was bedfast, blind, and unable to move or assist himself in any way. So constant and conscientious was her care and nursing of him during all those years that never once did he become distraught nor suffer even one bedsore.

Out of their marriage, eight children were born, seven of whom survive their mother.

Belle was a plain and humble woman. She never made much money, never bought herself a new dress, never lived in a fine home, never did anything to be accounted great or important as the world measures such things. But he had the qualities of character which truly endure. Qualities which the Apostle Paul calls the fruits of the Spirit, "love, joy, peace, patience, kindness, goodness, faithfulness, gentleness, self-control. . ." (Galatians 5: 12-23a)

Belle was a person of devotion and strength. When we think of strength, we often think of someone who is robust, muscular, powerful. But real strength comes from somewhere else, somewhere deep inside a person. And Belle, slight, frail, burdened, often undernourished, ill, distressed had IT. Strength is walking three miles to catch a truck and ride in the back fourteen miles to sew mattresses all day, and then ride 14 miles and walk 3 miles back at night, six days a week. And then come home to an invalid husband and a growing family. All to make $15 a month to support your family.

Strength is washing on a washboard, cooking on a wood stove, carrying water from a neighbor's. Strength is fixing meals, feeding your husband, feeding the children, and then eating what is left over, if anything. Strength is keeping your house immaculately clean through all of this even with small children underfoot. Strength was doing this day in and day out, with no days off.

Helen was lamenting this past week about the mental anguish her mother must have suffered during all those years, always doing for others, never for herself. But that is the miracle. It is not so much that Belle endured all the hardships, toil, and troubles; others have endured as much. No, the miracle is that Belle did all this day in and day out, with hardly a break, without ever becoming embittered or resentful or losing her sense of humor. That is the real miracle -- a miracle of Grace that made her life a benediction to anyone who knew her.

What a different world this would be if those with great responsibilities and great duties would fulfill them with the same devotion with which Belle fulfilled the responsibilities and duties that fell upon her. All of us who are married have promised to love, honor, cherish and serve one another through good times and bad, through health and sickness. What a witness of fidelity to those vows was Belle's 29 years of caring for Alvin from the onset of his disease until his death.

Belle leaves behind a great heritage - courage in the face of difficulty, cheerfulness in adversity, patience through suffering, a great capacity for friendship, a sense of joy and gratitude for the good that came her way (as little as it was). Someone remarked to me that they did not know anyone as much like Job as Belle. There is much truth in that statement. Surely Belle is in heaven, she has already endured her share of hell. She will be remembered as a patient, kind, unselfish, forgiving, and believing lady, who kept merriment always about her.

In the 31st Chapter of Proverbs, there is a description of a real lady and a good wife. It begins: "A true lady is hard to find; she is more precious than jewels..." And it ends by saying: "Give her the reward of her labor, and let the gates ring with praise of her deeds." Indeed, let the gates ring with praise of her deeds.

Belle never liked to be away from home. Carmon told me how he had once taken her to Houston hoping that she would stay with him awhile there. But no later than when they arrived, Belle wanted to come home to her little house in Big Lick. On August 15, 1989, Belle began the one final journey that we must all make. And we can now be reassured that she is finally home and at peace as she has never been before.

She is survived by: *[I read the list of survivors.]*

[I led an interim prayer and a hymn was played, and I closed the service with a Meditation and dismissal to place of burial for a committal service.]

JAMES WALTER "JACK" TOLLETT OBITUARY/ EULOGY – MARCH 3, 1990

[I did this whole service. The deceased was not a professing Christian. Other than not being a conventional believer, Jack was solid as a rock.]

OBITUARY/EULOGY

James Walter Tollett, known more simply to his friends and neighbors as "Jack," was born on December 13, 1923, in a little log house in the Big Lick community across the road from the home in which he died. He was the second child and first son of Kay and Bertha Sherrill Tollett.

As a young man he came calling on Anna Lou Nail riding one of the team of mares he used in his timbering work. And those who knew Jack well, who knew his love of animals and for the woods and the fields probably suspect that there were times when Anna Lou must have wondered which Jack loved the most - her or that mare. Be that as it may, on April 14, 1945, Jack and Anna Lou eloped to Rossville, Georgia, where they were married. To their union five children, two daughters and three sons were born, all of whom survive their father and live much as he did within a few miles of where they were born.

Jack was a worker - a sun-up to sun-down, seven days a week worker. Other than his family, he lived for his work, and sometimes it was his work that came first. But all of those who hold in high esteem those who make their living by the sweat of their brow and the skill of their hands; who understand the worth of manual labor – all those so inclined will mourn Jack's death. He was a man who valued his skill with a dozer and as a farmer above anything else he possessed. He was a man of honor and integrity who never pretended to be anything other than what he was and who always gave a full day's effort to any job he undertook.

There is a book of near-scripture that is included in some older Bibles but not in the ones we use today. It is called The Wisdom of Joshua ben Sirach. In the 39th chapter of his book, ben Sirach writes:

> "The wisdom of the scribe depends on the opportunity for leisure, And he who has little business may become wise.
> How can the one become wise who handles the plow, who gathers in the animals,
>
> Who works with teams and is occupied with their work, and whose talk is about the cattle?
> He sets his heart on plowing furrows and is careful to get feed for the heifers..."

He goes on to talk about the work of the craftsman, the blacksmith, and the potter, and then he writes:

> "All these rely upon their hands, and each is skillful in his own work.
> Without them a community cannot be established
> And people can neither visit nor live there. . .
> They keep stable the fabric of the world,
> And their prayer is in the practice of their trade."
>
> [MFS Translation]

Indeed, Jack's prayers, if any, were in the practice of his trade, and he was among those who helped to keep stable the fabric of the world.

Jack was country. Before, during and after country ever became cool, Jack was country. In the depth of his being, in ways that those who only pretend to live a country lifestyle will never be able to understand, Jack was country. And all of those who truly hold in high regard rural life and country values; those who believe in the beauty and honor of a genuinely country way of life; those who value the soil and those who work it; those who believe in the simple rural virtues of friendliness, neighborliness, hard work, simple living, a dollar's worth of effort for every dollar paid - all of those so inclined will mourn Jack's passing. With his death, we lose one more of the last generation of folks who were and are uncomplicatedly, uncompromisingly, unchangeably country - in outlook, in values, and in lifestyle.

Jack was a neighbor. Perhaps a point best made by one of his country neighbors who gave Anna Lou a note yesterday expressing how much Jack had meant to her as a neighbor. [I read the note at the funeral but no longer have it and cannot reprint it here.]

Among those who knew him best, Jack will be remembered for his unusual sense of humor, his neighborliness, and his virtues. He never drank any kind of alcohol, never smoked, never used foul language. He was stubborn and kept his own counsel. He could be rigid and unyielding in his attitudes, perhaps too much so, but it must be said that Jack Tollett lived as he believed. There was no hypocrisy in him.

He was stoic, strong, seemingly never sick, and for one who worked in timber, on a dozer, and as a farmer remarkably free of accidents. He never had a broken bone. Before his final illness he had spent the grand total of one night in a hospital - that was because of the one serious accident he did have which cost him the sight in one eye.

Jack never complained. For one who had little experience with ill health, who had been used to being active all the time, he made a very compromising patient - following his doctor's orders to a "T." Lana Sue said he became like a lamb during his illness - perhaps like a lion who became a lamb. He so impressed his doctors with his spirit and attitude that one of them called the family from Nashville to express what an impression Jack had made on him and how he had come to admire Jack over the past eighteen months.

Jack never lingered much over anything except dying. The long months of his final illness, the necessity of being hooked to a machine periodically, the forced inactivity, and the ravages of the disease which sapped the vitality from his once strong body may have gnawed at his inner spirit and may have caused him to welcome death, but they never caused him to complain. Though frustrated by the disease and the inability of his body and/or the doctors to do anything about it, Jack never gave in to the temptation of bitterness or remorse or recrimination. He accepted the inevitability of death with the same stoic determination, the same doggedness and fortitude with which he had faced life.

Jack died at home on March 1, 1990, 66 years, 2 months, and 15 days after he had been born at home in the little log cabin immediately across the road from the house in which he died.

He is survived by: *[I inserted a list of survivors.]*

The family wishes to thank everyone for all their kindnesses and expressions of sympathy during this time.

> *[I led an interim prayer, a hymn was played, and I closed the service with a Meditation.]*

ELMO "RED" BRADLEY OBITUARY/EULOGY – MAY 1, 1990

I did this entire service by myself.

INTRODUCTION

I stood on the porch at Elmo's last Sunday, two weeks after Easter, and looked over Lick Creek toward the hills beyond. The trees along the creek, maples, birch, beech are in full leaf. The oak leaves on the hills beyond are about the size of a squirrel's ear. Mother always said you were supposed to plant something when the oak leaves were the size of a squirrel's ear, but for the life of me, I can't remember what it is that you are supposed to plant.

Through the picture window by Elmo's kitchen table a hummingbird was visible, eating at the recently filled feeder. Beyond that the garden spot blossomed red with its crimson clover cover crop. There were signs of life all around - and signs of Elmo's hand. But that hand no longer stirred - the life that so animated this house - that had been so full, so rich, so vibrant, so vital - was no longer there.

And that absence brings us sorrow. Children played in these rooms last night, more or less oblivious to what was going on around us. Life goes on; the signs of life surround us, but today we think of death and there is sorrow. Sorrow is inevitable whenever we meet to give thanks for the life of one whom death has taken from among us. There is no shame in our tears. They water the eternal rose of love. Sorrow and grief are but the flip side of love. To love and be loved means inevitably to suffer sorrow and grief.

OBITUARY/EULOGY

Elmo "Red" Bradley - leader, lover, laugher, learner, listener, storyteller, inventor of language, Christian and churchman is gone, and we are the poorer for it.

This is not the first time I have done this - spoken a eulogy about Elmo Bradley. The first time was thirty years ago in a speech class my freshman year of college. All of us - the ten-twelve students in the class had to deliver a eulogy. It was one of the required speeches. Most spoke of famous people - Kennedy, Eisenhower, or a parent or minister or teacher - someone they looked up to.

I, too, spoke of someone I looked up to, but not someone famous. I spoke of Elmo. I had decided early on that I would speak about someone I knew, and I wanted to make the point that a person's worth is not a matter of how the world measures greatness. It is rather a measure of the quality of character and of the impact that a person has on those around him. It is not a matter of how much a person has but of what that person does with what he or she has.

It was "Red" who stood out most in my mind, and so it was "Red" who was the object of my eulogy. I don't remember much of what I said that day. I know I said some of the same things I will say today. I spoke about Elmo's wit and wisdom; his courage and capacity for caring; his leadership and other qualities of his character.

I was young then, naive, and less jaded by the realities of the world. My reflections came from a juvenile experience. But I have now lived as an adult with Elmo as my neighbor for the past sixteen years and have been his pastor for ten. I know things now that I never dreamed of then - both good and bad.

I know now how human Elmo was - how much he hurt sometimes and how much he could hurt others sometimes too. I know that he could be too bullheaded; that he made mistakes; that he did not always make the best decisions. I know that he was stained with sin, had failings and foibles and feet of clay just like the rest of us.

But I have never, not never, changed my mind that Elmo was one of the most unforgettable characters, one of the most honorable and impressive human beings, and one of the most gracious and conscientious Christians I have ever known.

I will miss him. And I will always regret that I never got around to getting him on tape - to recording some of his stories and recollections, his wit and wisdom. He had a unique way of making a thought take on life in the language he used - inventing new words almost as often as Shakespeare in order to make himself clearly understood. I am sad today.

But I cannot be sad for long, because there was so little in Elmo to be sad about. There was so little darkness in him, and I know what a rare privilege has been mine to have been, along with you and a few others - of all the people who ever lived - one of the few who really knew Elmo Bradley. We are among the few who were really close to him; one of a handful who shared an abiding familial love with him. Indeed, how privileged we are to grieve today.

Elmo Mitchell ("Red") Bradley was born on April 12, 1917, the youngest child of John Harrison and Elizabeth Houlette Bradley - born in the same house overlooking Lick Creek, in sight of the salt lick that gave Big Lick its name, the same house where he died. In 1940 he took a liking to a young nurse who had just moved to Big Lick. They soon fell to courting, and on October 2, 1942, Elmo and Anna Mary Everman were married. They lived together as faithful husband and wife until her death less than a year ago.

Upon their marriage, Red and Anna Mary immediately revealed the adventuresome spirit, the independence, the determination and quest for life that characterized much of their life together. The local draft board told Elmo that he was due to be drafted soon, and that he should not leave the county. Elmo told the draft board he figured the war would still be there when he got back and they could draft him then. He and Anna Mary took off on a two-month honeymoon trip that took them through Kentucky, Arkansas, Georgia, Alabama, North Carolina and Virginia - to wherever they could find relatives or friends to put them up and enough bootleg gas to get them there.

Upon their return, Elmo was indeed drafted in January 1943. He landed on the beaches of Normandy on June 7, 1944, D-Day + one. He served with distinction, winning a battlefield promotion to staff Sergeant (writing home to tell his parents that it was no big deal; all it meant was that all in front of him had been killed or wounded). In truth it was but the first of a long list of appointments that marked Elmo as a leader among men.

As he got older, Red, like many old soldiers, relished telling about his war experiences - the landing at Normandy with death all around, the thirty-pound German 88 shell that landed ten feet away, spun hissing, but failed to explode, stuffing straw in his boots that winter to keep his feet from freezing, his wounds - one of them in the "bung hole" as he expressed it. But he never dwelt on those experiences, for he was more a lover than a warrior, more a builder than a destroyer, more attracted to life than to death.

He returned to Big Lick where he homesteaded and repurchased the family farm through the Calvary Church Homestead Project. He began a remarkable career as husband, father, farmer, teacher, cooperator, neighbor, citizen, and community leader. Despite his eight-grade education but because of his innate intelligence, he was not only selected as a teacher for returning GI's, but earned the reputation as one of the best teachers in the program even though he sometimes had his students write words on the board for him because he was unsure of how to spell them.

He became an award-winning farmer (the first in Cumberland County whose fields produced 100 bushels of corn per acre). He took leadership roles in practically all the farm-oriented organizations in the county - the Fair Association, the Soil Conservation District, the Farm Bureau, and the Cumberland County Farmers' Cooperative which he helped organize and served over time as Board Member, Chairman, and Manager. He was a coop man, he said, and he remained unflinchingly loyal to the Coop. That was the way he was in everything he did - his church, his marriage, his friendships, his memberships, his leadership positions. Once Elmo made a commitment, you knew you could depend on him no matter what. His word was his bond, as much so as any person I have ever met. He loved life and people and liked to dance and play ball.

He was a Christian and a churchman. He made a profession of faith and united with Calvary Church of Big Lick on September 1, 1929, helped build the church in 1934-35, the Sunday school addition in 1954-55, and the kitchen in 1960. He was elected an Elder on January 29, 1961, and when he died was serving on the important Pastor Nominating Committee.

He is survived by:

> *[I read a list of survivors including a "shor-nuff" bunch of neighbors and friends.]*

Elmo died quietly, sitting at his kitchen table, without struggle and apparently without pain on the night of April 28, 1990, one day after he had so enlivened a community auction, by auctioning the shoes off his feet. He was as happy as he had ever been. He told me so earlier on the day of his death as I sat talking with him at his kitchen table.

Let us Pray: *[I led an interim prayer.]*

[A hymn was played.]

[I closed the service with a Meditation, that is also part Eulogy.]

ERNEST BLAYLOCK FUNERAL REMARKS – APRIL 30, 1994

I used Generic Meditation #2 printed at the end of this Collection after the Obituary/Eulogy.

"Blessed be the God and Father of our Lord Jesus Christ! By God's great mercy we have been born anew to a living hope through the Resurrection of Jesus Christ from the dead."

"Praise be to God, for we do not grieve as those who have no hope!" Jesus said, "I am the resurrection and the life. Those who believe in me, though they die, yet shall they live" "Come to me all who are burdened and heavy laden, and I will give you rest." "Blessed are those who mourn; they shall be comforted."

"Our help is in the name of the Lord who made heaven and earth!"

OBITUARY/EULOGY and MESSAGE OF HOPE and HEALING: WITNESS TO THE RESURRECTION

Ernest Martin Blaylock was born on November 12, 1895, in the southwestern edge of Cumberland County, near Thomas Springs or Erasmus or somewhere in that vicinity (in what had been a part of White County only 39 years earlier). He was the fourth child and second son of what would eventually be eleven children born to George Edward and Zenia Burgess Blaylock.

His was a life of historic proportions. Dying six months short of his 99th birthday, his life spanned the whole length of the 20th Century. Born five years before the beginning of the 20th Century, he died six years before the beginning of the 21st Century. Born the year radio was first introduced, five years after the Indian Wars ended at Wounded Knee; he was nine when the Wright Brothers finally got a plane off the ground at Kill Devil Hill in Kitty Hawk, North Carolina; fourteen when the first Model T rolled out of Henry Ford's shop in Detroit, and forty-six when penicillin was first introduced. From the horse and wagon to a man on the moon; from the bull-tongued plow to GPS controlled tractors, he rode the most inventive century in the history of humankind from beginning to end. He will probably be the last person I will ever help burry who was born before the turn of the 20th Century.

He served in the Navy during WWI. Shortly thereafter he married Flora "Viola" Cobble to whom he remained a loving husband for almost 72 years until her death four years ago. To their union three children, two sons and a daughter were born. Together they created a loving, close knit, supportive family.

Ern is survived by: *[I inserted a list of survivors.]*

He was preceded in death by his parents, his wife Vi and nine of his ten brothers and sisters

Ern was a plain and simple man, never accounted great as the world measures such things, but he was a person of a grand scale. Not only in physical size, but the size of his heart and his gregarious good nature. He was fun loving, friendly, gracious, giving, gentle man who loved people, was devoted to his family, and generous to neighbors. That latter I can personally attest to, having lived as his next-door neighbor for many years.

He was a person of upstanding character and impeccable integrity whom his neighbors trusted with considerable authority. He served as a deputy sheriff on three different occasions and at least once as a Justice of the Peace. He helped put the first prisoner in the "new" (now the "old") jail. He is the only and I know he is the last person I will ever help burry who in fact hunted down and arrested a real horse thief.

But the time I remember best is two hot, tense weeks in August 1954. Ern, duly deputized at the requests of his Neighbors, sat in his rocking chair with his shotgun by his side and helped patrol the roads at night – doing so to prevent a group of hell-raisers from interrupting the work being done on the Sunday School addition to the church by a group of young people which contained one very black young man. He did so to help protect the right of a person in America to go where he pleased and engage in the mission work he wanted to do no matter the color of his skin. A proposition that some people found unsettling if not downright worthy of mob violence.

Ern was many things in his life - coal miner, sailor, farmer, gardener. He helped to make airplane propellers during WWII. He worked as a security guard at the Wright-Patterson Air Force Base. But above all else Ern was a storyteller. And Ern did not tell little stories, he told whoppers.

He once said as a young man a bear was chasing him and rammed his fist down the bear's throat and yanked - thereby turning the bear inside out and causing it to run the other way.

But the story I remember best was told one Sunday afternoon when I was visiting my friend Major Hamilton. Ern and his family - Vi, Fred, Bob and Wanda - drove up from Winesap to Big Lick that afternoon to visit Ern's sister, Mabel, and her family. The car they were driving was not in the best of conditions. Ern said the car had a broken steering wheel, and that on the way he, Fred, and Bob had to take a turnabout. One of them would drive while the other two rode on the running boards and every time they came to a curve, one or the other of then would have to jump off and kick the wheel in order for them to turn the curve.

I think I have the bear story figured out. As for the car story, I was young and gullible then, and Ern swore it was true. The fact was that two of them were riding on the running boards, but I never saw one of then get off to kick the tires so they could turn into Ralph and Mabel's yard. One older gentleman upon hearing the story said, "Well if Ern Blaylock told it, it must be true." I will never know whether it was truth or fiction or a little bit of both.

Ern traveled a lot - Kentucky, West Virginia, Ohio. Perhaps that is why he joined the Navy. It was not just the going that Ern liked but meeting new people and visiting old friends. But when Ern was my neighbor for the better part of the first eighteen years of my life, I remember how he loved to sit on his front porch and watch the world go by. And so, I find this poem appropriate. It is entitled "The House by the Side of the Road," by Sam Walter Foss:

"I see from my house by the side of the road,
By the side of the highway of life:
The men who press with the ardor of hope;
The men who are faint with the strife.
But I turn not away from their smiles nor their tears,
Both part of an infinite plan –

> *Let me live in a house by the side of the road*
> *And be a friend to man."*

We live in a world in which the forces of darkness and death often seem to overshadow the forces of light and life. Yet the Apostle Paul wrote to the Romans: "We know that in everything God works for good with those who love him, who are called according to his purpose." (Rom. 8:28)

We look for evidence – something more that the thunder of the sun that fills this day; something more than the brilliance of the dogwoods that brighten this season. We look for some more substantial evidence that indeed God works for good with those who love him, for something that demonstrates that light will overcome the darkness and life will outlast death.

I suggest to you that we are gathered today to give thanks for just such evidence.

> *"This perishable nature must put on the imperishable, and this mortal nature must put on immortality" Paul wroth to the church at Corinth, "When the perishable puts on the imperishable, and the mortal puts on immortality, then shall come to pass the saying that is written: 'Death is swallowed up in victory.' 'O death, where is your victory? O death where is your sting?'. . . But thanks be to God, who gives us the victory throughout Lord Jesus Christ. Therefore, my beloved brethren, be steadfast, immovable, always abounding in the work of the Lord, knowing that in the Lord your labor is not in vain." (1 Corinthians 15: 53 - 58)*

Amen and Amen.

Let us Pray.   *[I led an interim prayer.]*

[A hymn was played.]

[I concluded with the Generic Meditation # 2 printed at the end of this Collection.]

[Benediction and dismissal to place of burial for a committal service.]

MARY BLAYLOCK FUNERAL REMARKS – MAY 4, 1994

I was charged with doing only one of the two eulogies for this service. The other was done by a grandson of the deceased. He also opened the service.

OBITUARY/EULOGY

"Praise be to God for we do not grieve as those who have no hope."

Thanks be to Almighty God for the life of Mary Hyder Blaylock. For 90 years God has blessed and brightened little bits of His world with the life of Mary Hyder Blaylock. As of May 1, 1994, that has changed.

Think of the year 1903: Theodore Roosevelt was in his first term as President.
In Detroit, Henry Ford was tinkering around with a motorized bicycle.
Five years later his first Model T would roll out of his shop.
In December of that year, two other bicycle mechanics, Orville and Wilbur Wright, on a stretch of beach below Kill Devil Hill in Kitty Hawk North Carolina, made a very short trip on a machine that would come to be called an airplane.
Crossville was three years old and had six laws, three against whiskey and three against prostitution.
There were no cars in Cumberland County.

There was a boom in timber with forty mills
operating.

Two Crossville homes had running water and indoor
plumbing.

J. E. Taylor was operating a boarding house. Eighteen
years later he would convert it to the Hotel Taylor.

And on November 19 of that year in the Vandever Community, Isaac and Elzada Campbell Hyder had a baby girl. They gave her a Biblical name, Mary.

Of all these events that birth has meant more to us than any of the other events. Among other things funerals are for remembering. And it is good to remember that what really matters in this world is the content of the character and the strength of the spirit of those we count as loved ones, neighbors, and friends.

Her life spanned virtually the entire 20th Century. We should remember the past with thanksgiving, although we cannot go back there to live. We should remember that it is the quality of Mary's character and the spunk of her spirit not merely the length of her years which makes today not a low point in our own journey from the cradle to the grave, but rather a day of rare privilege. Indeed, how fortunate we are to grieve today because it means that we loved and were loved by Mary Blaylock. A love she passed down to her children and they to their children. Mary was blessed with those qualities which in the Bible are called "Fruits of the Spirit: love, joy, peace, patience, kindness, goodness, faithfulness, gentleness, self-control." (Galatians 5: 22-23)

On December 17, 1924, at the age of 21 she married Isaac Blaylock with whom she lived as a loving wife until his death. Of their union five children were born. Mary was a mother. Left alone by the tragic death of her husband when her youngest child was only a few weeks old and the eldest but 12, she raised all of them, with help from her brothers and sisters, to be persons of high moral character and spiritual strength. And then she helped to raise several of her grandchildren, being, as Daryl has noted, like a second mother to them.

Mary joined Calvary Presbyterian Church of Big Lick the same year she was married. At her death she had been an active member of that church for years, longer than anyone else ever has. (It helps to join as a young woman three years after the church is founded and live to be 90.)

In the 12th Chapter of his letter to the Romans, the Apostle Paul defines the life of a Christian this way:

"Let love be genuine; hate what is evil, hold fast to what is good; love one another with brotherly [sic] affection; . . . never flag in zeal, be aglow with the Spirit, serve the Lord. Rejoice in your hope; be patient in tribulation, be constant in prayer . . . practice hospitality . . . Rejoice with those who rejoice; weep with those who weep. Live in harmony with one another; do not be haughty but associate with the lowly; never be conceited . . . If possible, as far as it depends on upon you, live peaceably with all . . . Do not be overcome by evil, but overcome evil with good."

(Romans 12: 9-21, Selected Verses)

Paul would have been glad to have had Mary as a friend. Mary died on May 1, 1914, after a lingering illness.

She is survived by: *[I read a list of survivors.]*

Mary was a patient woman. She took her time with whatever she did - cooking, sewing, visiting with a friend. But perhaps she lingered too long over dying. I do not know why some people linger so over dying. It happened, too, with my mother. It seems to our way of thinking that it would have been more merciful had Mary been spared the pain and distress of her last days. Perhaps it was that she was one of those people whose example is so exemplary that God was reluctant to take her from among us.

I do know part of the reason that Mary confounded the medical experts, and lived so much longer than they thought she would. It was that she spent her last days at home where she received such loving care from Mabel, Oliver, Diane, Daryl, Larry, Frances, and other members of her family, neighbors, and friends. In a time when we hear so much about what is wrong with families, what a witness this was to what is good and right about families.

And I further believe with all my heart that Mary died at peace and took with her the only thing of value any of us can take out of this world. Mary died secure in the knowledge that she was loved.

Let us pray.   *[I led an interim prayer, and a hymn was played.]*

[A message of hope and healing, a witness to the Resurrection followed, led by another pastor.]

[Dismissal to the place of burial for a committal service.]

JESSIE ROY RHEA OBITUARY/EULOGY – FEBRUARY 14, 1996

I shared this service with another pastor. My charge was primarily the Obituary/Eulogy, and I pretty much stuck to that except for two short sentences at the end.

As the snow thawed last week, I noticed new shoots of spring flower poking through the ground. Buds on the forsythia are straining at the husks surrounding them. In Jessie's flower bed along the edge of her yard yesterday I noticed the plant we know as a hen and chickens already awakened from its winter nap, popping out of the ground. That particular plant seemed especially appropriate as I remembered Jessie. In the same hospital where you so recently gathered to grieve a loss, others came to celebrate a birth. At the house yesterday and in this room last night there were a number of infants and toddlers. We are surrounded by the signs of life.

But for now, there is sorrow. There is no shame in our tears. Sorrow and grief are but the flip side of love. To love and be loved means inevitably to suffer sorrow and grief.

Death intrudes on us all. Its intrusion dulls life's brightness and casts a shadow of heartbreak on our souls. Indeed, there is sadness here today. But let us rejoice also - rejoice in thanksgiving for the life of Jessie Rhea and for the graciousness of God offered us in Jesus Christ, and so abundantly reflected in Jessie's life.

Yesterday at Jake and Jessie's I could sense Jessie's spirit hovering over that room like a mother hen over a brood of chickens. That is the way Jessie was.

How full of joy your hearts must be to have had the rare privilege to have loved and been loved by such a unique and remarkable woman.

Jessie was born on June 29, 1923, to John and Stacy Myers Roy, who named her Jessie Louise after an aunt. On late spring day in 1948, she took a box of cakes and pies and who knows what else to a pie supper held at the old Bethel school house. Jake Rhea and Buster Winingham were bidding on her box. Jake bought her box partly to keep Buster from getting it. Jessie who loved to cook had met her match in Jake who loved to eat. Jake is the only remaining principal in that little Big Lick love story. The old Bethel school house is falling down and Jessie and Buster are gone.

They were married on Christmas Day, 1948, and for over 47 years, Jessie was Jake's faithful wife, friend, and helpmate. For 30 of those years, from 1955- 1985, she was also co-provider for their family, working at Mosier Laces (later Roselon), the hospital, and finally Denison Carter. In the words of one of her grandchildren, "She was a strong woman before women were supposed to be strong." Indeed, although she excelled at and took pride in the domestic arts, she was a liberated woman before that term came into common usage.

She was a much beloved member and Elder of Calvary Presbyterian Church of Big Lick, an active member of Farm Bureau Women, a caring neighbor, a dependable nurse to sick family and friends, a respected leader in her community, and above all else a loving wife, mother, grandmother, and sister.

Images of Jessie flit through my memory like a butterfly on a warm spring day. I remember her as a bride, standing with Jake in the living room of the old Presbyterian Manse with my father presiding and my mother, my aunt Ruth, myself, and our dog Missy as witnesses. (Only Jake and I have that privilege - we are the only two left of the seven who were there that day.) Though I was only seven, I can see it in my memory's eye as clearly as if it happened a few months ago. It is one of my clearest childhood memories.

I remember her from my youth as a Sunday school and Bible school teacher and recreation leader, as an adult 4-H leader, and most clearly as one of those remarkable people who fill my memories of childhood with nostalgia.

I remember her from more recent years, a more mature woman, a friend and neighbor, a fellow worker in the church, one who was instrumental in getting the first Big Lick Homecoming together. Most of all I remember her life, her laughter, her love, and her loyalty.

She was full of life and lived a full life. She had enormous strength and energy and vitality. She thought sleeping later than 6 AM was almost a sin. She was up some mornings at 3 AM and often called her sister before 6 AM. Her grandchildren remember that no matter how early they got up - even in an effort to fool her - she was always up before them and had breakfast waiting. Listening to a litany of all that Jessie did in a single day is enough to make one tired.

She accomplished all this by being highly organized and she wanted others to be organized. She was curator of the family museum and archives; conservator of all forms of family and community history. She constantly kept in touch with family, neighbors, and friends, keeping up with everything that was happening in her community. Losing Jessie is like losing part of our own memory because her death has taken from us a storehouse of information that cannot be replaced.

In her church, she was one of the group of people, essential to every church, that James Glasse called the "chicken fryers." The chicken fryers are those who are always present and willing to do whatever task must be done, no matter how lowly or dirty or unrecognized. Jessie was always there to prepare the meals, to clean up the dishes, to serve refreshments at Bible school, to handle all the correspondence for the first Homecoming, to do whatever it was that had to be done. Already the women of the church are wondering who will bring the chicken and dumplings to church dinners.

I don't know whether Jessie really loved to cook, but I do know she understood the importance of good food to good fellowship whether in her family, among neighbors, or in the church. Like the early church members who it is reported in Acts partook of food in each other's homes with "glad and generous hearts," Jessie always did her part to make sure that good food was available. And she did so with a "glad and generous" heart.

Jessie was a person of good humor and warm laughter. I don't often specifically remember a person's laughter, but I remember Jessie's. It enlivened her conversations and filled her presence with a sense of ease and acceptance.

Jessie had a special capacity for love and loyalty. She was one of the least judgmental, most accepting and forgiving persons I have known. She tolerated the weaknesses, shortcomings, and failures of others, and she accepted those she knew to be less than perfect more graciously than most of us do. Though she thought everyone could and should live with the same moral rigor and vigor that she displayed in her life, she did not cast out those who failed to meet her standards. She always expected more of herself than she did of others. To be loved by Jessie was to know something of the love of God, because you could never fall completely from Jessie's grace. She had a fierce loyalty to those she loved - family, church, neighbors, friends. Once you were inside Jessie's circle of love, you could never get completely outside it. No matter what you did, no matter how far you strayed, the power of her love would eventually reach out and encircle you again.

Her love and loyalty were especially strong toward her family - parents, sister, brothers, children, grandchildren and great grandchildren. She took great pride in her children and their children and their children's children. She insisted on being involved in their lives. It was her way of loving. I know that those of you who have been the object of this intense scrutiny have, at times, experienced it as annoying. But as you talked with me yesterday you seemed to grasp what it really was - Jessie's way of loving and one of her most endearing and enduring qualities.

The writer of the last chapter of Proverbs might have had someone like Jessie in mind when he/she wrote:

> *"A [true lady] is hard to find;*
> *She is far more precious than jewels...*
> *She delights to work with her hands...*
> *And goes to work with a will...*
> *She opens her hands to the unfortunate,*
> *And stretches out her arms to the poor.*
> *She does not fear for her family when it snows,*
> *For all of them are doubly clothed...*
> *She makes her own bedcovers...*
> *Her clothing is of good quality and dignified;*
> *She has no worry about tomorrow.*
> *When she opens her mouth she speaks wisely,*
> *And kindly instruction is on her tongue...*
> *Her children rise to pronounce blessings on her;*
> *Her husband, too, sings her praises:*
> *'Many women have proved their worth*
> *But you have surpassed them all.'*
> *Charm is deceitful and beauty is fleeting,*
> *But the wise woman who fears the Lord is to be praised.*
> *Give her the reward of her labor,*
> *And let the gates ring with praise of her deeds."*
> [Proverbs 31: 10-31, Selected verses]

Jessie died in a tragic automobile accident on February 12, 1996. She is survived by:

[I read a list of survivors.]

Bob told me a story Monday night. It's about a man who died and was on his way to heaven. He begged the angels to let him take something from this world with him. They agree saying, "You can take one little satchel, but you will have to show it to St. Peter before you pass through the Pearly Gates." So, the man took one little suitcase with him. At the Pearly Gates, he opened it to show St. Peter. Inside were several gold bricks. Noticing that St. Peter looked concerned, the man asked, "Is something wrong?" "I can understand your bringing something with you," St. Peter replied, "but what I don't understand is why you brought paving bricks."

Whatever Jessie may have taken with her, it was not paving bricks. She never had much of it. What she did take is all that any of us can take with us out of this world - the love and affection of family, friends, and neighbors; the warmest recommendation of her fellow church members; and the certainty of being held in the everlasting arms of God.

If we could only hear what Jessie is saying to us today, it might go something like these words from Isla Pascal Richardson's poem "To Those I Love." It goes in part:

> *"If I should ever leave you whom I love*
> *To go along the Silent Way,*
> *Grieve not,*
>
> *. . .*
> *Please do not let the thoughts of me be sad,*
> *For I am loving you just as I always have.*
>
> *. . .*
> *We cannot see Beyond, But this I know:*
> *I loved you so – t'was heaven here with you."*

"Life in Christ is eternal. Love is immortal. Death is only a horizon, and a horizon is nothing but the limit of our sight." 1 We cannot know what is beyond that horizon, but we know who is there, and the risen Christ is enough.

Let us pray.   *[I led an interim prayer.]*

[A hymn was played.]

[Another minister delivered a Meditation of Hope & Healing: Witness to the Resurrection.]

[Dismissal to place of burial for a committal service.]

NOTES

1. William Penn, 1644-1718, in a prayer recorded in "The New South Wales Council of Churches Selected Christian Prayers PR006L," date unknown (but prior to 1923), and in Father Bede Jarrett, O. P., ed., Book of Prayers, date unknown, where these words are credited to "a prayer written by William Penn 1644- 1718." Secondly, Rossiter W. Raymond, 1848-1918 wrote a poem using the same words, date of publication unknown (but prior to 1923). Thirdly, Carly Simon wrote and sang a song using the same words published in her album "Have You Seen Me Lately," in 1990. I am using only one line from the prayer/poem/song. I originally got this line from William Sloane Coffin, Jr. who used it in an Easter sermon at Battell Chapel of Yale University in 1966. For forty years I thought Coffin was the originator of the line. For more information, see Appendix A at the end of this Collection.

OLIVER ESTILLE BURGESS FUNERAL REMARKS – OCTOBER 3, 1996

I was charged with doing only the Obituary/Eulogy for this service. Another minister gave the Message of Healing and Hope and Witness to the Resurrection.

Blessed be the God and Father of our Lord Jesus Christ. By His great mercy we have been born anew to a living hope by the Resurrection of Jesus Christ from the dead.

What a great honor and high privilege it is to be here today for this victory celebration – the celebration of good over evil, grace over sin, faith over futility, life over death. We are gathered to celebrate and give thanks to Almighty God for the life of Estille Burgess, and to rejoice in the promise of life eternal. Praise be to God who gives us the victory.

OBITUARY/EULOGY

He was born on March 7, 1913, the second child and first son of Vance and Amy Siever Burgess. They named him Oliver Estille, but he never used his first name, going by O. E. or simply Estille. Most of us came to know him, to love him, and maybe, at times, to fear him as Estille or Mr. Burgess.

He grew up in Big Lick and was married to Dora Bradley on April 8, 1934. Together they lived as loving husband and wife for 62 years, and reared two children, Wayne and Carol. He was a farmer, bus driver, mechanic, school transportation director, a member of Calvary Presbyterian Church of Big Lick.

He died quietly and peacefully after a lingering and debilitating illness on October 1, 1996. He is survived by:

[I inserted a list of survivors.]

Such are the meager details of a life well lived – until we dig deeper. The very first Psalm proclaims:

> *"Blessed is the man who walks not in the counsel of the wicked,*
> *Nor takes his stand with sinners, nor sits in the seat of the*
> *mockers; But his delight is in the law of the Lord, and on His law*
> *he meditates day and night.*
> *He is like a tree planted by streams of water, that yields its fruit*
> *in its season*
> *And its leaf does not wither."* [Psalm 1: 1-3]

Estille was that man. He was sturdy, strong, steadfast in every way that counts. His enormous skill and ability went beyond those of a craftsman. He was a competent farmer, carpenter, and mechanic. (I used to marvel at his giant forearms forged by years of yielding a wrench. When I shook hands with him for the last time, his grip was still firm and powerful.)

He was one of the first two drivers of county owned school buses, beginning in 1942, and from the very beginning he was also chief mechanic and Director of Transportation. With only an eighth-grade education, he was an able administrator who mastered the intricacies of budgeting and finance so that every one of his 35 years, his department ended up with a surplus. Dora used to say that he worked three jobs but only got paid for one. He became one of the most efficient managers of what became and remains one of the largest transportation systems in the State of Tennessee, all the while also working as a bus driver and chief mechanic.

To say that he was particular or meticulous or a perfectionist is an understatement. He took care of everything entrusted to his care as if his life depended upon it. Anything worth doing was worth doing well according to Estille. And he held himself to a very high standard. For 35 years Estille cleaned his buss every night and every morning with such diligence that it used to be said you could eat off of the seats and most days off of the floor without fear of picking up any dirt. I know, because, like many of you, I rode that bus five days a week, nine months of the year for four years.

He was a man of courage who stood tall for what is right. In 1954 when there were threats of mob violence in Big Lick, Estille was among those who quietly patrolled the roads at night - at some risk to himself - to protect the rights of a young black man to remain peacefully and securely in the neighborhood.

He was an extraordinary Christian and churchman. He accepted Christ, was baptized and became a member of Calvary Church of Big Lick in 1931. When the church was built, he donated more time than anyone except the minister and one Elder. In 1949 he was elected an Elder and served in that capacity for 47 years. He served the church at every level - local, in the regional Presbytery, in the multi-state Synod, at the national level. He served on two Pastoral Nominating Committees, as a church Trustee, as a Trustee of the Calvary Church Homestead Project, as a cemetery trustee. For over fifty years there was hardly anything of any importance that happened at the church in which Estille was not a leader.

He was an exemplary citizen of his community. When I was young, Estille was a leader in every organization I thought was important. By example, he taught me a lot about what it means to be a good citizen. He served as a member of the Election Commission, in the Centennial Celebration leadership, and a number of other organizations. He served on the Red Cross Board for 50 years and as a Red Cross volunteer for many of those years. He virtually built the Blood Bank Program in Cumberland County serving as its Chairman, chief cheer leader, and primary volunteer for many years.

He was a consummate husband, father and grandfather. Married for 62 years, he always wanted his children to do well, but was even more concerned that they do good. He was always there for them when they needed him. He was a beloved neighbor and friend. His friendship was steadfast, immovable, lifelong. It was Estille who most warmly and enthusiastically welcomed me back to Big Lick when I returned in 1974.

Punctual like a clock. So punctual that he was always ahead of time. He was organized, had time for everything, and always got things done on time (or ahead of time), and he expected others to do likewise. His life was regulated much like that of the Preacher in Ecclesiastes who proclaims that there is a "time for every matter under heaven." (Ecclesiastes 3: 1b).

Estille was never late for anything except dying, over which he perhaps lingered too long, but that was out of his control.

Dora would sometimes say that Estille was "born old," meaning that he did not care much for frivolity, lighthearted recreation, "foolishness" he used to call it. But he was not without a sense of humor (he could even laugh at himself at times), nor did he live a joyless life. It was just that he found his greatest joy and took his greatest pleasure in: A job well done; Devotion to duty; the fulfillment of responsibility; service to others, to his church, and his community.

I do not want to diminish the importance of recreation, lightheartedness, frivolity and fun. They have an important part to play in our lives. But no community can thrive unless there are some who find their joy and take their pleasure where Estille did.

It is a rare privilege to have known someone who was such a sterling example of both those characteristics we identify with good citizenship: Honor; Courage; Integrity; Hard Work; Dependability; Trustworthiness; Responsibility; devotion to duty; servant to his community – and at the same time such a good example of those characteristics that the Apostle Paul identified as the "Fruits of the Spirit: Love; patience; joy; peace; kindness; goodness; faithfulness; gentleness; self-control." (Galatians 5: 22- 23a)

Estille traveled a good bit in his life. As a young man he worked for a time in Florida. He went to many out-of-county and out of state meetings as a representative of his church and community. But he never really moved his place of abode much. He lived most of his life on the same farm where he was born. He lived in the same modest house for 62 years. He remained married to the same woman for 62 years.

But today he makes the one final move that we must all make. And in the church, we have a word more fitting than dying or deceased to describe this move. When a church member moves from one church to another, we say that person has transferred their membership.

So, it becomes our responsibility and privilege to announce today the transfer of our beloved brother, Oliver Estille Burgess, with the highest recommendations of his brothers and sisters in Christ, from the church temporal and transient located in Big Lick, Tennessee, to that church triumphant and eternal located in that "city which has foundations, whose builder and maker is God." (Hebrews 11: 10)

Please let your hearts by comforted by the following familiar and beloved Psalm:

[I read the 23rd Psalm.]

Let Us Pray: *[I offered an interim prayer and a hymn was played.]*

[The other minister had his say, and we removed to the place of burial for a committal service in which I participated.]

MYRTLE MAE ROBERTS DYE OBITUARY/EULOGY – JANUARY 22, 1997

I did this whole service

OBITUARY/EULOGY

Myrtle Mae Roberts Dye was born on February 17, 1912, the first daughter and second of eight children born to Joseph Houston and Mary Ledford Roberts.

At age 12 she accepted Christ as her Lord and Savior and was baptized in the Tellico River, joining a Baptist Church. She was active in churches all her life, taking great satisfaction that she had helped to resurrect one church and start another one.

When she was about 20, she moved with her family to another community in Loudon County where she fell among a group of young people who walked the railroad tracks to church on Sundays. Among this group was a young man who seemed interested in her, but he was a little too glib for her. He made some smart aleck remarks that caused her not to talk to him until he apologized the next Sunday. He immediately suggested that they kiss and make up. She didn't talk to him for another week. They eventually made up - or so it seems, since they were married on July 2, 1934, and spend 62 years together as loving husband and wife.

Mr. Dye's tales makes it sound as if they fought like the couple for whom Mammy's Creek and Daddy's Creed or name according to folklore. But the truth is they seldom had crosswords and the devotion between them was a shining example of the best that married love can and should be. As a contemporary country song says it: "The Keeper of the stars knew what he was doing when He joined those two hearts." Their love and affection for each other was so infectious that it spilled over not only upon their children and their children's children and their children's children's children, but also upon their neighbors and their neighbor's children, and on all who fell within their reach. I know from living as a neighbor to them for 20 years.

Mrs. Dye loved to garden and work with flowers. She worked for many years as a floral arranger. Even in her retirement, her artistic touch frequently showed up in the floral arrangements she put together for weddings, funerals and other events. She loved to sew but saying that she was a seamstress is akin to saying that Picasso was a painter. A needle in her hands became the instrument of an artist.

She was a quiet, unassuming, modest woman, never accounted great as the world measures things, but great in those qualities of character that truly endure - those which the Apostle called the fruits of the Spirit - joy, peace, patience, kindness, goodness, faithfulness, gentleness, self-control.

She had a smile that came from somewhere deep down in her soul and radiated out the corners of her mouth like the sunrise in a clear blue sky the morning after a thunderstorm. Even in her last days that warm, sly, sparkling smile with which she always welcomed guests never failed to light up the room.

When her parents named her Myrtle, they probably did not realize what an appropriate name it would become. The plant from which her name is derived occurs in over 100 varieties, all of them hardy, long living, evergreen scrubs that brighten the world with their beautiful blossoms. Many of them have berries that are good to eat, and their heartwood is as strong as gnarled hickory.

Beyond that it is a plant with spiritual - at least scriptural significance. One of the great heroines of the Old Testament, one of two women for whom books of the Bible are named, was named Myrtle. We know her by her Persian name, Esther, but her Hebrew name was Myrtle, and she was in many ways similar to the Myrtle whose life we celebrate and whose death we mourn today.

Myrtle in the Bible is a symbol of God's presence and power. When Zachariah experiences his great prophetic vision, it comes to him as he is standing among the myrtle bushes. Isaiah speaks of the things that will happen when the day of the Lord arrives.

> He writes: "For you shall go out in joy, and be led forth in peace; the mountains and the hills before you shall break forth in singing and all the trees of the field will clap their hands. Instead of the thorn shall come up the cypress; instead of the briar shall come up the myrtle; and it shall be to the Lord a memorial; an everlasting sign that you shall not be cut off."

One of the things we can say on this day of celebration and mourning is that this Myrtle lived up to her name.

Myrtle dye passed from this world on January 19, 1997, one month short of her 85th birthday.

She is survived by: *[I read a list of survivors.}*

Praise be to God for giving her life and for sharing her with us.

Let us Pray: *[I offered an interim prayer and a hymn was played.]*

[I closed the service with a Meditation, Prayer, and Benediction.]

[Dismissal to place of burial for a committal service.]

ROY T. HALL FUNERAL REMARKS – JUNE 22, 1997

I was charged only with doing the Obituary/Eulogy for this funeral. Even that I did differently than I did any other Obit/Eulogy. I spoke primarily to the deceased. You had to know the man to know why I did it this way.

A little over eight years ago many of us gathered at another place on another occasion to speak of you Roy. A little less than a year ago some of us met again to speak of you on the occasion of your receiving the Exchange Club's Book of Golden Deeds award. At that time, I said to you: "We're gonna have to stop meeting like this, or I'm gonna run out of stories." Roger Thackston summed up much of what made you unique when he remarked that you faced every day convinced that this is a wonderful life. And Don Hinch said you were like the seven-year itch - for every few years we had to get together to honor you. Well, Roy, this time it has been less than a year, and this time the itch is hard to scratch. This time you are up for an award greater than any of us can bestow. And this time I am somewhat, but not totally, at a loss for words.

It is not because there is not more to say - though much of what I say has been said before. It is partly that it is just harder this time. Levity, lightheartedness, and laughter seem out of place this time, yet it is so hard to speak of you without some humor, joy, and laughter in our hearts because that is the way you were. And it is partly that I must refrain from saying all that could be said. So let me remind those gathered here of a few of the things that many of us have heard before and maybe a few that some have not heard so frequently.

How you were born on February 10, 1914, the first son and second child of Albert H. And Verdie Croft Hall - born "78 steps from Daddy's Creek in Big Lick" as you used to say. Both that place and that creek meant a lot to you. How you went to Indiana because of ill health. How there you regained your health and became a big-time cowpoke for the Ball family (the ones that made Mason Jars - or something like that), and how you earned your keep breaking, training and riding horses - over 1000 - by your count at the time - on a big ranch. How you came home the first time with these stories and a stylish mustache. And how the boys back home made you shave off the mustache and sent you back to Indiana, you threatening them that you might never come back to Big Lick again.

How upon your return to Indiana, you met, fell in love with, married Betty Van Slyke and with her adopted son David. How, despite your earlier threat, you returned to Big Lick in 1951 to run the store, start a Boy Scout troop, and try to establish a large horse farm.

How then you tried several jobs and businesses, but none of them seemed to suit you until you became the "Voice of the Plateau," not just on radio, but through the 16 years you served as President and/or Executive Secretary of the Chamber of Commerce. You served during its formative years and helped lay the groundwork for the development that has occurred here over the past 30 years and helped create the Cumberland County we know today.

However, since 1957 when you served as Vice-President of the Cumberland County Planning Group, you have been a member - and more often than not, served as Secretary of virtually every organization dedicated to the improvement of Cumberland County and the Plateau – including but not limited to the Fair Association, the Livestock Association, the Upper Cumberland Development District, the Hull-York Lakeland Resource Conservation and Development District, the Farm Bureau, the Scottish Rite Club, the Soil Conservation District, the Tennessee Cattlemen's Association, the Board of Education, the Exchange Club, and the Chamber of Commerce. It tires me out just to list them.

How even these last few weeks some have sought your counsel and your signature on important papers. How you continued to serve virtually to the very end - attending meeting even after you were no longer able to drive

- Wilanna having to drive you. It is no wonder, Roy, that you became short of breath at the end, but we know how you came to be one of the best loved, most renowned, most respected, and most honored of local citizens.

But, Roy, beyond all that, I know some other things that illustrate the quality of your character. How you loved people and refused to make distinctions between the high and the lowly, the meek and the mighty, treating them all with the same dignity and respect. How you loved this mountain, especially a little place called Big Lick. How, though you were sometimes a sceptic, you were a dedicated member and Elder of Calvary Presbyterian Church of Big Lick. How you served your church faithfully at the local level and beyond. How for many years did you teach the interdenominational Sunday morning fellowship class in Crossville.

I remember your generosity of spirit - how you always thought of others (every time I visited you recently, wasting away in a hospital bed, you wanted to know about others who were sick or, as you said, "In bad shape." Or how your sister-in-law remarked to me yesterday that you were always a gentleman - even in your last days you never failed to thank people for even the smallest kindness.

I remember how you loved and honored traditions of the past but were always open to new thoughts, new ideas, new ways of doing things. I remember your eternal optimism - how you approached every day, as Roger Thackston has said, with the conviction that this is a wonderful life. Your infectious good humor inoculated those around you against pessimism, defeatism, and ill-temper.

I remember how you never met a stranger - only a potential new friend; how you never sought personal gain from your public service; how you were never ill-tempered, antagonistic, or acrimonious. And I remember how you loved a good-natured argument; how you liked to ask hard questions, especially in Sunday School and Bible Study, and how you were never satisfied with easy answers to tough questions. I remember how you mastered the fine art of disagreeing without being disagreeable, and how you never attacked those with whom you disagreed.

In this time when too often what passes for civic leadership is little more than acrimonious fault-finding, backbiting, and accusatory name-calling, how much better off we would be if more of our civic leaders displayed the same respect for others, abandonment of self-interest, generosity of spirit, humility, harmony, hope, and helpfulness that characterized your years among us.

I remember yet other things, Roy – more personal things – things buried deep in your life experiences that fewer people know about – things about which we seldom spoke, but which I must note today because they speak even more tellingly about the content of your character and the quality of your journey from the cradle to the grave. Things which make your years with us even more remarkable.

I remember how you overcame ill-health, frailty of body and an incomplete formal education. How you were virtually blind as a child and spent two terrifying, tormented, homesick years in a Knoxville hospital. How another illness in your teens caused you to lose half your stomach and almost your life – your family thought you might not make it to adulthood.

And I remember how you suffered from and yet overcame deep melancholy and a sense of hopelessness after the death of your son David, exacerbated by the grief of your wife. I remember how you suffered personal loneliness which none of your activities, memberships, or friendships could overcome after Betty's death.

But then I remember, too, how you were rejuvenated, reborn really by your marriage to and life with Wilanna. How she brought personal joy back into your life. And how through her and her children you were able to fill the greatest emptiness in your life – your deep desire to be a father and grandfather. How you were finally able to patch the hole left in your heart when David died. How you loved those children, and how they loved you.

W. C. Fields, a great cynic, is reputed to have said, "Never trust a man who loves children and dogs." But another eternal optimist, a great friend of Roy's, my father, taught me that one of the truest tests of a person's heart is the degree to which she or he loves and is loved by children and pets. By that test, Roy, you pass with flying colors. I suspect that if Roy had been asked to trade parts of his life, he would have traded all the accomplishments, all the accolades, all the honors for the last few years he had with those children.

In George Orwell's fable about the foolishness of dictatorships, "Animal Farm", the pigs, which have the power, are prone to saying, "All animals are equal, but some are more equal than others." That's a bit of foolishness, although Roy would have gotten the satire in it, but in life we can truthfully say that all individuals are unique, but some are more unique than others.

We will go on. That is what life demands, and Roy would expect no less. We will know, respect, honor, and yes, even love others. But we will never know another Roy Hall.

Indeed, how blest we are today! How great our joy must be, even in the midst of sadness and loss. For we have the great and rare privilege of having known and worked with, loved and been loved by Roy T. Hall. Praise be to God for giving him life and for sharing that life with us.

Roy died quietly at home on June 20, 1997, after a lingering final illness.

He was preceded in death by: *[I read the names of Roy's family members who had preceded him through death's door.]*

He is survived by: *[I read a list of survivors;]*

The first time I visited Roy on his last trip to the hospital, he told me some things that I cannot say to you. But I remarked to him how much he reminded me of his father. He was honored by that because of the thousands of people he had met and the hundreds he had gotten to know well, the one he respected and revered the most was his father. On the occasion of his father's funeral, I used the following Scripture and poem. I think they are appropriate again today, and I know that Roy feels honored by their use.

The poem first: *[I read the poem, The House by the Side of the Road, by Sam Walter Foss. The first verse of this poem may be read in its entirety in Appendix A at the end of this collection.]*

I will close with the 15th Psalm:

> *O Lord, who shall you invite to your house?*
> *Who shall come to live on your Holy Hill?*
>
> *He who walks blamelessly; who does what is right;*
> *Who seeks truth with his heart; who can be trusted to speak honestly;*
> *Whose word can be trusted. Who speaks no slander;*
> *And does no evil to a friend; nor repeats gossip against his neighbor;*
> *Who sticks by his word, even if it causes him harm;*
> *Who is dependable, trustworthy, and not two-faced;*
> *Who will not cheat nor harm the innocent for any amount of money.*

Let Us Pray: *[I led an interim prayer.]*

[The song "Go Rest High On that Mountain" by Vince Gill was played.]

[A message of witness to the Resurrection was presented by another pastor.]

[Dismissal to the place of burial for a committal service.]

WANDA ROSE BREWER HALL OBITUARY/ EULOGY – SEPTEMBER 28, 1998

I did this whole service

"Have you not known? Have you not heard? The Lord is the everlasting God, the Creator of the ends of the earth. He does not grow weary . . . He gives power to the faint, and to him who has no might, he increases strength. Even youths shall faint and be weary, and young men shall fall exhausted; but they who wait for the Lord shall renew their strength, they shall mount up with wings like eagles, they shall run and not be weary, they shall walk and not faint."

Jesus said: "Come to me all who labor and are heaven laden, and I will give you rest. Take my yoke upon you and learn from me, for I am gentle and lowly in heart, and you will find rest for your souls."

"Our help is in the name of the Lord who made heaven and earth."

Wanda shared with me a fondness for the columnist Lewis Grizzard with whom she shared an acerbic wit and a love for all things Southern. She had copies of all his books including such classics as: Shoot Low Boys, They're Riding Shetland Ponies; and Elvis is Dead and I don't Feel so good Myself; and

My Daddy was a Pistol and I'm a Son of a Gun; and the one about his heart operation: They Took Out My Heart and Stomped that Sucker flat.

At the time of her death, she was reading the last of Grizzard's book - published after his death. The title might serve as an epithet for Wanda. It is entitled: It Wasn't Always Easy, but It Sure Was Fun. Speaking of Wanda's sense of humor, Jeff was recalling how his mother always got them ready for church while Ern got the car ready. I was reminded of the story of the mother who laid the children's clothes out on the bed one Sunday morning and said to her husband: "You get the kids ready today, I'll go out and lean on the horn for you."

OBITUARY

Wanda Rose Brewer Hall was born on May 22, 1925, the daughter of Albert and Kate Brewer. From a very early age she knew that she wanted to be a nurse. That dream came true in 1947 when she graduated with a RN degree from the Fort Sanders Hospital Nursing Program. She loved being a nurse and had a passion for her profession. For over 40 years she was a Nurse at Cumberland Medical Center spending much of that time in the obstetrics ward. She was a bringer of life, helping to deliver 100's, perhaps 1,000's of babies. One of those who nurses human life into existence at one of its most fragile points.

I don't know what a nurse was doing at a square dance at the State Park in 1948, but Wanda was there, and there she met a young man who was recently out of the military. Shortly after they met, on October 3, 1948, they hastened off to Rossville, Georgia to be married - supposedly because they could not, did not have the time, or simply did not want to wait the three days necessary for a blood test in Tennessee. Ern Hall became the second love of her life, taking a back seat only to nursing. He became part of the center of her life for the next 50 years.

Three children, Tina, Jeff, and Joel were born from their union, and they and their children remained among her greatest joys. She was a loving and devoted mother and grandmother, who in their eyes, as one of her grandchildren told me yesterday, was "one of the best people you could ever meet."

Teeny wrote this:

[I read a one-page eulogy that Tina had written of her mother that is not included here.]

Wanda loved to read and enjoyed traveling to see new parts of the country, though she did not get to do as much as she would have liked. But she was always happy to be back home on this mountain. A woman of faith, Wanda's health began to seriously deteriorate three years ago, and she spent her last on earth unable even to sit up in her favorite chair.

But she surprised even her family with her courage and strength in the face of her final illness which wrecked her body but never destroyed her spirit.

She had hoped to sit up in her favorite chair on her 50th wedding anniversary, but, alas, that was not to be. Wanda died peacefully on September 26, 1998, seven days prior to her and Ern's 50th wedding anniversary.

She is survived by:

[I inserted a list of survivors.]

LAURA BRADLEY KERLEY OBITUARY/ EULOGY – DECEMBER 8, 1998

I did this whole service

OPENING REMARKS:

"Praise be to God, for we do not grieve as those who have no hope!"

Jesus said, "I am the resurrection and the life. Those who believe in me, though they die, yet shall they live"

"Come to me all who labor and are heavy laden, and I will give you rest."

"Blessed are those who mourn; they shall be comforted."

"Our help is in the name of the Lord who made heaven and earth!"

We are gathered to take account of change, to pay attention to sorrow; to grieve a loss and celebrate a homecoming: to remember, and to thank God for the life of Laura Bradley Kerley; and to witness to the Resurrection and rejoice in the victory over sin and death which is ours in Jesus Christ. One of visitors last night put today in perspective when he said: Laura got an early Christmas present: Eternal Peace.

We thank God today for the life of Laura Bradley Kerley and for sharing her life with us. Laura was born in White County on Feb. 16, 1910, the 5th daughter and 11th child of J.H. and Elizabeth Bradley. At the tender age of 5 months, she moved (the 1st of several times) with the rest of her family to Cumberland County and shortly thereafter to the community of Big Lick.

She liked to recall her years growing up as part of a large family and as a neighbor of other large families. But perhaps her fondest memories were of one young man who often came by her house visiting her brothers or some of their neighbors, so he said. But the truth came out on Oct. 9, 1932, when Laura and Leslie (Let) Kerley were married. They lived together as loving husband and wife until his death in 1989, one month short of their 57th wedding anniversary. From their union came one daughter, Gwen, whom they loved dearly and who loved them equally, and who was able to care for her mother throughout her last years and final illness.

Laura's obituary says she was a homemaker - and that she was, but she was more also. When the young men her age, including the younger brother she adored, went off to war, Laura went to work - on an assembly line in Detroit where she helped build the machinery that won the war and helped keep many of those young men, including her brother, alive. She loved the outdoors, liked to work in yard and garden, a love she passed on to at least one of her granddaughters. She was greatly pleased with one last trip she took through the autumn foliage less than a month before her death. She could and often did outwork many of the men in her life, even when they were half her age. She was a great communicator who loved people and kept in touch almost daily with many of her family and friends. Laura was a Christian who as a young woman had embraced Christ as her savior and Lord. She was a member of Calvary Presbyterian Church of Big Lick where she was an active participant until age and infirmity limited her ability to remain active. I can remember when Let and Laura never missed a Sunday service. Above all else she is remembered for her love of her family and her strength of both body and spirit.

Though sexist by today's standards, prior to 1911, Sam Walter Foss wrote a poem inspired by a line from the Greek Poet, Homer, which is entitled "The House by the Side of the Road" it captured some of what made Laura special. Part of it goes:

> *"I see from my house by the side of the road,*

By the side of the highway of life:
The men who press with the ardor of hope;
The men who are faint with the strife.
But I turn not away from their smiles nor their tears,
Both part of an infinite plan –
Let me live in a house by the side of the road And be a friend
to man." ¹

Laura died as she had lived, with quiet dignity on Dec. 6, 1998.

She is survived by: *[I read a list of survivors.]*

   [A hymn was played.]

   [I followed with a Meditation, Prayer, and Benediction.]

   [Dismissal to place of burial for a committal service.]

NOTES:

1. By Copyright law this is the maximum portion of the poem I can reproduce here. I think this verse captures the essence of the poem, but I encourage you to find the whole poem and read it. A further explanation may be seen and read in Appendix A at the end of this Collection.

DORA KERLEY WOOD OBITUARY/EULOGY - DECEMBER 29, 1999

I was the lead minister of two who participated in this service. This meant I was assigned primarily the Obituary/Eulogy. But as you will see I was, as often, unable to refrain from drifting into a Message of Hope and Healing: A Witness to the Resurrection.

"Praise be to God, for we do not grieve as those who have no hope!"

> *Jesus said, "I am the resurrection and the life. Those who believe in me, though they die, yet shall they live"*
> *"Come to me all who are burdened and heavy laden, and I will give you rest."*
> *"Blessed are those who mourn; they shall be comforted."*
> *"Our help is in the name of the Lord who made heaven and earth!"*

We are gathered to take account of change, to pay attention to sorrow; to grieve a loss and celebrate a homecoming: to remember; to thank God for the life of Dora Kerley Wood; to witness to the Resurrection, and to rejoice in the victory over sin and death which is ours in Jesus Christ.

A little over a year ago many of us gathered for the funeral of one of Dora's contemporaries, Laura Kerley. On that occasion someone said of Laura what we may now say of Dora - she received the most lasting of Christmas presents possible: Eternal Peace.

OBITUARY/EULOGY

We thank God today for the life of Dora Kerley Wood and for sharing her life with us. Dora was born on a little farm on the south bank of Lick Creek in the Big Lick Community of Cumberland County on October 23, 1909, the 3rd daughter and 6th child of Emmett and Zenia Selby Kerley.

She grew up there, became a young woman, accepted Christ as her Lord and Savior, united with Calvary Presbyterian Church of Big Lick, went off to the Alpine Academy in Overton County to high school where she graduated in 1932, and returned home where she met and married General Wood in 1934. They moved to a little farm on the north bank of Lick Creek in the Bethel community and lived there as loving husband and wife until his death in 1969. To their union 4 children, Loreda, Willene, Gerald, and Carlene, were born. Added to their household was her father who lived with them, watched over and cared for by Dora for the last 16 years of his life.

From the first nine years after she married, Dora remained at home, content to be a homemaker and mother to her three young children. But in 1943 the people of Bethel persuaded her to become their teacher so they could re-open their school that had been closed for lack of a qualified teacher. How soon we forget how difficult it was in the middle of this century to find qualified teachers and have good schools in rural communities. But Bethel got their teacher and Dora found her calling. And what a teacher she became. For 28 of the next 31 years when school was in session at Bethel and later at Big Lick Dora was there as one of, and sometimes the only teacher. She took three years off after her last child, Carlene, was born, but when Carlene was three, she started teaching again, taking Carlene to school with her. So it may be that Carlene is the smartest person ever to take 4 years to get through of first grade. Dora loved teaching and she loved her students.

That is how I first got to know Dora well. She was my 5th grade teacher, and I soon learned that we had something in common - an abiding interest in the study of history. She was the first to teach me the subject that would become my major in college. And there is something else I remember about that 5th year in school - perhaps it was partially the new subjects that held my interest or the fact that we were in a new school building, perhaps I was growing up a little - but I suspect it was mostly the way Dora taught and the way she managed her classroom, but that was the first time I went through a whole school year without getting a single whipping.

Dora liked to read and study her Bible. In a more harmonious time, she would have her students answer the roll by reciting a Bible verse. To which, I am told, Carlene, after hearing several other children quote one or another of the shorter commandments, "Thou shalt not do this or that," was known to answer, "Thou shalt not do anything."

After Dora became too sick and weak to read her Bible, she comforted her pastor by explaining to him that this was all right because she knew the passages she liked best by heart. During her last illness when her daughters would read to her from the Bible, she would often "read along,' mouthing the words silently as they read. And sometimes they would hear her repeating something which, though they could not make out the words, they could tell was some favorite scripture passage.

Dora, like all of her brothers, enjoyed singing, and she often sang as she worked around her house and garden. She was not only a student of history; she was a recorder of history. She kept notes on her calendar of events as they occurred - when her children graduated or got married, when a relative or neighbor got sick or died, when it snowed, when important events happened - the kind of record that most of us, as we get older, wish we had kept but which few of us find the energy or time to actually keep.

Dora was a country wife and mother who enjoyed and was renowned for her cooking. She loved her family and enjoyed having them around, and they often gathered at her house for reunions and other get-togethers. She took up crocheting after she retired from teaching and became quite good at it. She enjoyed telling and swapping stories with her friends and neighbor.

Dora died as she had lived with quiet dignity on Dec.27, 1999.

She is survived by: *[I read a list of survivors.]*

Ninety years is a long time. Sobering to realize that Dora was born almost midway between the Civil War and WWII. A few days before her death the space shuttle lifted off yet again, but Dora grew up in an age of horse drawn wagons and never learned to drive an automobile. She was 11 when radio was broadcast for the first time ever by station KDKA in Pittsburgh, Pa. 30 when TV was first introduced at the 1939 World's Fair; in her 40's when it first seen in Cumberland County; 32 when penicillin (the birth of modern medicine) was discovered. When I graduated from Seminary and began my life's work almost a third of a century ago, Dora was already the age I am today.

However, it is not the sheer magnitude of her years, but the content of her character and the strength of her spirit that make today not so much a low point in our own journey from the cradle to the grave as it is a day of rare privilege. Indeed, how fortunate we are to grieve today - because our grief means that we had the rare privilege of knowing - and loving - and being loved by Dora Kerley Wood.

Yes, 90 years is a long time. But not long enough. It is never long enough. It is a hard thing to lose someone who has been a part of our lives for so long. But we are not promised any number of days on this earth, and we cannot have permanence in this world. The best we can hope for here is to have our lives touched by the Hand of God - and next to that - the best that most of us ever experience in this life - is to have our lives touched by someone who is truly loving & caring, kind & generous, accepting and forgiving. To the degree that you had that with Dora-as mother, grandmother, mother-in-law, sister, loved one, neighbor or friend - then you know a little of what it is to be touched by the Hand of God. And your memory of that makes you as richly blessed as it is possible to be blessed in this life.

For, you see, beyond the grief and the tears, today is a victory celebration - not only because every Christian funeral is so, but especially because Dora in her life and in the courage and dignity of her dying bore such powerful witness to the victory which is ours in J. Christ - the victory of joy over despair, of peace over enmity, of kindness over meanness, of love over hate, of purity over corruption, of forgiveness over ridicule, of humility over self-righteousness, of faith over sin, and of all the forces of life over the forces of death.

Dora was an ordinary, plain, simple woman. I am reminded of a beautiful and poignant Shaker hymn which speaks to this occasion: It goes

> Tis the gift to be simple, tis the gift to be free
> Tis the gift to come down where we ought to be.
> And when we find ourselves in the place just right
> It will be in the valley of love and delight.
> When true simplicity is gained
> To bow and to bend, we will not be ashamed To turn and to turn
> will be our delight
> Til by turning, turning we come round right.

Dora never traveled far during her life. Oh she went off to Alpine to high school, and she went back and forth from Big Lick to Crossville and Cookeville frequently when she was working to get her teaching credentials. But she lived her whole life on one side or the other of Lick Creek in the Big Lick and Bethel communities. When she died, her home was within a half mile of where she was born. Today, however, she makes the one last trip that we must all make, and we can be comforted in knowing that while with us Dora turned, turned until she came round right, and today is in the valley of love and delight.

"Death, you see, is only a horizon, and a horizon is nothing - nothing but the limit of our sight."1 We cannot know what is beyond that horizon, but we know who is there, and the Resurrected Christ is enough to comfort and reassure those who trust in Him.

Blessed be the God and Father of our Lord Jesus Christ, for by God's great mercy we have been born anew to a living hope by the resurrection of Jesus Christ from the dead.

Let us Pray: *[I led an interim prayer, a hymn was played, and the Rev. Pete Ullmann delivered a message of hope and witness to the Resurrection.]*

NOTES

1. Penn, et al., Op. Cit. For more information, see Appendix A at the end of this Collection.

GRANVILLE DYE OBITUARY/EULOGY – AUGUST 29, 2000

I shared this service with the Rev. Pete Ullmann, Mr. Dye's pastor at the time. I was charged with opening the service and delivering the Obituary/Eulogy (which was my usual role). I stuck pretty much to this assignment except maybe for the last passage of scripture at the end of my remarks.

"Blessed be the God and Father of our Lord Jesus Christ! By God's great mercy we have been born anew to a living hope through the Resurrection of Jesus Christ from the dead."
"Praise be to God, for we do not grieve as those who have no hope!"

Jesus said, "I am the resurrection and the life. Those who believe in me, though they die, yet shall they live"
"Come to me all who are burdened and heavy laden, and I will give you rest."
"Blessed are those who mourn; they shall be comforted."

"Our help is in the name of the Lord who made heaven and earth!"

We are gathered to take account of change, to pay attention to sorrow; to grieve a loss and celebrate a homecoming; to witness to the victory over sin and death which is ours in Jesus Christ; to rejoice in the Resurrection to Eternal Life; to remember and to thank God for the life of one whom many of us first came to know and love as "ole man Dye." That's the way this gregarious, out-going, marvelously positive man who never met a stranger introduced himself to me when I first met him almost 30 years ago, and it was the only way I ever heard him introduce himself - with those words, a smile on his lips, and a twinkle in his eye.

Friends, today is a victory celebration - not merely because every Christian funeral celebrates the victory over sin and death which is ours in Christ Jesus, but also because in his life, Granville Dye, gave such eloquent witness to the victory of love over hate, of joy over bitterness, of hope over despair, of kindness over hard-heartedness, of goodness over mean-spiritedness, of gentleness over harshness, of faith over sin, and of life over death.

Funerals are historic occasions because they are one of the ways that most of us mark time on our own journey from the cradle to the grave. 92 years is a long time. "Ole man Dye" may have been joking when he introduced himself that way, but like "Ole Man River" he just kept rolling along - for almost a century. His life spanned almost the entire 20th century. However, it is not the length of his life - but the size of his heart; it is not the weight & quantity of his years, but the quality of his character and the strength of his spirit that help to make this not so much a time of mourning as a day of celebration.

OBITUARY/EULOGY

Granville Dye was born October 15, 1908, the third son and third of seven children born to Genis and Nancy Ferguson Dye.

As a young man he accepted Christ as his Lord and Savior, thus beginning a spiritual journey that led him into a faith that grew deeper and more vibrant as he grew older. A few years ago, when his eyesight began to fail he acquired a large print NT and read it repeatedly so that by the time his eyesight no longer permitted him to see the words, he had many of the passages committed to memory. When he got so he could not see well enough to read or watch TV, he listened regularly to a radio station which carried his beloved Gospel music and religious programing. He listened to the preachers there, and was so familiar with many NT passages that he frequently called his son to check on a preacher he thought had misquoted or misused scripture. He was a beloved member of Calvary Presbyterian Church of Big Lick where for several years he served as song leader.

He loved to tell stories, and one of his favorites was about the events that led up to his and Mrs. Dye's marriage. As Mr. Dye told it, when he was in his early 20's, he ran with a crowd of young people who walked the railroad tracks to church every Sunday. On the first Sunday that a new young lady, Myrtle Mae Roberts, joined the group, Granville took to her right away, and, as was his style, began to joke and kid around with her. He said something which she thought was out of line and she refused to speak to him again until he apologized. When she accepted his apology the next Sunday, he immediately suggested that they kiss and make up. She did not speak to him for another two weeks or so. Apparently, they did eventually kiss and make up, for they were married on July 2, 1934, and spent 62+ years together as loving husband and wife. To their union two sons, Charles and Kenneth, were born.

Mr. Dye's tales about his and Mrs. Dye's courtship reminded me of the tales I had heard from childhood about how two of our local creeks, Mammy's and Daddy's, got their names. As the story goes, a group of early settlers were crossing this plateau. They camped one night on the bank of a certain creek, and that night Mammy won the nightly argument, thus they called it Mammy's Creek. The next night as they camped along another creek, Daddy won the argument, hence Daddy's Creek got its name.

But the truth is the Dyes seldom had crosswords and the love and devotion between them was a shining example of the best that married love can and should be. Mr. Dye was devoted to his wife and children, but especially to his wife. Much is sometimes made these days of the fact that men should accept more responsibility for household chores that are necessary to keep a family going. The fact is that Mr. Dye did all that - learned to cook and clean and can and do all the chores that are required to keep a rural household together - not because it was politically correct but out of love for and devotion to his wife. During Mrs. Dye's last few years when she suffered from various infirmities, he cared for her with such devotion and diligence that it turned what could have been a time of despair into a blessed time of togetherness.

When they were married as Mr. Dye told the story, Mrs. Dye was making $12/week working in a hosiery mill, and Mr. Dye was making $0.50/day working on a farm, leading some to suggest that perhaps he married her for her money. However, in 1943 Mr. Dye took a job at the K-25 plant in Oak Ridge (when it was still part of the Manhattan Project), where he worked for 30 years until his retirement.

In 1963 (10 years before he retired), he bought a piece of land in Big Lick. Upon his retirement in 1973, he and Mrs. Dye moved there and turned it into the Dye Farm. He loved farming and gardening, and he had a gift for it. With his gentle touch, the land blossomed and produced abundantly. He was especially renowned for the quality and quantity of his potatoes. When

Charles embarked on a new and uncertain career, Mr. Dye encouraged him to go ahead, assuring him that if things did not work out, "You can always come home. We've always got taters." Thus, was underscored an understanding in the family that taking risks to improve your situation was ok, because if you failed, you could always "come back home and raise taters."

He loved his farm and his new neighbors, and they grew to love him. He was a friendly and generous neighbor - a fact I can attest to personally from all the times I borrowed tools from him, from the vegetables we took home from his farm, from his generosity to our children – including the time he graciously gave cats to both of them, thereby launching us into the cat farming business until after the kids were out of high school.

He was full of mirth and joy and a self-effacing sense of humor which put everyone in his company at ease. He had a beautiful voice and loved to sing. He sang with spirit and vigor and his voice could lift a whole congregation. He sang more privately also - to his family and friends. And notwithstanding his steadfast devotion and unwavering loyalty to Mrs. Dye, he remained a wee bit of a lady's man all his life. He loved to joke and kid around with the ladies. At times during the last few years, he would call some of the ladies in the neighborhood and serenade them with Gospel tunes over the phone. One of the women who also came from a singing family sometimes joined him singing old time gospel songs over the phone.

Thinking of Mr. Dye, I am reminded of Francis of Assisi who like Mr. Dye's forsook material wealth to live a simple life close to nature. Mr. Dye was a living example of one of the fundamental truths of the Christian life, a truth perhaps first codified by Francis in the rules for the order that took his name. This is that even if we live alone, we live for others. Visiting with Mr. Dye in his house just off the side of the road, just out of sight of Hwy 127, experiencing his love for and enjoyment of people and his always positive, upbeat, uplifting spirit sometimes reminded me of a poem by Sam Walter Foss entitled The House by the Side of the Road.

It goes in part . . .

[I read two verses of the poem, but in order to comply with Copyright law I can print only the following one here.]

"I see from my house by the side of the road,
By the side of the highway of life:
The men who press with the ardor of hope;

The men who are faint with the strife
But I turn not away from their smiles nor their tears,
Both part of an infinite plan –
Let me live in a house by the side of the road
And be a friend to man."

Mr. Dye died much as he had lived, quietly and peacefully, on August 28, 2000, barely six weeks short of his 92nd birthday. Having been fiercely independent and fearing, perhaps more than anything else, that he might lose his independence and become a burden to someone else, he died as he would have chosen - stricken while performing one of the fundamental acts of personal independence, cooking his own meal, he died after a short final infirmity without extended pain or suffering, without ever becoming a burden to anyone, without ever having to leave the farm he loved. We are left not so much to mourn as to ponder how his "ole man Dye" routine will go over when he introduces himself to Methuselah.

He is survived by: *[I read a list of survivors.]*

As I sat with some of you at Mr. Dye's house the other day, I could see through the open door the hummingbirds darting around his feeders. I remembered how Mr. Dye loved the birds, and I was reminded of the following passage from the naturalist, Loren Eiseley. Eiseley wrote it after arising from a brief nap in a forest glade. He told how he awoke one day in a glade in the wood to see a raven devour a nestling song sparrow. He tells the story at some length and then he writes: "It was then that I saw the judgment. It was the judgment of life against death. I will never again see it in notes so tragically prolonged. . . the crystal note of a song sparrow lifted hesitantly in the hush; then another joined in and then another. . .They sang because life is sweet and sunlight beautiful. They sang under the brooding shadow of the raven. In simple truth they had forgotten the raven, for they were the singers of life, and not of death."[1]

Granville Dye was a Singer of Life.

> *"What then shall we say to this? If God is for us who is against us? He who did not spare his own Son, but gave him up for us all, will he not also give us all things with him? Who shall bring any charge against God's elect? It is God who justifies; who is to condemn? Is it Christ Jesus, who died, yes, who was raised from the dead, who is at the right hand of God, who indeed intercedes for us? Who shall separate us from the love of*

Christ? Shall tribulation, or distress, or persecution, of famine, or nakedness, or peril, or sword? [Shall sorrow or change?] . . . NO! In all these things we are more than conquerors through him who loved us. For I am sure that neither death, nor life, nor angels, nor principalities, nor things present, nor things to come, nor powers, nor height, nor depth, nor anything else in all creation, will be able to separate us from the love of God in Christ Jesus our Lord." (Romans 8: 31- 35; 37-39)

Let us Pray: *[I led an interim prayer.]*

[A hymn was played.]

[The Rev. Pete Ullmann presented a message of hope and witness to the Resurrection.]

[Dismissal to place of burial for a committal service.]

NOTES:

1. In compliance with Copyright law I have reproduced here only seven lines of Eiseley's description of the event.

CORA BURGESS OBITUARY/EULOGY – FEBRUARY 21, 2002

I was charged with doing only the Opening and the Obituary/ Eulogy for this service, but as you will see I got into a message of hope and healing; witness to the resurrection more than perhaps I should have.

OPENING SCRIPTURE and REMARKS

> *"Praise be to God, for we do not grieve as those who have no hope!"*

> *Jesus said, "I am the resurrection and the life. Those who believe in me, though they die, yet shall they live"*

> *"Come to me all who are burdened and heavy laden, and I will give you rest."*

> *"Blessed are those who mourn; they shall be comforted."*

> *"Our help is in the name of the Lord who made heaven and earth!"*

We are gathered to take account of change; to pay attention to sorrow; to grieve a loss and celebrate a homecoming; to remember and to thank God for the life of Cora Wilbanks Burgess; to witness to the Resurrection, and to rejoice in the victory of eternal life over sin and death which is ours in Christ Jesus.

OBITUARY/EULOGY

Have no doubt about it, grief and tears notwithstanding, today is a victory celebration - not merely because every Christian funeral is such, but especially because Cora throughout her life and in the courage and dignity of her last days bore such powerful witness to the victory which is ours in Jesus Christ - the victory of joy over despair, of peace over enmity, of kindness over meanness, of love over hate, of faith over falsehood, of purity over corruption, of forgiveness over vindictiveness, of humility over self-righteousness, of true righteousness over sin, and of all the forces of life and right over the forces of death and destruction.

You may ask, "Preacher, if today is a victory celebration, why are our hearts so heavy?" We grieve because life is good, and change is hard, and parting is such sweet sorrow. We grieve for our loss - not for Cora. We grieve partly because we had her for so long. Cora lived a long, useful, fruitful, fulfilled life. I truthfully do not know how long, and even if I did, I am sworn to secrecy and could not reveal it to you. But as long as it was, it was not long enough. It is never long enough. There are always things left undone and incomplete. It is hard to part with one who has been a mainstay of our lives for so long.

By the same token, however, we also rejoice not only because of the length of her years but because the length of her years was matched by the quality of her life. She lived a remarkable life, full of spirit and spunk until the very end. And it is not merely the magnitude of her years with us, but the content of her character and the strength of her spirit that makes today not so much a low point in our own journey from the cradle to the grave as it is a day of rare privilege. Indeed, how blessed we are to grieve today - for it means we had the privilege of loving and being loved by one of God's great people.

We are not promised any number of days on this earth, and we cannot have permanence in this world. The best we can hope for here is to have our lives touched by the Hand of God - and next to that - the best that most of us ever experience in this life - is to have our lives touched by someone who is straight & true, loving & caring, kind & generous, accepting & forgiving. To the degree that we had that with Cora - as mother, granny, mother-in-law, sister, loved one, neighbor or friend - then we know a little of what it is to be touched by the Hand of God. And our memory of that makes us as richly blessed as it is possible to be blessed in this life.

A few years ago, there was a book written entitled "It Takes a Village to Raise a Child." Cora may stir in her coffin at this reference for the book was authored by a person of the wrong political persuasion, and a person whom Cora did not particularly respect. I have not read the book, and cannot speak for its contents, but I know that those of us who were reared in the Big Lick community in the 1940's and 50's should resonate to the truth of the book's title. We were reared by a village, and we had several mothers and fathers, each of whom cared almost as much for each of us as they did for their own children, and each of whom took an active role in parenting us, each of whom rejoiced in our successes and grieved our failures almost as much as our own parents. Cora was one of our mothers. I had already decided to mention this today, but it was reinforced last night by three other individuals who reminded me of this fact. Big Lick was a remarkable and wonderful place to grow up in during those years, and it was so because of Cora and others like her.

Cora Evelyn Wilbanks was born in Pleasant Hill sometime in the first quarter of the 20th century. No one knows exactly when, and if I knew I could not tell you. I am sworn to secrecy. She was the 2nd of 7 daughters born to Eston K. and Emily Elmore Wilbanks. As a young woman she pursued her own career, securing certification as a registered nurse. She was working at this career in the old hospital at Pleasant Hill in the fall of 1937 or the spring of 1938 when a young man was admitted with appendicitis. He was from a community on the other side of the county (a "fer" piece in those days), and was, at the time, working on the "new" road from Crossville to Rockwood (Hwy 70E).

He had a somewhat unusual first name, but an engaging personality. They came to know and like each other during his stay in the hospital, and even more so over the days and weeks that followed. He used the money he made on the road to buy her some rings, and she and Eucle Burgess were married in June, 1938. So it was that Cora Wilbanks became Cora Burgess and left her job at the hospital in Pleasant Hill and moved into her husband's family home in Big Lick.

Thus, begins today's remarkable story. It has been said that some people are an enigma wrapped in a riddle. That cannot be said of Cora. There was not much mystery about her. You never had to wonder much about what Cora was like or what she thought or what she felt to be important. She was straightforward and forthright and honest and sometimes blunt. No, what was confounding about Cora was that she was somehow successfully two persons molded into one whole that was greater than its parts.

She was on the one hand the quintessential rural farm wife and mother, who moved into her husband's family home with her mother-in-law and made a success of that relationship. She was in all ways her husband's helpmate -

waiting on his every need as wives were once expected to do - working beside him as farm boss and field hand - sweating beside her mother-in-law making a huge garden - rearing their children - and in later years when Eucle's work kept him away from home much of the time, she ran not only the household but the farm as well. In this mode, she reared not only the three children born of their union but also helped to rear some of her grandchildren as well.

Her relationship with her mother-in-law, Amy, is particularly worthy of note. They not only made a success of their situation but did so with such grace and harmony that their families not merely survived but flourished. Her brother-in-law, Marvin, who was about 10 when Cora moved into their home, made special note of this in his booklet about his early years.

Their relationship reminds me of another mother- and daughter-in-law, and the spirit of Cora's relationship with Mrs. Burgess is well summed up in the words of that daughter-in-law, Ruth, when she said to her mother-in-law Naomi, "...where you lodge, I will lodge; your family will be my family, and your church my church; where you die, I will die, and there will I be buried." It is interesting to note that Cora did die almost exactly where Mrs. Burgess had died (and where Cora had so lovingly cared for her during her final illness). Both women had a "green thumb" and enjoyed gardening together.

At the same time that she was this model mid-20th century rural farm wife and mother, Cora was also, on the other hand, a modern, up-to-date, 21st century kind of woman who was ahead of her time in many ways. She had an independent streak and pursued her own career at a time when such was rare for women, and she regularly practiced her profession, at times for pay, and at times for free among her neighbors. Among other things she served for several years as a community nurse in Big Lick.

She was a strong-willed person who had a mind of her own. She read widely and kept up avidly with local, state, national, and international events. She had a keen mind and sharp memory. She was active in her community and in her political party. She had her own opinions - opinions about almost everything - about what was happening with the people she knew and loved - about national and world events - about what was happening in her church - and she was not reticent about sharing them with her children and grandchildren, friends and neighbors, and anyone else she thought needed to hear them.

Perhaps it was her nursing training - perhaps it was just her personality - perhaps a bit of both - but she had this wonderful combination of being tough minded and tender hearted. She had the ability to speak the truth in love, even when the truth was hard. She was quick to make tough decisions and calm in the midst of crisis. She was a very practical woman who disliked things that seemed impractical. She followed a demanding moral code and expected others to do likewise, but she was seldom judgmental and almost always gentle, loving, and forgiving.

In the 31st chapter of Proverbs, there is a passage that reads, in part:

"A true lady is hard to find;
She is far more precious than jewels...
She delights to work with her hands...
And goes to work with a will...
She opens her hands to the unfortunate,
And stretches out her arms to the poor.
She does not fear for her family when it snows,
For they are all more than adequately clothed...
She makes her own bedcovers...
Her clothing is of good quality and dignified;
She has no worry about tomorrow.
When she opens her mouth she speaks wisely,
And kindly instruction is on her tongue...

Her children rise up to pronounce blessings on her;
Her husband, too, sings her praises:
'Many women have proved their worth,
But you have surpassed them all.'
Charm is deceitful and beauty is fleeting,
But the intelligent woman who fears the Lord is to be praised.
Give her the reward of her labor,
And let the gates ring with praise of her deeds."
[Proverbs 31: 10-31; MFS translation]

Thus, may it be said of Cora. She lived her faith. Not just in her practice of daily Bible reading and prayer. Not just in her reciting of the 23rd Psalm every night before she went to sleep. Not just in her faithful church attendance and taking active responsibility in the life of Calvary Presbyterian Church, where she was an active member from 1940 until her death. But equally in the important aspects of her daily life - in her relationship with her family and her neighbors - in her dealings with friends and strangers - in her efforts to build people up and not tear them down. Her sister called her an "intercessory prayer warrior" because she cared so deeply for others and regularly carried those cares to God in prayer.

Cora died at home on February 18, 2002.
She is survived by: [I read the list of survivors.]

[One of her former pastors sang Lead Kindly Light.]

When Sherry called me Monday morning to tell me that her mother had died, the next thing she said to me was, "Yea, she's gone out back, to the beautiful place." It was a reference to something Cora had said while I was visiting on the Saturday before. Linda had asked her mother if she wanted to go lie in bed. Cora said, "No." and then she said either, "I want to go out back to the beautiful place" or "I want to go back to the beautiful place" (as if she were referring to someplace she had previously been). I was sitting closest to her at the time, and I am not sure which she said. In either case, it was clear what she meant. Cora's spirit had already departed this world (and perhaps glimpsed what lay ahead), and Cora was urging her body to follow. It was so clear to me that I momentarily thought Cora might actually die at that moment.

As was said of my own mother, Cora never lingered much over much of anything except dying. For her, it took too long to travel the final road out of this world. She came at times to scold God for not responding quickly enough to her prayers to be transported to the "beautiful place out back." She even told one of her doctors that she did not think God was listening to her prayers. When she, in turn, was reminded by one of her daughters that she should not be telling God what to do but rather asking God what she should do, she adjusted her prayer life. But even then, she indicated that in doing so, she thought that might hasten that for which she wished.

I am not so sure that Cora was rightly corrected about the nature of her prayers. Perhaps it was that she was just somewhat confused and had forgotten the training that she had received at church and needed a little reminder. On the other hand, perhaps it was that her spiritual discipline over the years had been so intense, her prayer life so regular that she had come to be so comfortable in speaking with God that she could speak to God freely - even remonstrate with God about her feelings that God was not doing what she thought God should do. If that is the case, she was in good company: Abraham, Sarah, Moses, Job, Jeremiah, David and other psalmists, and perhaps Jesus himself when he quoted from the 22nd Psalm from the Cross did the same thing. Maybe it was not evidence of an insufficient faith or inadequate spiritual discipline but in fact, the very evidence of just how deep and thorough her faith and spiritual life actually was.

Considered these words which the Apostle Paul wrote to the Corinthians:

> *"We know that if this earthly shack we live in is destroyed, we have a house built by God - not made with human hands, but eternal and spiritual. Here, indeed, we groan and can hardly wait to get into our spiritual dwelling, so that we will not be found naked and exposed to the elements. For as long as we remain in this earthly shack, we have many worries and anxieties. It is not that we wish to be without a house, but we want a better dwelling - so that our dying may be swallowed up by life in Christ Jesus. God himself is preparing us for this very thing and has given us the Holy Spirit as a guarantee."*
> (2 Corinthians 5:1-5)

In 1954 Stewart Hamblin wrote what became the top country songs of that year, based in part upon St. Paul's image of our body as a ramshackle house in which our spirit dwells here on earth and which is to be replaced by a more splendid dwelling upon our departure from this world. Though hardly the kind of music normally heard at funerals, this song has a message appropriate for a Christian funeral. My father thought so. Cora herself might not have considered this appropriate for a funeral, but knowing how she loved and respected my father, I think she would defer to his judgment. Moreover, it seems particularly suited to Cora in view of the fact that she happily spent most of her life in a house that was probably already eligible for listing on the National Historic Register when she moved in. Some of you may remember the tune of this song-upbeat, uplifting, joyous-fully appropriate for a victory celebration such as a Christian funeral. It is entitled "THIS OLD HOUSE" and the chorus goes:

> *"Ain't goin'need this house no longer; Ain't goin' need this house no more; Ain't got time to fix the shingles; Ain't got time to fix the floor;*
> *Ain't got time to oil no hinges;*
> *Nor mend the broken window panes. Ain't goin' need this house no longer, I'm gettin' ready to meet the saints."* [1]

We will soon take the house that Cora lived in here on earth to its final resting place, but she's not there anymore - she's gettin' ready to meet the saints.

Let us pray: [I led an interim prayer, and a hymn was sung or played.]

[The Rev. Pete Ullmann continued and ended the funeral service with a Meditation.]

[A hymn was played, and we were dismissed to the place of burial for a committal service.]

NOTES:

1. I read one verse in addition to the chorus in the service, but using the chorus only enables me to comply with Copyright regulations.

AMANDA HICKS BELL OBITUARY/EULOGY MARCH 8, 2002

I did this complete service.

OPENING

> *"Praise be to God, for we do not grieve as those who have no hope!"*
> *Jesus said, "I am the resurrection and the life. Those who believe in me, though they die, yet shall they live"*
> *"Come to me all who are burdened and heavy laden, and I will give you rest."*
> *"Blessed are those who mourn; they shall be comforted."*
> *"Our help is in the name of the Lord who made heaven and earth!"*

We are gathered to take account of change; to pay attention to sorrow; to grieve a loss and celebrate a homecoming; to remember and to thank God for the life of Amanda Hicks Bell; to witness to the Resurrection, and rejoice in the victory of eternal life over sin and death which is ours in Christ Jesus.

Shortly before Christmas 2000, I was involved in another funeral. One of the visitors at that occasion said of the deceased, "Laura received an early Christmas present-eternal peace." Remembering that statement and the fact that eggs have long been used as symbols of the Resurrection-thus their association with Easter, we may say of Amanda-in the year 2002, she received an early Easter basket-filled with the joys of the Resurrection.

"Fear not, for I am with you, be not dismayed, for I am your God. I will strengthen you, I will help you, I will uphold you... Fear not, for I have redeemed you; I have called you by name, you are mine. When you pass through the waters I will be with you, and through the rivers, they shall not overwhelm you. When you walk through fire you shall not be burned, and the flames shall not consume you. For I am the Lord your God, the Holy One of Israel, your Savior." (Isaiah 41:10; 43:1b-3)

Have no doubt about it, grief and tears notwithstanding, today is a victory celebration-not merely because every Christian funeral is such, but especially because Amanda, throughout her life, bore such powerful witness to the victory which is ours in J. Christ-the victory of joy over despair, of peace over enmity, of kindness over meanness, of love over hate, of faith over falsehood, of purity over corruption, of forgiveness over vindictiveness, of humility over self-righteousness, of true righteousness over sinfulness, and of all the forces of life and right over the forces of death and destruction.

You may ask, "Preacher, if today is a victory celebration, why are our hearts so heavy?" We grieve because life is good, change is hard, and parting is such sweet sorrow. We grieve for our loss - not for Amanda. We grieve partly because we had her for so long. Amanda lived a long, useful, fruitful, fulfilled life. And at its end, she could say with the Apostle Paul in his words to Timothy "...I am already on the point of [death]...I have fought the good fight, I have finished the race, I have kept the faith. Henceforth there is laid up for me the crown of righteousness, which the Lord...will award me...and not only to me but also to all who have loved his appearing." (2 Tim. 4:6-8).

OBITUARY/EULOGY

We thank God today for the life of Amanda Hicks Bell and for sharing her life with us. Amanda was born in Putnam County on November 14, 1907, the third daughter and fourth of six children born to Haywood and Belle Webb Hicks. She was married for over 30 years to Carson Bell who preceded her in death.

Amanda was a teacher all of her life-and for 42 of her years, she even got paid to do the job she loved. Amanda loved children, and having none of her own, she simply adopted the many who came into her classrooms and loved them as her own. She was a great communicator and after her retirement form, the classroom used the phone extensively to keep in touch with former students, co-workers, and friends. For someone who lived alone, she was seldom lonely, at least not until after her sister Kathleen died. She was close to her family, and although she had many other close relatives, the death of her last sibling left her lonely at times.

She loved the farm and the farm way of life. She got great joy out of tending to the cattle and hogs that she kept on her place until age and health forced her to give up the daily chores that such required.

She had an independent streak and did not much like to ask for help. She experienced good health most of her life and was seldom sick until her final few years when the heart that had been so strong for herself and for others finally began to give out. She lived alone, taking care of herself until her very last illness. She had a keen mind and kept up with what was happening in her community, in the world, and in the church both locally and nationally, and she often raised those issues when we were visiting.

Her life was not without pain and hardship. What was largely missing from her life was any hint of bitterness. She seemed always in a good spirit and had a marvelous sense of humor; she saw the humor in situations that others might have seen as mundane or humorless and was able to laugh at herself. She joked and laughed frequently. Even the last time I visited with her, shortly before her death, she was joking and laughing. Chief among the physical characteristics I shall always remember about Amanda is her laugh.

Amanda lived a long remarkable life, full of spirit and spunk until the very end. But we rejoice today not merely in the magnitude of her years but more so because the length of her years were matched by the quality of her character. And it is the content of her character and the strength of her spirit that makes today not so much a low point in our own journey from the cradle to the grave as it is a day of rare privilege. I grieve today, but I grieve in joy. Indeed, how blessed we are to grieve today - for it means we had the privilege of loving and being loved by one of God's great people.

Ninety-four years is a long time. But not long enough. It is never long enough. It is hard to lose someone who has been a part of our lives for so long. We are not promised any # of days on this earth, and we cannot have permanence in this world. The best we can hope for here is to have our lives touched by the Hand of God-and next to that-the best that most of us ever experience in this life-is to have our lives touched by someone who is straight & true, loving & caring, kind & generous, accepting & forgiving. To the degree that we had that with Amanda, then we know a little of what it is to be touched by the Hand of God. And our memory of that makes us as richly blessed as it is possible to be blessed in this life.

Though it lasted longer than most of ours will, Amanda's physical heart finally failed her body, and she left this realm of space and time. However, Amanda's spiritual heart never weakened. By the world's measure, Amanda lived and died poor-deriving her only income from small social security and teacher's pension checks. And such was her generosity that much of the treasure she might have stored up on earth she had given away. On several occasions, she told me about a relative who would say to her, "Amanda, you'd be rich if you hadn't given it all away." I personally witnessed at least one occasion when Amanda offered what little money she had saved to another whose need she saw as greater than her own.

But the irony is that Amanda was rich - Rich in those qualities of character and strength of spirit that truly endure - dependability, honesty, integrity, trustworthiness, steadfastness. She was faithful and true, kind, generous, loving, and forgiving. She was Rich in those qualities the Apostle Paul called the fruits of the Spirit; Joy - Peace - Patience - Kindness - Goodness - Faithfulness - Gentleness - Self-control. And she was Rich in friendships and in the rewards of service forged over a lifetime of teaching and living and loving.

I am reminded of what another person I once knew said near the end of his life. He was a person of considerable abilities who had chosen to spend his life in a relatively obscure place and work when his talents and abilities would have fitted him for more visible and lucrative positions. When it was suggested by someone that he had wasted his life, he replied, "The life that was wasted has been full...Perhaps that is what life is for in the economy of God - to be wasted for others."

The 15th Psalm (slightly revised):

> "O Lord, who shall you invite to your house
> Who shall come to live on your Holy hill?
> She who walks blamelessly
> Who does what is right
> Who speaks truth from her heart;
> Who does not slander with her tongue, and does no evil to a friend,
> Nor repeats a derogatory report against her neighbor . . .
> She who sticks to her word (promise) and does not change
>   even if it causes her hardship;

> Who does not seek a profit from what she gives,
>> And will not cheat the innocent.
> She who does these things shall never be moved."

Amanda died quietly on March 6, 2002. She is survived by:

[I read a list of survivors.]

[I led an interim prayer and a hymn was played.]

[I completed the service with a Meditation, Prayer, and Benediction.]
[Dismissal to place of burial for a committal service.]

ALBERTA BURGESS GIBSON OBITUARY/ EULOGY - JULY 19, 2002

I was charged only with the Opening and the Obituary/ Eulogy for this service, but as you will see I drifted well beyond that. Pete Ullmann was the minister charged with doing the message of hope and witness to the Resurrection.

OPENING:

> *"Praise be to God, for we do not grieve as those who have no hope!"*
> *Jesus said, "I am the resurrection and the life. Those who believe in me, though they die, yet shall they live"*
> *"Come to me all who are burdened and heavy laden, and I will give you rest."*
> *"Blessed are those who mourn; they shall be comforted."*
> *"Our help is in the name of the Lord who made heaven and earth!"*

We are gathered to take account of change; to pay attention to sorrow; to grieve a loss and celebrate a homecoming; to remember and to thank God for the life of Alberta Burgess Gibson; to witness to the Resurrection, and rejoice in the victory of eternal life over sin and death which is ours in Christ Jesus.

Have no doubt about it, grief and tears notwithstanding, today is a victory celebration-not merely because every Christian funeral is such, but especially because Alberta, throughout her life bore such powerful witness to the victory which is ours in J. Christ-the victory of joy over despair, of peace over enmity, of kindness over meanness, of love over hate, of faith over falsehood, of purity over corruption, of forgiveness over vindictiveness, of humility over self-righteousness, of true righteousness over sinfulness, and of all the forces of life and right over the forces of death and destruction.

You may ask, "Preacher, if today is a victory celebration, why are our hearts so heavy?" We grieve because life is good, change is hard, and parting is such sweet sorrow. We grieve for our loss - not for Alberta. We grieve partly because we had her for so long. Alberta lived a long, useful, fruitful, fulfilled life. And at its end, she could say with the Apostle Paul in his words to Timothy, "...I am already on the point of [death]...I have fought the good fight, I have finished the race, I have kept the faith. Henceforth there is laid up for me the crown of righteousness, which the Lord...will award me...and not only to me but also to all who have loved his appearing." (2 Tim. 4:6-8).

OBITUARY/EULOGY

Alberta Burgess Gibson was born a few days before Christmas on the 18th of December, 1918, the fourth child and second daughter of Vance and Amy Sevier Burgess.

Early in life she learned (I suspect from her mother) a bit of scripture which she often repeated. It is the words Paul and Silas spoke to the Philippi jailer the morning after the jail was opened, but none of the prisoners escaped. By the time she was 10, she had probably committed these words to heart. In any case, she had taken them to heart because on Sept 1, 1929, 3 months before she turned 11, she accepted Christ as her Lord and Savior and was baptized into the membership of Calvary Presbyterian Church of Big Lick, where she remained a member all her life. Oh yes, Paul and Silas' words to the Philippi jailer: "Believe in the Lord Jesus Christ and you will be saved."

As a young woman she attended the Mossop School in Harriman and then the High School in Crossville. Then, at a time when such was uncharacteristic of women, she displayed the spirit, courage and drive that characterized her life by going far from home to attend Berea College.

It was there, in the late 1930's while washing dishes as part of her required work program, that she first came to know a young man from Raceland, Ky., who would harass her while she worked. This young man was bouncing off a failed love affair and was drawn to the buoyant and vibrant young woman from Tenn. According to his accounting, she paid him no attention at first, wouldn't give him the time of day, but he persisted and she relented.

So it was that on July 6, 1940, a little over 62 years ago, at the encouragement of the preacher, Everett and Alberta slipped away from a party at her brother's house, sneaked back into her mother's house through a window to change into their good clothes, and went with those at the party to Calvary Presbyterian Church and became the first couple ever married in that church. Afterwards, they treated their guests to a wedding supper of hamburgers and fries at the West Side Café in Crossville. You may remember the nursery rhyme that has a phrase, "where will the wedding supper be?" Well, in this case, it was at the West Side Café. I have been to many wedding suppers some with mariachi' bands and six-foot-tall wedding cakes and dancing and banquet tables laden with food, but I was never to one at the West Side Café. I will always harbor the suspicion that I thereby missed something special. Alberta returned to Berea where she became the first married student to be permitted to continue her education there.

Alberta was a vivacious person who was physically limber and supple. She could stand on the hearth at her home, bend over without bending her knees and place the palms of her hands flat on the carpet four inches lower than her feet. Perhaps it was her nimbleness of foot that led her as a young woman to enjoy folk dancing. Though I suspect it caused her mother considerable consternation, she and Christine Hall Thompson returned from Mossop School to teach other young people in Big Lick how to do "singing games" (folk dances in which the music is provided by the dancers singing). In 1985 when we held the first Big Lick Homecoming, it was Alberta whom we turned to, to teach us some of those old dances. She enjoyed singing and was not afraid to take the lead. For as long as I can remember, hymns at Calvary Church began with Alberta's voice leading the way. She enjoyed sitting on her front porch and looking at the mountains and reminded me of my father's saying: "The mountains give you something to rest your eyes against."

Alberta was a teacher all of her life - and for 27 years from 1953-1980 she even got paid to do the job she loved. She was still serving as a Sunday school teacher at the time of her death. She was a child of Vance and Amy Burgess: stubborn, strong-willed, determined, set in her ways, and as straight and true as the day is long. Like her mother before her, she was a worrier who could often envision bad things happening. But she was always prepared. She was renowned for her frugality. She wasted nothing. Mary Nina has been going through some of the things Alberta stored away over the years because they might be useful later, and I think Mary Nina has about decided that nothing that came into her mother's house ever left. It's all stored away somewhere, neatly folded and packed - in drawers and boxes and five-gallon lard cans.

Alberta died on July 16, 2002. She died peacefully as she would have chosen-after a brief final illness and without any prolonged lingering or suffering. She is survived by: [I read a list of survivors.]

The other night Mary Nina told me about the crow that crashed into Letha's windshield on her way to visit Alberta, and Everett told of the night bird that called three times at his door almost at the very moment that Alberta died. Mary Nina reminded me of the Native American legend that birds (especially crows and ravens) represent spirits from the world beyond. I thought of the birds that fed Elijah and also of the dove that represents the Spirit of God. But mostly, I was reminded of the poem "To Those I Love" by Isla Pascal Richardson. Perchance if those birds did represent Alberta's spirit, maybe this is what they were trying to say:

> If I should ever leave you whom I love
> To go along the Silent Way,
> Grieve not,
>
> . . .
> Please do not let the thoughts of me be sad,
> For I am loving you just as I always have.
>
> . . .
> We cannot see Beyond,
> But this I know:
> I loved you so – t'was heaven here with you." [1]

Eighty-three years is a long time. But not long enough. It is never long enough. It is hard to lose someone who has been a part of our lives for so long. We are not promised any number of days on this earth, and we cannot have permanence in this world. The best we can hope for here is to have our lives touched by the Hand of God-and next to that-the best that most of us ever experience in this life-is to have our lives touched by someone who is straight & true, loving & caring, kind & generous, accepting & forgiving. To the degree that we had that with Alberta as wife, mother, grandmother, sister, teacher, co-worker, neighbor or friend then we know a little of what it is to be touched by the Hand of God. And our memory of that makes us as richly blessed as it is possible to be blessed in this life.

The 15th Psalm:

> "O Lord, who shall you invite to your house
> Who shall come to live on your Holy hill?

[She] who walks blamelessly; Who does what is right;
Who speaks truth from her heart;
Who does not slander with her tongue, and does no evil to a friend,
   Nor repeats a derogatory report against her neighbor; . . .
[She] who sticks to her word (promise) and does not change
   even if it causes her hardship;
Who does not seek a profit from what she gives,
   And will not cheat the innocent.
[She] who does these things shall never be moved."

Alberta was a devoted and disciplined follower of Jesus Christ throughout her life. She lived her faith, not just in her practice of Bible reading and prayer. Not just in her faithful church attendance and taking active responsibility in the life of her Church where she taught Sunday school and served as an Elder. But equally in the important aspects of her daily life - in her relationship with her family and her neighbors - in her teaching - in her dealings with friends and strangers - in her efforts to build people up and not tear them down.

As I visited with Everett and Mary Nina the other night I was struck by the peace they had in their decision to trust Alberta to God's hands rather than subject her to any of the death-prolonging interventions of which modern medicine is capable. As we talked, I was reminded of some things my father said in a sermon he preached on Sept 15, 1957, the week after my sister had almost died and while she was still in guarded condition following a risky operation. The sermon is entitled "Reflections in A Day of Trouble." Alberta was among those who heard this sermon when it was first delivered, and she was among those who comforted and strengthened my family during those days of trouble.

In that sermon, my father said, in part: "soon or late a day of trouble, a day of personal and family distress and sorrow comes to all of us. 'Suffering is the common lot and all the devices of man are unable to make him completely immune from it. Sooner or later, it tracks out our footsteps and discovers our hiding places.'...

"The Bible and the Christian faith does not run away from the terrible reality of these days of trouble. How could it? How can we? One of the remarkable things about the Bible is its account of how [people] have found their faith raised to the highest level at precisely that point where one expects them to lose it...

"[The promise of God in the day of trouble] finds beautiful expression in [these] words from the prophet Isaiah:

"'Fear not, for I am with you, be not dismayed, for I am your God. I will strengthen you, I will help you, I will uphold you...Fear not, for I have redeemed you; I have called you by name, you are mine. When you pass through the waters I will be with you, and through the rivers, they shall not overwhelm you. When you walk through fire you shall not be burned, and the flames shall not consume you. For I am the Lord your God, the Holy One of Israel, your Savior.' (Isaiah 41:10; 43:1b-3)

"In these word is no promise that those who trust God will escape the storms and fires of life, no promise of freedom from a day of trouble, no suggestion that the circumstances will be made less terrible. But there is the assurance of God's presence and concern, and herein lies the difference...

"Think finally of Jesus Christ...when we think of that figure on the Cross, we know that he, too, had to cling to trust in the face of despair. He still calls out 'My God, My God', even in the moment he feels utterly forsaken. And it is only because He can pass through this moment of dereliction that he is able to say, at the end, 'Father, into thy hands I commit my spirit.'...these final words of Jesus...point to another truth...This is: Nothing is lost when we make an offering of it. We can never lose a loved one whom we have committed to God's care...The amazing truth is that the moment we let go, the instant we stop trying to push reality, life is enriched instead of being impoverished. It is at this point that we find the difference between the person who demands and the person who trusts. The most precious things in life cannot be reached by seizing and demanding - the love of a wife or a child [or a mother] - friendship - the forgiveness of God [or another] . . . What we really need is the assurance that despite all the perils which surround us, and despite the mystery of death which stands at the end of the road, we belong to a fellowship within which we can find abundant life...this assurance comes to the person who has a trust similar to that expressed in these word of an [ancient] prayer:

> 'In those moments when we seem to have reached the end of our own strength, teach us to commit our lives and all that we hold dear to Thy keeping, in the knowledge that Thy wisdom is more certain than all human plans, and Thy mercy is deeper than all human reckoning.'" [2]

Alberta, at various times has complimented me on funeral services I had helped conduct, but she would remind me that "It was almost as good as your Daddy used to do. He could make people feel blessed at a funeral." She particularly had fond recollections of the funeral service my father conducted for her mother. I close with another quote from my father, this one an excerpt from that funeral address for Mrs. Amy Burgess delivered on April 21, 1958. You can substitute Alberta's name and thoughts of her in those places where Mrs. Burgess is mentioned in this excerpt:

"Mrs. Burgess was a devout and faithful member of the Church, never missing a service except for illness. She was a woman of prayer, carrying her family and her neighbors to the throne of grace. She was willing to bear reproach in her witness to Jesus Christ. The pew which she always occupied is now vacant, but really is vacant only to physical sight, for her spirit of faith and love and faithfulness will ever hover near, an unseen but deeply experienced inspiration to others who seek to follow her example in living for Christ. She has not left the church but journeyed, at the call of God, to assume a larger ministry with the multitudes who worship and serve the Lord in heaven and on earth. [3]

> 'There is no death
> To those whose hearts are set
> On higher things than this life doth afford;
> How shall their passing leave one least regret,
> For those who go to join their Lord.'" [4]
>   — John Oxenham

Let Us Pray: [I offered an interim prayer and a hymn was played.]

[The Rev. Pete Ullmann delivered a message of hope and witness to the Resurrection.]

[Benediction and dismissal to place of burial for a committal service.]

NOTES:

1. In the service, I read the whole poem. These eight lines, however, capture the essence of the poem and are all I am permitted to print by Copyright law.

2. I hold the Copyright to this material.

3. I hold the Copyright to this material.

4. In the service, I may have read more of this poem, but these five lines are sufficient to give the reader an idea of the content of the poem and are within the parameters of what is permitted by Copyright law.

LENA MAE TOLLETT OBITUARY/EULOGY FEBRUARY 19, 2003

I did this entire service by myself.

OPENING

"Praise be to God, for we do not grieve as those who have no hope!"

Jesus said, "I am the resurrection and the life. Those who believe in me, though they die, yet shall they live"

"Come to me all who are burdened and heavy laden, and I will give you rest."

"Blessed are those who mourn; they shall be comforted."

"Our help is in the name of the Lord who made heaven and earth!"

We are gathered to take account of change, to pay attention to sorrow; to grieve a loss and celebrate a homecoming: to remember; to thank God for the life of Lena Mae Tollett; to witness to the Resurrection, and to rejoice in the victory of eternal life over sin and death which is ours in Christ Jesus.

If there is one thing you hold onto from today, I hope you will hold on to these words from Isaiah:

Thus says the Lord: "Fear not, for I am with you, be not dismayed, for I am your God. I will strengthen you, I will help you, I will uphold you...Fear not, for I have redeemed you; I have called you by name, you are mine. When you pass through the waters I will be with you, and through the rivers, they shall not overwhelm you. When you walk through fire, you shall not be burned, and the flames shall not consume you. For I am the Lord your God, the Holy One of Israel, your Savior." (Isaiah 41:10; 43:1b-3)

OBITUARY/EULOGY

We thank God today for the life of Lena Mae Tollett and for sharing her life with us. Lena Mae was born near Melvin in the Sequatchie Valley on March 28, 1922, the third daughter and youngest of eight children born to Waymon and Eliza Swafford Henry. At the age of 18 she married Johnnie Tollett and moved to Big Lick where she lived for the remainder of her life. To their union, 4 daughters were born - Burdeen, Sandra, Lillie, and Mary Jean - all of whom survive their mother.

As I grew up, I knew Lena Mae as the mother of a classmate and other schoolmates and as a regular attendee of Calvary Presbyterian Church in Big Lick. As I grew old, I came to know of Lena Mae as a determined and strong woman who defied the predictions of her doctors and lived longer than anyone expected her to. Until yesterday, however, I did not know that she and I shared a passion and some skill for basketball. In her youth, she had started playing on the Melvin H. S. varsity when she was in 8th grade.

Though she worked at times at Lay's and the Ben Franklin 5 & 10 stores, Lena Mae was at heart a country wife, mother, and homemaker. She loved to cook and will be fondly remembered for her morning biscuits and chocolate pies. She loved flowers and was a skilled seamstress who made most of her children's clothing when they were young, even making her own patterns and taught at least one of her daughters to be a good seamstress also. She was also a gifted quilter and made quilts for all her children and grandchildren before she had to give up that art. She loved children, often saying that every child is a blessing, and she often comforted and reassured her children and grandchildren, telling one, for instance, not to worry about her freckles because every freckle was a kiss from God. I am reminded of a passage from the 31st chapter of Proverbs where it is written:

> "A good woman is hard to find;
> She is far more precious than jewels...
> She delights to work with her hands...
> And goes to work with a will...
> She opens her hands to the unfortunate,
> And stretches out her arms to the poor.
> She does not fear for her family when it snows,
> For all of them are doubly clothed...

She makes her own bedcovers...
Her clothing is of good quality and dignified;
She has no worry about tomorrow.
When she opens her mouth she speaks wisely,
And kindly instruction is on her tongue...
Her children rise to pronounce blessings on her;
Her husband, too, sings her praises:
'Many women have proved their worth
But you have surpassed them all.'
Charm is deceitful and beauty is fleeting,
But a good woman who fears the Lord is to be praised.
Give her the reward of her labor,
And let the gates ring with praise of her deeds."
[Proverbs 31: 10-22; 25-31; MFS Translation]

Lena Mae was a resourceful mother. We talk today about multitasking, but I am told that she would iron while keeping one of her daughters in tow by standing on the daughter's skirt and singing "In The Garden." I'm not saying which of her daughters that was, but those of you who have known the girls as long as I have can probably guess.

Lena Mae was a plain and simple woman. Never accounted great as the world measures such things, but great in those qualities of character which truly endure. And it is the quality of her character and the content of her soul that make this not so much a day of sadness as it is a day of rejoicing for those who loved her. Indeed, how blessed we are to grieve today - because it means that we had the great rare privilege of knowing, loving and being loved by Lena Mae Tollett. There are millions of people who never have the privilege of knowing - let along loving and being loved by someone like Lena Mae. So as you grieve today, grieve also for them - they and not Lena Mae who rests today in the everlasting arms of God - they are the ones for whom the angels weep.

Lena Mae loved her family, and oh Lena Mae, how you were loved you in return. Your husband and children loved you so much in life, and they would not forsake you during your final illness. They were with you through it all until the end. They were constantly at your bedside even when all they could do was hold your hand, even when it was almost unbearably painful for them to see you in that condition. Though saddened by your departing, they are filled with joy at knowing you loved them through it all.

If we could choose our path between this world and the next, most of us would choose to die at home, surrounded by the mementoes and memories that give meaning to our life and cared for by the people we love most. Lena Mae got to walk that path.

If she could speak across the barriers of time and eternity, Lena Mae's words to you today might be summed up in these words from a poem entitled "To Those I Love" by Isla Pascal Richardson. A portion of it goes:

> *If I should ever leave you whom I love*
> *To go along the Silent Way,*
> *Grieve not,*
>
> . . .
>
> *Please do not let the thoughts of me be sad,*
> *For I am loving you just as I always have.*
>
> . . .
>
> *We cannot see Beyond,*
> *But this I know:*
> *I loved you so – t'was heaven here with you."*[1]

Eighty-one years is a long time. But not long enough. It is never long enough. It is a hard thing to lose someone who has been a part of our lives for so long. But we are not promised any number of days on this earth, and we cannot have permanence in this world. The best we can hope for here is to have our lives touched by the Hand of God - and next to that - the best that most of us ever experience in this life - is to have our lives touched by someone who is truly loving & caring, kind & generous, accepting & forgiving. To the degree that you had that with Lena Mae - as wife, mother, grandmother, mother-in-law, loved one, neighbor or friend - then you know a little of what it is to be touched by the Hand of God. And your memory of that means that you are as richly blessed as it is possible to be blessed in this life.

Lena Mae died on February 17, 2003, after an extended illness.

Lena Mae is survived by: *[I read a list of survivors.]*

> *[I led an interim prayer and a hymn was played.]*
> *[I completed the service with a Meditation, Prayer, and Benediction.]*
> *[Dismissal to place of burial for a committal service.]*

NOTES:
1.   In the service I read the whole poem. These eight lines, however, capture the essence of the poem, and are all I am permitted to print by Copyright law.

VESTIL HASSLER FUNERAL REMARKS APRIL 10, 2003

This is one of the funerals I did in which the Obituary/Eulogy is inseparable from the Message of hope and healing. The deceased may or may not have been a believer. He was not a church member, and though not his pastor, I was the closest thing he had to a pastor. I included no real witness to the Resurrection. I am including it with the Obituary/Eulogies because it more nearly belongs there than with the Meditations.

"Praise be to God, for we do not grieve as those who have no hope!"

Jesus said, "I am the resurrection and the life. Those who believe in me, though they die, yet shall they live"

"Come to me all who are burdened and heavy laden, and I will give you rest."

"Blessed are those who mourn; they shall be comforted."

"Our help is in the name of the Lord who made heaven and earth!"

We are gathered to take account of change, to pay attention to sorrow; to grieve a loss and celebrate a homecoming: to remember; to thank God for the life of Vestil Hassler; to witness to our belief in the Resurrection, and the triumph of eternal life over sin and death which is ours in Christ Jesus.

If there is one thing you hold onto from today, I hope you will hold on to these words from the 43nd chapter of Isaiah: (Here is no promise that we will be spared the difficulties - the trials - the travail that comes to all persons - only that in such times God will strengthen us, help us, uphold us.)

"Thus says the Lord," it is written there: ". . . Fear not, for I have redeemed you; I have called you by name, you are mine. When you pass through the waters I will be with you, and through the rivers, they shall not overwhelm you. When you walk through fire you shall not be burned, and the flames shall not consume you. For I am the Lord your God, the Holy One of Israel, your Savior." [Isaiah 43: 1b-3;]

OBITUARY, REMARKS and MESSAGE

We gather today to give thanks to Almighty God for the life of Vestil Hassler (Hos'ler - it was unique - there were other Hasslers - but only in Big Lick were they Hos'lers). Vestil was born in the Burke Community in the head of the Sequatchie Valley on May 1, 1909 (making him 3 months older than my mother). He was the baby boy, the fifth son and seventh child of George Buhl and Martha Rhea Hassler (Hos'ler). As a young child he moved with his family from Burke to Big Lick, where he lived the rest of his life (except for a brief sojourn in Jamestown during WWII). In 1930 he married Lela Tollett, and to their union four children were born all of whom except Wilma survive their father.

Vestil was tough and hardy, plain & simple, and down-to-earth country to the core of his being. Before, during, and after it ever become "cool," Vestil was country. He is one of the last reminders of what Big Lick was like in my youth, and those who see value & beauty & honor in a genuinely country way of life, those who value rural virtues - friendliness, neighborliness, simple living, satisfaction with sufficiency, the ability to make do with less than the best - they should mourn Vestil's passing - because with his death we lose one of the last of those who were uncomplicatedly, uncompromisingly, unchangeably country - in outlook, values, and lifestyle.

Vestil was honest and straightforward - with Vestil what you saw was what you got. His satisfaction with a plain and simple life reminds me of an old Shaker hymn that goes:

Tis a gift to be simple, tis a gift to be free
Tis a gift to come down where we ought to be
And when we find ourselves in the place just right
T'will be in the valley of love and delight.

Vestil was a pleasant and friendly man who seemed to always have a smile on his face. He liked to joke with family and friends, and he loved his garden.

His family knew something was badly wrong this spring when he did not take a real interest in his garden and failed to joke with them about how the work they did in tilling his garden and mowing his yard was O.K., but not as good as he would have done it.

As a young man he worked in sawmills - the only thing that ever took him out of Big Lick was to work at a sawmill in Jamestown during WWII. However, most of his working life was spent as a truck driver, primarily for the county. For a brief time, he worked (along with Burkett Swafford) as a trash collector in Tansi. I am reminded of a passage from the 38th chapter of Joshua ben Sirach's Wisdom (a Book in the Apocrypha of the Old Testament - RSV). The book is primarily filled with wise sayings and extols the greatness of those who study and teach and expound on the scriptures and the law and the prophets. However, in one passage, the author turns his attention to common workers (farmers, blacksmiths, artisans, potters - we must add truck drivers, trash collectors, and many others). What kind of place would we live in without trash collectors and truck drivers? Of these he writes:

> *"Without them a city cannot be established,*
> *and people can neither sojourn nor live there.*
> *Yet they are not sought out for the council of the people,*
> *nor do they attain eminence in the public assembly.*
> *They do not sit in the judge's seat,*
> *nor do they understand the language of lawyers;*
> *They cannot expound religious doctrine or judgments of the*
> *high courts;*
> *And they are not found quoting great proverbs;*
> *But they keep stable the fabric of the world,*
> *And their prayer is in the practice of their trade."*
> [Ecclesiasticus, or The Wisdom of Joshua Ben Sirach 38: 31-34]

Vestil really was not much a "joiner" of any kind. He enjoyed his life alone with his family in a little house more or less removed from the bustle of life. But he was not a loner. He had a strong sense of community. In 1974 when the school at Big Lick was closed, Vestil was one of those who recognized the threat this presented to the cohesiveness of the community and joined in an effort to prevent its closing. Last Saturday, we had a working at the Big Lick cemetery. It is an annual event - in preparation for Decoration Day. Though folks often accuse me, correctly, of getting there too late to be of much help, I have been to many of these workings (at least 45 by my reckoning). Vestil was not there last Saturday. It was the first time I can remember not seeing him there.

Though he was not much of a churchgoer, I am told that Vestil had accepted Christ and was among those saved from the tentacles of sin and death. Be that as it may, in some Jewish communities, there is a tradition that God preserves the world because of 36 righteous non-believers that exist somewhere in the world. Even if he had not been a believer, Vestil would have been among the 36 righteous ones. And in at least one way, Vestil was like Jesus - or rather like the Risen Christ. Vestil's hands were gnarled in such a way that his little fingers and ring fingers were drawn permanently toward his palms. As long as I can remember, Vestil's hands were like that. You noticed when he reached out to shake your hand, as he invariably did. I don't know what caused Vestil's hands to be in such condition - whether injury or disease or arthritis. I do know that he never complained, and it never stopped him from working. And I also know that those hands were what Jesus' hands looked like after the crucifixion - that's what crucifixion did to hands. When the Risen Christ showed his hands to Thomas in that Upper Room, they looked a lot like Vestil's.

Vestil died after a brief but difficult final illness on April 8, 2003, 22 days before his 94th birthday.

He is survived by: *[I read the list of survivors.]*

Ninety-three - almost 94 years is a long life. 73 years is a long time to be married. But not long enough. It is never long enough. But we are not promised any length of days on this earth, nor is it guaranteed that we will have loving, supportive, wholesome family, loved ones and friends while we are here. Many people do not. The tears you shed today are but the flip side of love. To forego them today, you would have had to forego your love for and your being loved by Vestil all the long years past. Indeed, how fortunate you are to grieve today, for it means that you loved and were loved by your husband, father, grandfather, neighbor and friend for lo these many years.

The Bible has several beautiful, and a few scary, images of what life beyond death may hold for us. I do not claim knowledge of what awaits any of us beyond - I think we have enough to worry about in keeping ourselves straight in this life, over which we have some control, and can best leave worrying about the beyond to God. But I do believe the promise of the Psalmist in the 139th Psalm where he/she writes:

> *"If I ascend to heaven, you are there.*
> *If I make my bed in Sheol, you are there.*

If I take the wings of the morning, and dwell in the uttermost parts of the sea,

Even there your hand shall lead me, and your right hand shall hold me.

If I say, 'Let only darkness cover me, and the light about me be night,'

Even the darkness is not dark to you, the night is bright as the day;

For darkness is as light to you." [Psalm 139: 8-12]

There is nowhere any of us can go that is beyond the reach of God's love and care.

Let us Pray: *[I led a closing prayer and a hymn was played.]*

   [Benediction and dismissal to place of burial for a committal service.]

DR. J. T. CAMPBELL OBITUARY/EULOGY AUGUST 9, 2003

I was charged with doing only an Obituary/Eulogy for this funeral. However, the deceased had been my personal physician, and I revered him for the way he practiced medicine. At the end, I wandered very briefly into some Remarks about hope, healing, and witness to the Resurrection.

"Praise be to God, for we do not grieve as those who have no hope!"

Jesus said, I am the resurrection and the life. Those who believe in me, though they die, yet shall they live

Come to me all who labor and are heavy laden, and I will give you rest. Blessed are those who mourn; they shall be comforted.

"Our help is in the name of the Lord who made heaven and earth!

Yesterday, Betty was remembering how some people compared Dr. Campbell to Marcus Welby of TV fame, but it was another TV doctor, Dr. Kildare, who on one of his programs in 1963 interpreted the function of a funeral by saying to a grieving relative of a patient who had died, The purpose of a funeral is to pay attention to sorrow and to take account of change.

So it is that we gather to pay attention to sorrow, and to take account of change; but also to grieve a loss and celebrate a homecoming; to thank God for the life of J. T. Campbell; and to rejoice in the victory over sin and death which is ours in Jesus Christ.

OBITUARY/EULOGY

James Truen, J. T. Campbell, remembered by many of us simply as Dr. Campbell, was born in Greenville, TN on July 18, 1920, the first child and only son of J. T. and Maude Pence Campbell.

He was a freshman at Tusculum College and working in a drugstore in Greenville when his life changed. Mary Pauline Hardin had recently moved to town with her family. Her father was Superintendent of a Methodist children's home there. Mr. Hardin enjoyed smoking a cigar every morning, but he would not smoke at the children's home for fear of corrupting the youngsters there. So every morning Mary Pauline drove him to the local drugstore where he smoked his daily cigar. So it was that

J. T. and Mary Pauline met. It was apparently a happy coincidence for both of them for on Sept 15, 1942, Mary Pauline Hardin became Polly Campbell, and she and J. T. shared a life together as loving wife and husband for almost 60 years.

Early in WWII, J. T. interrupted his college career to volunteer for the U.S. Army Air Corps (it was not yet the Air Force), where he became a pilot and a pilot's instructor. After discharge, he wanted to become a commercial pilot, but was persuaded by his father to follow the family profession, so he set out to become a doctor like his father and grandfather before him. He finished college at UT under the GI Bill and then medical school at UT's Memphis campus. He interned at Temple, Texas where he focused on obstetrics and gynecology. He worked in a VA hospital and as a doctor for TVA and in his own medical practice in Dandridge, TN. In 1965 at the behest of Dr. Stuart Seaton, Dr. Campbell came to Crossville and joined the Cumberland Clinic Foundation. It was a move for which hundreds of Cumberland County families will always be grateful. He practiced in Crossville until his retirement about 10 years ago.

J. T. was the descendent of Scotch-Irish Calvinists and French Huguenots, and he remained a Presbyterian all his life. True to this heritage, in his retirement, J. T. read the Bible daily. He read it systematically from "In the beginning God created...to John the revelator's benediction at the very end, "The grace of the Lord Jesus be with all the saints. Amen." And when he finished, he read it again, every word, every begat, every blessing, every curse, every sentence, every verse, every chapter, every Amen. And when he was done, he read it again. He was particularly intrigued with the book of Job and its wrestling with questions of good and evil and of how righteous people can deal with unjust suffering.

J. T. was relieved of the prolonged suffering of his final illness and released from this world on August 7, 2002. He was preceded in death by his beloved son, John Hardin.

He is survived by   *[I inserted a list of survivors.]*

J. T. was a doctor. Medicine was his consuming passion. He practiced as if there were no tomorrow (at least not for him). He gave it his every ounce of energy, every day. Through the pain that often racked his own body, through the grief that frequently nagged at his spirit, especially after the death of his son, but also after the deaths of many of his patients, through it all he never stopped and seldom paused. When you were sick at home and couldn't get out of bed, Dr. Campbell was there. When your father was dying, Dr. Campbell was there every day. When you took your child to the emergency room late on a Sunday evening with a gash in their chin or forehead, Dr. Campbell met you at the door. He was devoted to his patients to the exclusion of almost everything else.

He was gruff, grumpy, demanding, often difficult to work with, and I expect, at times difficult to live with. To those who were the object of his wrath he could seem downright mean. But he had a steel trap mind, and a wry sense of humor, both of which were still functioning to the very end. He would joke with visitors about his attending physicians or kid them about something they had just said. He was still prescribing the correct palliative treatments for himself shortly before he died. His gruff and grumpy exterior may have been partly because of the pain, often excruciating, from which he frequently suffered. It was partially his impatience with those he perceived as applying themselves less diligently or less competently than he thought they could or should. But I have long suspected that it was largely a cover-up for the tenderness inside. The gentleness of his spirit hid behind the gruffness of his exterior, the kindness in his soul hid behind his grumpy demeanor.

Surgeons and other medical specialists are often able to experience a satisfying sense of success in their work. Their final contact with a patient is often to celebrate the success of a procedure or diagnosis which has returned the patient to good health. But family and general practitioners have to develop some mechanism for coping with the emotional strain not only of daily dealing with sick and dying people, but also the frustration of the final failure of their best efforts. In the end, the efforts of the doctor who is closest to you, all of those effort, no matter how dedicated, no matter how skilled, no matter how heroic - in the end, they all fail.

Some doctors may deal with this by creating an emotional screen between themselves and their patients - so that they never become emotionally engaged with their patients. Dr. Campbell was never able to do that. Despite his best efforts, he became emotionally entangled with his patients - caring for them not only as patients but as persons. And he suffered with them when they were in pain, and he grieved for them when they died.

When Polly and Betty told me that Dr. Campbell had been a pilot and primarily a pilot's instructor during WWII, I was reminded of another person who recently died - Ted Williams. Ted Williams was renowned not only as a baseball player but as a wartime pilot. He flew 39 combat missions in Korea as a wingman for John Glenn. However, during WWII, when he earned his reputation as a pilot, he never flew in combat. He was so good that instead of risking him in combat, the Army made him a pilot's instructor.

We have all heard the tired and trite saying: Those who can, do, and those who can't teach. Well, when it comes to combat flying (and I expect to lots of other things), the truth is, those who can, do, and those who can do best, teach.

I was struck by other similarities between the world-renowned baseball player and the small-town doctor known only by those he served. The two of them shared

- A similar intensity
- A similar dedication to excellence
- A similar striving for perfection in their chosen craft
- A similar gruff and grumpy exterior
- A similar impatience with those they perceived as doing less than their best
- A similar loneliness and disdain for the accolades of the crowd.

During our lives we all have contact with several practitioners of various professions: Teachers, Preachers, Doctors, et.al. I have learned that we can count ourselves very fortunate if among these contacts there are a few individuals who are truly excellent at their craft: a widely informed, creative, exciting teacher; an insightful and inspiring preacher; a doctor who is both a skilled diagnostician and a caring, persistent practitioner. Those fortunate enough to have had J. T. Campbell as a family physician should count themselves blessed.

The Apostle Paul wrote to the Corinthians: We know that if this earthly shack we live in is destroyed, we have a house built by God - not made with human hands, but eternal and spiritual. Here, indeed, we groan and can hardly wait to get into our spiritual dwelling so that we will not be found naked. For as long as we remain in this earthly shack, we have many worries and anxieties. It is not that we wish to be without a house, but we want a better dwelling - so that our dying may be swallowed up by life in Christ Jesus. God himself is preparing us for this very thing and has given us the Holy Spirit as a guarantee. [2 Corinthians 5:1-5]

In 1954 Stewart Hamblin wrote what became one of the top country songs of that year, based in part upon St. Paul's image of our body as a ramshackle house in which our spirit dwells here on earth and which is to be replaced by a more splendid dwelling upon our departure from this world. It's not necessarily the kind of song Dr. Campbell would have enjoyed, but perhaps he will forgive us for quoting it here. It seems especially appropriate given the difficulties Dr. Campbell suffered with his own body through much of his life. Moreover, my father once said that he would like this song sung at his funeral. For whatever reason, we failed to get that done. But my father was right. Though hardly the kind of music normally heard at funerals, this song has a message appropriate for a Christian funeral. Some of you may remember the song, and if you do you may also recall that it has a rousing, uplifting, joyous tune - appropriate for a victory celebration such as a Christian funeral. It is entitled "THIS OLD HOUSE" and in part the lyrics are:

> "Ain't goin'need this house no longer;
> Ain't goin' need this house no more;
> Ain't got time to fix the shingles;
> Ain't got time to fix the floor;
> Ain't got time to oil no hinges;
> Nor mend the broken window panes.
> Ain't goin' need this house no longer,
> I'm gettin' ready to meet the saints."[2]

The body in which Dr. Campbell dwelt here on earth will soon be taken to its final resting place, but he's not there anymore - he's gettin' ready to meet the saints.

Dr. Campbell has passed beyond the veil which no human eye can pierce, but "death is only a horizon, and a horizon is nothing but the limit of our sight."[1] We cannot see what is beyond that horizon, but those of us who live by faith know who is there, and the resurrected Christ is sufficient to dry every tear, steady every shaky knee, sooth every aching heart, and reassure every troubled soul.

Let us Pray: *[I led an interim prayer and a hymn was sung.]*

   [The Rev. Pete Ullmann delivered a Message of hope and witness to the Resurrection, and we were dismissed to the place of burial for a committal service.]

NOTES:

1. Penn, et al., Op. Cit. For fuller explanation see **Appendix A** at the end of this Collection.

2. To stay within the bounds of Copyright law, I have printed only the chorus here. I read slightly more at the service. See **Appendix A** for further explanation.

DORA BRADLEY BURGESS OBITUARY/ EULOGY - DECEMBER 14, 2003

I was charged with doing only the Obituary/Eulogy for this service, but I wandered some at the end into a few words of healing.

OPENING SCRIPTURE and REMARKS

"Praise be to God, for we do not grieve as those who have no hope!"

Jesus said, "I am the resurrection and the life. Those who believe in me, though they die, yet shall they live"

"Come to me all who are burdened and heavy laden, and I will give you rest."

"Blessed are those who mourn; they shall be comforted."

"Our help is in the name of the Lord who made heaven and earth!"

Friends, this is a victory celebration - not only because we gather as Christians and every gathering of Christians should be a celebration of Christ's victory, but especially because Dora, throughout her life, to the very end, bore such powerful witness to the victory of all that is good over that which is evil-of joy over despair, of peace over enmity, of kindness over meanness, of love over hate, of faith over falsehood, of purity over corruption, of forgiveness over vindictiveness, of humility over self-righteousness, of true righteousness over sin, and of all the forces of life and right over the forces of death and destruction.

OBITUARY/EULOGY

You may ask, "Preacher, if this is a victory celebration, why do our hearts seem so heavy?" We grieve because life is good, and change is difficult, and parting is so hard. We grieve for our loss-not for Dora. We grieve partly because we had her for so long.

When we met here to celebrate the life of Dora's sister-in-law Cora, I told you I was sworn to secrecy and could not reveal Cora's age, even if I knew it (which I did not). Well, today, Dora would probably come back to haunt me if I did not mention her age. She was proud of it, and her only regret was that she did not live to count 3 digits on her age. Like her grandmother Frazier before her she died a few days short of 100.

Dora lived a long, useful, fruitful, fulfilled life. And at its end, she could say with the Apostle Paul in his words to Timothy "...I am already on the point of [death]...I have fought the good fight, I have finished the race, I have kept the faith. Henceforth there is laid up for me the crown of righteousness, which the Lord...will award me...and not only to me but also to all who have loved his appearing." (2 Tim. 4:6-8).

Ninety-nine years - 7 months short of 100 years - is a very long time indeed. But not long enough. It is never long enough. Especially not with someone like Dora. It is hard to lose someone who has been a mainstay of our lives for so long. But we are not promised any # of days on this earth, and we cannot have permanence in this world. The best we can hope for here is to have our lives touched by the Hand of God - and next to that - the best that most of us ever experience in this life - is to have our lives touched by someone who is straight and true, loving and caring, kind & generous, accepting & forgiving. To the degree that we had that with Dora-as mother, Grandmother, mother-in-law, sister, loved one, neighbor or friend-then we know a little of what it is to be touched by the Hand of God. And our memory of that makes us as richly blessed as it is possible to be blessed in this life.

We do not rejoice merely because of the magnitude of her years but because that quantity of life was matched by its quality. Dora lived a remarkable life, full of joyous spirit and spunk until the very end. And it is the content of her character and the strength of her spirit, not merely the magnitude of her years, that makes today not so much a low point in our own journey from the cradle to the grave as it is a day of rare privilege. Indeed, how blessed we are to grieve today - for it means we had the privilege of loving and being loved by one of God's great people.

Shortly before another Christmas, on Dec 8, 1998, we gathered here to celebrate the life of one of Dora's sisters, Laura. On that occasion, one of the visitors said of Laura what we can say of Dora today, "Dora received an early Christmas present - eternal peace."

"If you can't say something good about somebody, don't say anything at all." Dora's frequent admonition to her children and her students is not hard to observe today. There is nothing but good to say. However, it is harder to live up to her creed as she did. She saw every individual as a person of worth, thought everybody could do something worthwhile, and never gave up on anybody. Many of her students became more than they thought they could partially because of Dora's confidence in and encouragement of them.

Dora was born in White County, Tennessee on June 9, 1904, the fourth daughter and ninth of fourteen children born to J. H. and Elizabeth Houlette Bradley. In the summer of 1910, at age 6, she moved with her family to Cumberland County and shortly thereafter to the community of Big Lick. There she remained for the rest of her life.

As a young woman, she earned her teaching certificate and undertook her lifelong profession. One of her first students was a young man she had known all of her life. His name was Estille Burgess, and a few years after their encounter in the classroom, they were married on April 8, 1934. They lived together as loving husband and wife and mother and father of Wayne and Carol for 62 years until his death in 1996. She was asked on occasion why she, a mature woman of 30, would marry a man 9 years younger. On at least one occasion, she answered by saying, "Oh, Estille was born old." She meant it not as a put down but as a compliment to his exceptional maturity and serious mindedness.

Dora was a teacher all of her life-and for 37 of her years, she even got paid to do the job she loved. Carol was remarking the other day about how she could never get away from her mother who was also her school teacher, her SS teacher, and her Bible School teacher. Such was the case for a whole generation of children who grew up in Big Lick in the '40's and '50's.

The Big Lick community was a remarkable place to grow up in during those years. Those of us who were reared there at that time had a multitude of mothers and fathers, each of whom cared almost as much for each of us as they did for their own children, and each of whom took an active role in parenting us, rejoicing in our successes and grieving our failures almost as much as our own parents. Dora was one of the primary mothers for that generation.

Little Jimmy Dickens used to say, "I'm little but I'm loud." Dora was also small of stature, and though she was not loud, she had a presence about her that demanded respect. Through all her years in various classrooms, I don't know that Dora ever had a discipline problem (even in the early years when she was teaching boys almost as old as and considerably bigger than she).

Dora never learned to drive. As a young woman, she never thought it necessary. She could walk anywhere she wanted to go - as much as 3 miles each way to teach at various schools, a mile or so to church, and wherever she needed to go to visit or to care for sick or dying neighbors.

Dora was positive, optimistic, fun-loving. She greatly enjoyed family and community get-togethers, dinners, and celebrations. She was patient and determined. A wonderful gardener, she has been known to work a year to successfully get a cutting to root. She was a resourceful care giver and sometimes spent months, day and night, nursing a sick child back to health. She was a great cook who was revered by her family and friends for her various cakes and deserts with which she blessed them at Christmas time and at community dinners. She had a quick and agile mind and remained alert even into her final illness. She had an independent streak and lived alone until her final illness. She was virtually never sick and seldom went to a doctor. At the age of 98, when she did finally go to a doctor, the doctor asked her how it was that she had lived so long. She replied, "By never coming to see you all." She lived well on little because she was renowned for her frugality, she wasted nothing and saved everything that might come in useful later.

Linda wondered aloud the other day about why someone as good as Dora would have to lay and linger and struggle so hard at the end of her life. She answered her own question by surmising that it was because Dora was so determined, so strong willed that she simply would not give in to the forces of death. That is part of the story. But I suspect that the rest of the story is that the forces of life and the God that created them are just very reluctant to see the earthly end of a life so well lived as Dora's.

Though it lasted longer than most of ours will, Dora's physical heart finally failed her body, and she left this realm of space and time. However, Dora's spiritual heart never weakened. By the world's measure, Dora lived and died poor. In truth, Dora was rich in things that really count. Rich in those qualities of character and strength of spirit that truly endure - dependability, honesty, integrity, trustworthiness, steadfastness. She was faithful and true, kind, generous, loving, and forgiving. And she was rich in those qualities the Apostle Paul called the fruits of the Spirit: Joy - Peace - Patience – Kindness - Goodness - Faithfulness - Gentleness - Self- control.

In the 15th Psalm it is written:

> "O Lord, who shall you invite to your house.
> Who shall come to live on your Holy hill?
> She who walks blamelessly;
> Who does what is right;
> Who speaks truth from her heart;
> Who does not slander with her tongue, and does no evil to a friend,
> Nor repeats a derogatory report against her neighbor;
> She who sticks to her word (promise) and does not change
> Even if it causes her hardship;
> Who does not seek a profit from what she gives,
> And will not cheat the innocent.
> She who does these things shall never be moved."

Dora died as she had lived, with quiet dignity, on June 11, 2003

She is survived by: *[I read the list of survivors including "a host of neighbors, friends and former students."]*

Dora never moved around much in her life. As a young girl, she moved to Big Lick and never left. In 1934 she married Estille and moved into the house she lived in the rest of her life. As a young woman, she united with Calvary Presbyterian Church and remained a faithful and beloved member there until her death. Today she makes the one final move that we all must make. In the church, we have a term far more fitting than "deceased" to describe this event. When a Christian moves from one church to another, we say she has "transferred" her membership. So now it becomes our responsibility and privilege to announce the transfer of our beloved sister, Dora, with the highest recommendations of her friends, neighbors and fellow church members, from the church temporal to the church eternal and triumphant, located in that city not made with human hands, whose builder and maker is God.

When Estille and Dora built their house, the house they lived in for the rest of their lives, shortly after they were married, the one thing that Dora wanted were windows without sticks. So, though it was expensive and rare in those days in the midst of the Depression, she got windows with balances that would remain open without sticks. Dora wanted and maintained a comfortable and cozy house all her life. But she cared more and took more care to maintain her spiritual dwelling.

She resonated to the words of the Apostle Paul to the Corinthians: "We know that if this earthly shack we live in is destroyed, we have a house built by God - not made with human hands, but eternal and spiritual. Here, indeed, we groan and can hardly wait to get into our spiritual dwelling so that we will not be found uncovered. For as long as we remain in this earthly shack, we have many worries and anxieties. It is not that we wish to be without a house, but we want a better dwelling - so that our dying may be swallowed up by life in Christ Jesus. God himself is preparing us for this very thing and has given us the Holy Spirit as a guarantee." (2 Corinthians 5:1-5)

In 1954, a popular country song reflected on this image of our body as a ramshackle house in which our spirit dwells here on earth and which is to be replaced by a more splendid dwelling upon our departure from this world. Though hardly the kind of music normally heard at funerals, this song has a message appropriate for a Christian funeral. Some of you may remember this song and if you do, you may also recall that it has a rousing, uplifting, joyous tune - appropriate for a victory celebration such as today. It is entitled "THIS OLD HOUSE" and in part the words are:

> "Ain't goin'need this house no longer;
> Ain't goin' need this house no more;
> Ain't got time to fix the shingles;
> Ain't got time to fix the floor;
> Ain't got time to oil no hinges;
> Nor mend the broken window panes.
> Ain't goin' need this house no longer,
> I'm gettin' ready to meet the saints."
> By Stuart (or Stewart) Hamblin

We will soon take the "house" that Dora lived in here on earth to its final resting place, but she's not there anymore - she's gettin' ready to meet the saints.

Let us Pray: *[I led an interim prayer, and another minister delivered a Meditation, prayer, benediction, and dismissal to place of burial for a committal service.]*

ERNEST HALL FUNERAL REMARKS DECEMBER 26, 2003

I was invited to help conduct this funeral, although I was given a Eulogy to read. I did the Obituary and read the Eulogy. I then ended my part of the service with some words of healing. Another minister did the Meditation.

MY REMARKS AT ERN HALL'S FUNERAL

> *"Praise be to God, for we do not grieve as those who have no hope!" Jesus said, "I am the resurrection and the life. Those who believe in me, though they die, yet shall they live"*
> *"Come to me all who are burdened and heavy laden, and I will give you rest."*
> *"Blessed are those who mourn; they shall be comforted."*
> *"Our help is in the name of the Lord who made heaven and earth!" "The grass withers, the flower fades, but the word of our God will stand forever."*

Thus it is that we gather to pay attention to sorrow and to take account of change, to grieve a loss and commemorate a homecoming; to thank God for the life of Earnest H. Hall, and above all to celebrate the victory over sin and death which is ours in Christ Jesus.

OBITUARY

Earnest H. Hall was born on June 13, 1924, the youngest son and 6th of seven children born to Albert H. and Verdie Croft Hall. As a young man, he accepted Christ as his Savior and united with Calvary Presbyterian Church of Big Lick where he remained a member all his life. He served in WWII during which he saw action in Italy, but he never dwelt on it much. He was more a lover than a warrior - far more attuned to compassion than to vengeance.

Shortly after returning from service in 1947, he began working at Trade-A-Plane where he remained employed for 40 years until his retirement in 1987. It was at a square dance at the State Park in 1948 that he first met a young nurse by the name of Wanda Brewer. They took an instant liking to each other and on October 3, 1948, the hustled off to Rossville, Georgia, to be married, unable or unwilling to wait the three days than required in Tennessee.

They lived together as devoted husband and wife for 50 years until her death in 1998, and became the loving parents of Tina, Jeff, and Joel.

Earn was quiet, unassuming, friendly, and patient, especially with his children and grandchildren, who remained one of his greatest joys. He was a plain, humble man, never accounted great or important as the world measures such things, but he had those qualities of character which truly endure. He bore witness to those things the Apostle Paul called the "fruits of the Spirit:" "love, joy, peace, patience, kindness, goodness, faithfulness, gentleness, self-control."

On behalf of herself, her brothers, and all their children, Tina wrote the following remembrance which I now share with you: [I read Tina Hall O'Conner's three-page Eulogy.]

[Upon finishing said eulogy I ended my part of the service as follow.]

Ern died as he had lived, with quiet dignity, on October 14, 2003.

He is survived by: *[I read a list of survivors.]*

Seventy-nine years-7 months short of 80 years-is a long time, but not long enough. It is never long enough. It is hard to lose someone who has been a mainstay of our lives for so long. But we are not promised any # of days on this earth, and we cannot have permanence in this world. The best we can hope for here is to have our lives touched by the Hand of God-and next to that-the best that most of us ever experience in this life-is to have our lives touched by someone who is straight & true, loving & caring, kind & generous, accepting & forgiving. To the degree that we had that with Ern - as father, Grandfather, father-in-law, brother, loved one, fellow worker, neighbor, or friend-then we know a little of what it is to be touched by the Hand of God. And our memory of that makes us as richly blessed as it is possible to be blessed in this life.

Indeed, how blessed we are to grieve today because it means that we had the rare privilege of loving and being loved by one of God's great gentle spirits.

And if Ern could speak to you today across the gap between time and eternity - this is what he might say (in the words of poet Isla Pascal Richardson):

> *If I should ever leave you whom I love*
> *To go along the Silent Way,*
> *Grieve not,*
>
> *. . .*
>
> *Please do not let the thoughts of me be sad,*
> *For I am loving you just as I always have.*
>
> *. . .*
>
> *We cannot see Beyond,*
> *But this I know:*
> *I loved you so – t'was heaven here with you."*[1]

Let us Pray: *[I led an interim prayer.]*

[The Rev. Pete Ullmann delivered a message of hope and witness to the Resurrection.]

[Benediction and dismissal to place of burial for a committal service.]

NOTES:

1. To conform to Copyright regulations, only a portion of the poem is printed here. At the service, I read the whole poem. I encourage you to find it and read it all.

JOHN WESLEY (JAKE) RHEA OBITUARY/ EULOGY - DECEMBER 29, 2006

My charge for this service was primarily the Obituary/ Eulogy. And that is mostly what I did though I did slip in one small passage of hope and healing at the very end.

OPENING SCRIPTURE and REMARKS

> *"Blessed be the God and Father of our Lord Jesus Christ! By God's great mercy we have been born anew to a living hope through the Resurrection of Jesus Christ from the dead."*
> *"Praise be to God, for we do not grieve as those who have no hope!"*
> *Jesus said, "I am the resurrection and the life. Those who believe in me, though they die, yet shall they live"*
> *"Come to me all who are burdened and heavy laden, and I will give you rest."*
> *"Blessed are those who mourn; they shall be comforted."*
> *"Our help is in the name of the Lord who made heaven and earth!"*

We are gathered to take account of change; to pay attention to sorrow; to grieve a loss and celebrate a homecoming; to remember and to thank God for the life of Jake Rhea; to bear witness to the victory of eternal life over sin and death which is ours in Christ Jesus.

OBITUARY/EULOGY

How blest we are to grieve today because it means we had the rare privilege of knowing, loving and being loved by Jake Rhea.

John Wesley (JAKE) Rhea began his remarkable life on August 31, 1909, in a little cabin just off the banks of Lick Creek in the Big Lick community, the youngest son and ninth child of John Wesley and Florence Fryar Rhea. He came of age in the near frontier conditions that prevailed in Big Lick in the years leading up to and following World War I.

When Carolyn called me to tell me about the arrangements for Jake's funeral, she reached me on a cell phone. I was in Kentucky, but I could have been virtually anywhere in the world. Jake was six when the first transcontinental phone call was completed and 48 by the time that he (and most of the rest of Big Lick) had regular phone service.

A few days before Jake died, the space shuttle landed safely, returning a crew from outer space. When Jake was born, the Wright brothers were still tinkering with their flying machine. Only six years earlier, they had flown for the first time.

Some of you will remember Jake as a kind, gentle, peaceful, warm- hearted elderly gentleman with a quick smile and hearty laugh. But for many of us, Jake takes with him a part of our memory. Ninety-seven (97) is a remarkable span of years, and Jake's equally remarkable ability to recall details from those years (even to the end) made him a source of information for three generations of people seeking knowledge about the past.

Details like the time in 1928 that he and Roy Hall trapped a few mangy critters and sold the hides to get enough money to send off for some high top, lace-up leather boots so that they could get across the creek to visit their girlfriends.

- Or like the time Tommy Burgess rode a horse into the social room at church.
- Or what it was like on the streets of Dayton during the Scopes trial.

I feel lonely today. Jake takes with him the last of those families - the Burgesses, Bradleys, Blaylocks, Halls, and Rheas - that circled my life as a youth and helped make growing up in Big Lick so special.

However, as remarkable as they are, it is not the quantity of Jake's years but the quality of his life that makes this a time for rejoicing. Just as it is not the quantity of time, but the quality of life that makes eternity so promising.

Never overanxious or in a hurry, Jake was a quiet, calm, kind, gentle, even-tempered soul who seldom, if ever, raised his voice in anger and never said a bad word about anyone. He loved music and could play any stringed instrument. He continued to play a harmonica almost to the end, playing it the last time with the carolers who visited shortly before Christmas.

He worked for years with the ASCS and retired from the Tennessee Dept. of Transportation. But above all else, he was a farmer who loved the farm where he spent his entire life. Perhaps his greatest contribution came through his volunteer work in the church and community. He was a beloved member and longtime Elder at Calvary Presbyterian Church of Big Lick, and for more years than any of us can remember, the managing trustee of the Big Lick/ Hillcrest cemetery. When we lay him to rest today, he will be among friends, for he helped to bury most of the people in that cemetery.

He was almost always in good humor, smiled easily, and laughed readily. Though never accounted great as the world measures such things, he was great in those qualities the Apostle Paul calls the "fruits of the spirit:" "Joy, Peace, Patience, Kindness, Goodness, Faithfulness, Gentleness, Self- Control."

When Carolyn called me Wednesday morning to tell me about arrangements for Jake's funeral, I was sitting at a table in the Inn at Shaker Village in Pleasant Hill, Kentucky. Shaker Village is a restored community of the Society of Shakers, a 19th century American religious movement known more formally as the United Society of Believers in Christ's Second Appearing. They had some beliefs that most of us would find strange. But the unifying principles of their community, we would almost universally find admirable. They believed that the following should be reflected not only in their society but in their souls:

Purity, Simplicity, Honesty, Utility, Order, Economy.

Jake would have liked the Shakers, and they would have like him. Like Jake, they loved music and dance, even incorporating dancing into their worship services.

The Shakers are remembered in the larger society, the "world" they called it, primarily by two things. One is the simple, practical, sturdy, carefully crafted and beautiful furniture that is still called by their name.

The second is a beautiful little hymn that captures the essence of their beliefs and the longings of many of us. It is called Simple Gifts. I first used it as part of a funeral eulogy at the service for Jake's sister, Ida. It is equally appropriate today. It goes in part:

> Tis a gift to be simple, tis a gift to be free,
> Tis a gift to come down where we ought to be, And when we
> find ourselves in the place just right, It will be in the valley of
> Love and delight.

Perhaps Jake's greatest joy came from his children, grandchildren and great-grandchildren. He loved them all unconditionally and lavished his attention on them.

Jake's death brings to an end one of the great love stories in Big Lick's history. It began at a pie supper in the old Bethel School House one spring night in 1948. Jake outbid Buster Winningham for the box prepared by Jessie Roy Campbell. Thus, it was that Jake who loved to eat, met his match in Jessie who loved to cook. All the principals in that drama are gone now - the old Bethel School, Buster, Jessie, and now Jake. For many of us, our lives have been forever shaped by the outcome of the bidding contest that night.

Jake and Jessie were married on Christmas Day, 1948. Of those who were there, I am now the last surviving witness to that ceremony. I had never attended a wedding before, and though only 7 at the time, I still have vivid memories of Jake and Jessie standing together to take their vows.

Jake died as he had lived, calmly, peaceably, at peace with himself, his family, his fellow human beings, and his God, on December 26, 2006, one day after what would have been his and Jesse's 58th wedding anniversary.

He is survived by:
    2 Sons: *[I read the names of surviving children.]*
    1 Daughter:
    11 Grandchildren
    27 Great Grandchildren
    His Brothers and Sisters at Calvary Church of Big Lick And numerous other neighbors and friends.

He was preceded in death by: Wife: Jesse
        Parents: John Wesley and Florence Fryar Rhea
        Three Sisters: Ola Wilson, Polly Dixon, Ida Parham

Four Brothers: Floyd, Frank, Roy, Oscar, Wilburn
(The older members of the congregation and family members may remember them better as Ollie, Polly, Priss, Cat, Fuzzy, Tobe, Tater, and Bill)

Jake lived his whole life on the farm in Big Lick near the forks of Lick Creek and Daddy's Creek. But today he makes the one last move that we must all make. In the Christian tradition of which Jake and I are a part, we have a far better word than deceased to describe this event. When a church member moves from one church to another, we say he/she has transferred his/her membership. So it becomes my privilege today to announce the transfer of our beloved brother Jake from the church temporal to the church triumphant, "located in that city whose builder and maker is God.) [Hebrews 11: 10]

Let Us Pray.   *[I offered an interim prayer here.]*

[The Rev Pete Ullmann gave a Meditation of Hope and Witness to the resurrection.]

Dismissal to place of burial for a Committal Service and Benediction.

WAYNE LINCOLN BRADLEY – JANUARY 30, 2007

I was to do only the Obituary/Eulogy for this service. But Wayne was a childhood friend and we had been close so I ended up delivering two pages of Remarks on Healing at the end. It was inevitable in light of who Wayne was to me.

"Blessed be the God and Father of our Lord Jesus Christ! By God's great mercy, we have been born anew to a living hope through the Resurrection of Jesus Christ from the dead."
"Praise be to God, for we do not grieve as those who have no hope."
Jesus said, "I am the resurrection and the life. Those who believe in me, though they die, yet shall they live."
"Come to me all who are burdened and heavy laden, and I will give you rest."
"Blessed are those who mourn; they shall be comforted."
"Our help is in the name of the Lord who made heaven and earth!"

We are gathered to take account of change; to pay attention to sorrow; to grieve a loss and celebrate a homecoming; to remember and to thank God for the life of Wayne Bradley; and to bear witness to the victory of eternal life over sin and death which is ours in Christ Jesus.

Wayne is not the first of my childhood friends to die, but he is the first one with whom I am indelibly linked in some peoples' memories like an ornery pair of mules. Though most of them are gone now, there was a time when practically all the older folks in Big Lick had a Wayne & Mike or a Mike &

Wayne story. We have become the "old folks" now, but in a lot of ways we were like brothers. Our mere presence could lift the spirits of the other.

However, as I told his family on Sunday, I won't be telling everything I know about Wayne (and I know more than most). The truth is, a lot of those Wayne & Mike stories were known to only two people on earth. One of them is now gone, and I ain't talking.

As a young man, Wayne was a bit of a daredevil and roustabout. One of his high school classmates recalled how he was once caught trying to sneak out of a class on his hands and knees - a crime that Sheila paid for 20 years later when she had the same teacher in college. I once drove from the Church in Big Lick to the old high school in about 8 minutes. I was quite proud of that feat until I realized that I never once had reached the speed at which Wayne regularly drove that same stretch of road.

But those are not the things I most want to remember today because I revere Wayne not for the child he was but for the man he became.

OBITUARY/EULOGY

Wayne Lincoln Bradley, like his namesake, was born on February 12 in a log cabin. Unlike Abe's, his birth came in 1942 and in Big Lick, Tennessee. It was six months after I had entered this world of wonder and weeping. A fact that would help shape both of our lives.

He was the 8th child of Lee and Elsie Wright Bradley, and according to the attending nurse, weighed 6 ½ pounds at birth. By account of that same nurse, he was doing well one month later, but his mother was not. She would not recover and died from a weak heart on April 15, 1942, when her new son was barely two months old.

On April 2, 1942, the nurse recorded that Wayne, not yet six weeks old, was "taken to Dora Burgess' home" and by July 1 that year, she wrote he was "Doing nicely." He did nicely indeed in that home where, though never formally adopted, he grew up as the son of Estille and Dora Burgess.

There has always been a debate about which is more important in shaping who we become - nature or nurture - the genes we inherit or the way we are reared. All I will say is that Wayne Bradley, without a drop of Vance or Amy Burgess's blood in him turned out to be more like the Burgesses than some of their blood descendants. Wayne was a cook, a citizen, a cowman, a crook catcher, a companion and a churchman; a friend, a husband, a father and a grandfather, a storyteller and a softball player. He was loyal, dependable, determined, trustworthy, tender and tenacious. That list reminds me that Wayne and I were once part of a Boy Scout troop that Roy Hall tried to start in Big Lick. That Boy Scout troop never made it, but it seems Wayne got all the characteristics of the Scout oath anyway.

I have often thought that were I in a dangerous situation in which I needed someone to watch my back, Wayne would be high on my list of recruits. Though he could be timorous in the face of certain unrealistic fears, he was absolutely loyal and unfailingly dedicated to; tenacious and fearless in the defense of his family, friends, and the community and institutions he cherished.

It has been said, and rightly I think, that courage is not the absence of fear (the absence of fear is foolishness). Courage is the ability to go on in spite of our fears. By that definition, Wayne was one of the more courageous people I have ever known. There were things which Wayne feared, hated, and detested. He was fearful of speaking before crowds - his knees shook and his voice trembled, but when I was installed as Pastor at Calvary Church, there he was before a church full of people leading the affirmation of the congregation. Why did he do it? Because I had asked him and I was a friend.

He loathed computers, and wished they had never been invented, but he learned to use one and used it regularly in his work. Why? Because his work demanded it and his family depended on his work.

Wayne despised being stuck with a needle. He fiercely resisted getting his immunizations when he was young. They sometimes had to run him down. He distrusted doctors, despised hospitals, couldn't stand the thought of being stuck with a needle, but he endured them all - stuck and poked, prodded and pricked and hospitalized - endured them all. Why? He did it for those he loved. Wayne was not afraid of dying, he faced it with great courage, confidence in his faith and determination, he just regretted leaving those he loved behind.

Dylan Thomas wrote of death:

> *"Do not go gentle into that good night...*
> *Rage, Rage against the dying of the light."*

Wayne did not rage, but he fought the grim reaper to a standstill in a valiant toe-to-toe battle for two years after the doctors had given him six months to live.

Wayne liked to cook, and he was good at it. But he enjoyed being outdoors more. He never grew up to be the cowboy that he and I dreamed about as we chased mythical badmen over the hills and through the woods of Big Lick in the years after WWII. But he did grow up to be a cowman - a knowledgeable and proficient producer of cattle. He enjoyed working with his cattle. They helped restore his sanity. After working in a world that often seemed to him insane, he found tranquility, peace, and fulfillment in working on the farm and with his cattle. Next to time with his family, it may have been the thing Wayne liked the best. One of the things that bothered him most about his illness was the inability to be outside working on his farm.

Wayne was an active and faithful churchman. If there was anything happening at church Wayne was there. Next to his home, his fields and perhaps a softball diamond, it was the place where Wayne most enjoyed being. Wayne was the kind of member and leader that a pastor hopes to have. He was untiringly faithful, dependable and trustworthy. If you asked Wayne to do something and he agreed, you could cross it off your list. It was as good as done.

He was a leader in the church and community, an officer of all the continuing community institutions in Big Lick, an Elder of Calvary Church, a Trustee of the Calvary Church Homestead Project, a leader in the Big Lick Homecoming, and a Trustee of the Big Lick/Hillcrest Cemetery Association. He was an active citizen and a leader in his political party. A true and blue (or perhaps we should say "red" these days), died-in-the-wool Republican, he was so respected in his party that when Lamar Alexander walked across Tennessee in his famous plaid shirt and stopped in Cumberland County, he spent the night with Wayne and Faye.

About two weeks ago, when I became convinced that in spite of my prayers and those of others, Wayne was going to leave this world, two thing popped into my mind. They seemed incongruous at first, for they represent attitudes that were the direct opposite of how I remember Wayne. Then I realized that it was this contrast that made them so poignant. They are both thoughts that I have seen printed on tee shirts. The first of them goes: "I love my job; it's the work I can't stand."

Wayne stood that comment on its head. He had some jobs that he did not like, but it was not the work that bothered him. The work he did willingly with care and competence. It was rather the systemic failures and petty politics that accompany large bureaucracies and the apparent worthlessness of some individuals that bothered Wayne. As straightforward and true as a gymnast's tightrope, Wayne was sometimes flabbergasted by what went on around him in some of the jobs he held.

The second saying is like the first. It goes: "I love humanity, it's people I can't stand." Again, Wayne stood this on its head. There were certain parts of humanity for whom Wayne had no love. But face-to-face, on a personal level, Wayne never met a person to whom he was not friendly, hospitable, loving, generous, charitable, honorable and kind.

Someone who did not know Wayne might have concluded after hearing some of his comments at a SS Class or elsewhere, that he was disgruntled, judgmental, uncharitable, and mean-spirited. They couldn't have been more wrong. Wayne was one of those rare people who walk a better Christian life than they talk. He walked the walk, even if he didn't always talk the talk of a devoted follower of Jesus Christ.

When he was younger and in better health, Wayne loved to play softball. One of his favorite memories was of the time he and a bunch of other Big Lick teenagers entered the Cumberland County Softball League for the first time and won the whole shebang. Asked once if he could hit a home run, he said, "Yea, maybe, if I can hit the ball three times." He meant hitting the ball as far as he could, going to the spot where the ball landed and hitting it again, and then doing the same a third time.

He was not a power hitter, but he had some of the best bat control of anyone I ever saw play. He could place a ball about wherever he wanted to, and he could do it consistently. And that, Wayne once said (quoting his Uncle Eucle I think), "That's the object of the game: To hit 'um where they ain't." His softball playing could serve as a metaphor for his life. Wayne refused to let his life be defined by the things he couldn't do. He just did the things he could do and did them well, with determination, dedication, dependability, and distinction. He did what was necessary even when it brought him no acclaim or fame.

Over thirty years ago, I began an article by writing: "I was born and grew up in Big Lick, Tennessee, near the Hell Hole and Devil Step holler, at the headwaters of Daddy's Creek and the Sequatchie River. That is the spot of the earth I still call home, and if such choices were ours, it is the place I would choose to die."

A few days ago, Wayne said it more simply. Confronted by the doctor with the possibility that he might have to remain in the hospital (for fear that he could not be cared for properly at home), Wayne told the doctor: "I was born in Big Lick and I want to die in Big Lick." Wayne got his last wish because of the loving care of Faye, Sheila and Larry, with some help from his best friend, Oliver Blaylock and his cousin Butch. Faye, Sheila and Larry have given up large chunks of the last two years of their lives and almost full time for the last two months caring for Wayne at home. It would not have been possible without the sacrifices they have made. Oliver's ministry to Wayne epitomizes what we mean when we say that not just the pastor but the whole church is minister. As for Butch, when Wayne got confused in his last days and thought he was somewhere other than home (perhaps in a hospital), he'd say, "Go get Butch. He's got a gun. He'll get me out of here."

When asked what he wanted for Christmas, Wayne said he had seen a ring at Walmart that said "Dad" on it and that was what he wanted. That was who he was and how he wanted to be remembered. Above all else, Wayne was a husband, a father, a grandfather. He loved children, but especially his granddaughters - the love that passed between them was palatable - so strong that you could feel it when you were around them - a love that has shaped and will continue to shape their lives into adulthood. Peyton and Kayla and the rest of you, I hope that you can see through the tears that we rightly shed today to understand that even though we grieve today, we grieve with joy. Not everybody has the good fortune in life to have a grandfather, or a father, or a husband, or a friend like Wayne Bradley. And the fact that you had him and all that he gave you is far more important than the fact that he is now gone. Our memories make us as blessed as it is possible to be blessed on this earth.

Wayne died at home on January 27, 2007, a little more than two weeks before his 65th birthday.

He is survived by: *[I read a list of survivors.]*

REMARKS ON HEALING

In the 11th chapter of his Gospel, John recalls what happened when Jesus went to the tomb of his friend Lazarus. He writes:

> *"Then Mary, when she came where Jesus was and saw him, fell at His feet, saying to Him, 'Lord, if you had been here, my brother would not have died.' When Jesus saw her and the others who*

came with her weeping, He was deeply moved in spirit and troubled; and he said, 'Where have you laid him?' They said to Him, 'Lord, come and see.' Jesus wept. So they said, 'See how He loved him!'. . . Then Jesus, deeply moved again, came to the tomb; it was a cave, and a stone lay over it. Jesus said, 'Remove the stone!'. . . So they took away the stone . . . [After he prayed] Jesus cried with a loud voice, 'Lazarus, come out!' The dead man came out, his hands and feet bound with body wrap, and his face wrapped with a cloth. Jesus said, 'Unbind him, and let him go!'" [John 11: 32 – 44; MFS Translation]

I remember that passage today not only because of the comfort it brings; not only because it is especially appropriate for a Christian funeral, but also because it contains the verse that Wayne so often recited whenever we were asked in Sunday school to quote a Bible verse from memory. Since his name began with a "B," Wayne got to go before most of us and got to this verse before the rest of us had a chance. It is John 11: 35, the shortest verse in the Bible: "Jesus wept." He wept for His friend Lazarus. So we can be sure that He also weeps for His friend Wayne today.

Wayne, bound by the tentacles of a disease that stole his spirit and sapped his strength. Trapped in a body that was no longer of any use to him. Wayne has heard the same blessing that Lazarus heard: "Unbind him and let him go!"

So Wayne can sing with the angels that old spiritual, "Free at last, free at last, Great God Almighty, I am free at last."

In Isaiah, it is written:" Thus Says the Lord:

Fear not, for I am with you, be not dismayed for I am your God. I will strengthen you, I will help you, I will uphold you . . . Fear not, for I have redeemed you; I have called you by name, you are mine. When you pass through the rivers, they shall not overwhelm you. When you walk through fire, you shall not be burned, and the flames shall not consume you. For I am the Lord your God, the Holy One of Israel, your Savior."

[Isaiah 41:10; 43: 1b-3]

Death intrudes on us all. No respecter of persons, it comes to all, rich and poor, famous and unknown, Christian and non-believer. Though it may come as a welcomed guest to one who has lived a useful life only to become enfeebled by illness or infirmity, it is never a welcome guest to those of us left behind. It is never fully expected. It always comes as a dreadful surprise. We are never completely prepared for it. It always brings sorrow and pain and loss, and its intrusion into our lives dulls life's brightness and casts a shadow of heartbreak on our souls.

However, while the outward experience is substantially the same, the inner reality is vastly different for those who are in Christ. In Christ, death assumes another face. It is no longer a frightening enemy, robbing us of all we hold dear, but merely the door into another room in the Father's house. It is no longer the darkness that empties life of its joy and meaning. It is rather the gladness of going home.

For the past 30 years, Wayne has struggled with health problems and botched medical procedures, yet he never became resentful or bitter, and he never gave up. He fought a long battle with cancer, and at the end, he could say with the Apostle Paul (who wrote to Timothy):

> ". . . I am already on the point of [death] . . . I have fought the good fight, I have finished the race, I have kept the faith. Henceforth, there is laid up for me the crown of righteousness, which the Lord . . . will award me . . . and not only to me but also to all who have loved His appearing." [2 Timothy 4: 6-8]

Shortly after I returned to Big Lick in 1974, Wayne took a job with Goodyear and moved from Big Lick (to where I do not remember). I grieved for him then because he had left Big Lick. But it didn't last long.

Fay says it was a week; Sheila says three days. My spirits soared when I saw him coming up the walk to church on their first Sunday back.

This time Wayne will not return to this world of time and space, and I grieve for losing him. But I do not despair because I know that Wayne is in that city which has foundations whose architect and contractor is God, where "death shall be no more, neither shall there be mourning nor crying nor pain anymore for the former things have passed away." [Revelation 21: 4]

> "What then shall we say to this?" the Apostle Paul wrote to the Romans, "If God is for us, who is against us? He who did not spare His own Son, but gave him up for us all, will He not give us all things with Him? . . . Who shall separate us from the love of Christ? Shall tribulation or distress or persecution or famine . . . or peril? . . . No, in all these things we are more than conquerors

through him who loved us. For I am sure that neither death, nor life . . . nor things present, nor things to come . . . nor anything else in all creation will be able to separate us from the love of God in Christ Jesus our Lore."

[Romans 8: 31-32, 35, 37-39]

"Life is eternal and love is immortal, and death is only a horizon – and a horizon is nothing but the limit of our sight."[1] We cannot see what is beyond that horizon, but we know who is there and the Risen Christ is enough to strengthen and sustain those who trust in him.

Let us Pray: *[I led an interim prayer and a hymn was played.]*

[The Rev. Pete Ullmann delivered a Meditation of witness to the Resurrection.]

[Benediction and dismissal to place of burial for a committal service.]

NOTES:

1. Penn, et al., Op. Cir. For clarification see **Appendix A** at the end of this Collection.

VICKEY KERLEY DAVIDSON – APRIL 14, 2007

> *I did this entire service by myself.*

"Blessed be the God and Father of our Lord Jesus Christ! By God's great mercy, we have been born anew to a living hope through the Resurrection of Jesus Christ from the dead."
"Praise be to God, for we do not grieve as those who have no hope!"
Jesus said, "I am the resurrection and the life. Those who believe in me, though they die, yet shall they live"
"Come to me all who are burdened and heavy laden, and I will give you rest."
"Blessed are those who mourn; they shall be comforted."
"Our help is in the name of the Lord who made heaven and earth!"

We are gathered to take account of change; to pay attention to sorrow; to grieve a loss and celebrate a homecoming; to remember and to thank God for the life of Vickey Ann Kerley Davisson; and to bear witness to the victory of eternal life over sin and death which is ours in Christ Jesus.

OBITUARY

Vickey was born on April 7, 1960, the third child and only daughter of Wendell and Velma Norrod Kerley. She enjoyed the outdoors, liked water and loved to water ski. She played first base for the Big Lick Women's softball team. She liked dogs and small children, which according to my light, makes her someone you can trust. She enjoyed gardening and loved to travel, especially to visit her grandchildren. She enjoyed working on building and remodeling projects. Today should be special for her since she so enjoyed collecting angels. She was a homemaker and a member of the Calvary Presbyterian Church of Big Lick. She was a warm and loving person who shared her love with her family and friends.

It is a hard thing to lose someone who should be in the prime of life. Parents should not have to bury their children. It seems to put everything out of order. But we are not promised any # of days on this earth, and we cannot have permanence in this world. The best we can hope for here is to have our lives touched by the Hand of God-and next to that-the best that most of us ever experience in this life-is to have our lives touched by someone who is loving & caring, kind & generous, accepting and forgiving. To the degree that you had that with Vickey-as daughter, granddaughter, mother, grandmother, mother-in-law, sister, loved one, neighbor or friend-then you know a little of what it is to be touched by the Hand of God. And your memory of that makes you as richly blessed as it is possible to be blessed in this life.

> The Apostle Paul wrote to the Corinthians: *"We know that if this earthly shack we live in is destroyed, we have a house built by God - not made with human hands, but eternal and spiritual. Here, indeed, we groan and can hardly wait to get into our spiritual dwelling, so that we will not be found naked. For as long as we remain in this earthly shack, we have many worries and anxieties. It is not that we wish to be without a house, but we want a better dwelling - so that our dying may be swallowed up by life in Christ Jesus.*
> *God himself is preparing us for this very thing and has given us the Holy Spirit as a guarantee."* (2 Corinthians 5:1-5)

One of the popular country and western tunes in 1954 was written by Stewart Hamblin and is based in part on St. Paul's image of our body as a ramshackle shack in which we live here on earth and which is to be replaced by a more splendid dwelling upon our departure from this world.

The song is entitled "This Old House," and in part it goes:

> *"Ain't goin'need this house no longer;*
> *Ain't goin' need this house no more;*
> *Ain't got time to fix the shingles;*
> *Ain't got time to fix the floor;*
> *Ain't got time to oil no hinges;*

Nor mend the broken window panes.
Ain't goin' need this house no longer,
I'm gettin' ready to meet the saints." [1]

We will soon take the house that Vickey lived in here on earth to its final resting place, but she's not there anymore-she's gettin' ready to meet the saints.

Vickey died after a long and valiant battle with cancer on April 11, 2007, four days after her 47th birthday. She is survived by

[I inserted a list of survivors.]

If Vickey could speak to each of you now, perhaps she might say something like this:

"To Those I Love" by Isla Richardson

If I should ever leave you whom I love
To go along the Silent Way,
Grieve not,
. . .
Please do not let the thoughts of me be sad,
For I am loving you just as I always have.
. . .
We cannot see Beyond,
But this I know:
I loved you so – t'was heaven here with you." [1]

[I led an interim prayer, a hymn was played, and I proceeded with a Meditation.]

NOTES:

1. I have printed here only a portion of this song and poem. That is all that Copyright Regulations will permit. I read more of both at the service, and I encourage you to find copies and read the whole song and poem.

OLIVER H. HALL OBITUARY/EULOGY – AUGUST 22, 2007

I did both an Obituary/Eulogy and a brief Meditation at this service.

> *"Blessed be the God and Father of our Lord Jesus Christ! By God's great mercy we have been born anew to a living hope through the Resurrection of Jesus Christ from the dead."*
> *"Praise be to God, for we do not grieve as those who have no hope!"*
> *Jesus said, "I am the resurrection and the life. Those who believe in me, though they die, yet shall they live"*
> *"Come to me all who are burdened and heavy laden, and I will give you rest."*
> *"Blessed are those who mourn; they shall be comforted."*
> *"Our help is in the name of the Lord who made heaven and earth!"*

We are gathered to take account of change; to pay attention to sorrow; to grieve a loss and celebrate a homecoming; to remember and to thank God for the life of Oliver H. (Ob) Hall; and to bear witness to the victory of eternal life over sin and death which is ours in Christ Jesus.

OBITUARY/EULOGY

Born on the 16th of September, 1921, in the Linary Community, Ob was the fifth child and third son of Albert H. and Verdie Croft Hall. In the rollicking years of the 1920's and the depression years of the '30's, he came of age mostly in the Big Lick Community along the banks of Daddy's Creek where his father ran a store and served as postmaster. His parents were leading members of the community and charter members of Calvary Presbyterian Church of Big Lick. Like all his brothers and sisters, Ob took Christ as his Lord and Savior as a young man and never forsook his faith.

He was a diligent and disciplined child who always completed his chores early, somewhat to the chagrin of his less disciplined siblings. He inherited his father's middle name (Harrison), disposition, and stature. Like his father, he seldom used the middle name, and the gentle spirit and calm disposition served him well throughout his life. As far as I know, Ob never raised his voice in anger, but he did get angry and exasperated at times. When he did, he would swear a hearty oath, the only oath that anyone can remember ever passing his lips. When angry or exasperated Ob was known to exclaim, "Dad burn it."

As for the stature, Ob would have preferred to have been larger, especially when he was ribbed about his size by his larger brothers and friends of more robust size like Elmo Bradley and Jake Rhea.

"There was a man named Zac . . . he was kind of short . . . so he climbed a sycamore tree to see Jesus . . . Jesus said, 'Zac, hurry up and get down out of that tree. I must visit with you today.'" [Luke 19: 2-5; MFS Translation]. There was a man named Ob. He was kind of short, but that's not what mattered. The content of his character, the size of his heart, and the strength of his soul far outweighed his small stature. One day, Jesus said, "Ob, come on up. I've got to visit with you today."

Many of us who grew up in the Big Lick community before the arrival of electricity, telephones, and all-weather roads, have a Halloween story or two to tell, but the tale told by Ob and his buddies of the 1930's tops them all. One Halloween they completely disassembled Uncle Tom Hale's buggy and reassembled it. No big feat, you say. Oh yea, but when they reassembled it, it was on top of Uncle Tom's barn.

Ob's experience during the Depression made him as tight as the spots on a blue tick hound, but he was generous with his family, always endeavoring to insure that his children and grandchildren had everything they needed to thrive in life.

A member of the "Greatest Generation," Ob was drafted into service during WW II and served 4 years in the Army. The business end of those years were spent as a member of the Reconnaissance Company of the 692nd

Tank Destroyer Battalion traipsing over the map of Europe from a landing at Cherbourg, France along a route that passed near Paris, on to the Rhine River, up the river and through Germany to the city of Munich.

Ob took to the military like a lab takes to water. He did not spend most of his life there (as ducks do), but he loved to splash in it every chance he got. He enjoyed it - its dedication and discipline, its honor and bravery, its love of country and comradery. He served for 30 more years in the National Guard, and was a charter member of local VFW Post.

Ob was determined and could be headstrong. He loved to work on his small farm, to hunt, and to work with wood. He was an excellent repairman and worked for years as a maintenance man for the Crossville Housing Authority. He was organized - had a place for everything and everything in its place. He enjoyed reading and devoured books, especially after his health restricted his freedom to spend time outdoors.

On June 4, 1954, Ob married Agnes Ford, and she and the children they adopted, Sheila and Greg, became the most precious things in his life. He adored his family and loved spending time with them. He laughed when they were happy and grieved when they were sad.

At 8 AM on Monday, August 20, 2007, Ob took his last breath on this earth. He died peacefully after several years of declining health and a final illness that reduced him to a shell of the man he once was. He was 26 days short of his 86th birthday.

He is survived by: *[I read a list of survivors.]*

   [I led an interim prayer and a hymn was played.]

   [I completed the service with a brief Meditation, a prayer, a benediction, and dismissal to the place of burial for a committal service.]

EVERETT L. GIBSON OBITUARY/EULOGY AND REMARKS - DECEMBER 9, 2007

"Blessed be the God and Father of our Lord Jesus Christ! By God's great mercy we have been born anew to a living hope through the Resurrection of Jesus Christ from the dead."

"Praise be to God, for we do not grieve as those who have no hope!"

Jesus said, "I am the resurrection and the life. Those who believe in me, though they die, yet shall they live"

"Come to me all who are burdened and heavy laden, and I will give you rest."

"Blessed are those who mourn; they shall be comforted."

"Our help is in the name of the Lord who made heaven and earth!"

OBITUARY, EULOGY and REMARKS

Everett L. Gibson - Husband, Father, Grandfather, soldier, sailor, farmer, quarryman, teacher, Thinker, talker, storyteller, writer, theologian, preacher is gone from among us.

We will grieve his passing and mourn his loss, but we must celebrate his life. We celebrate because his life was a long, full, useful, purpose filled life that demonstrated the importance of faith and self-discipline in overcoming some of the darker impulses of the human soul-a life that gave witness to the victory over sin and death that is ours in Christ Jesus. Friends, this is a victory celebration.

Everett Louis Gibson was born on August 21, 1916, in Huntington, W. VA., the 2nd son and 5th child of Grover Gerard and Jessie Mae Strait Gibson. At age 14, he moved with his family to Raceland in Greenup County, Kentucky, where he matured and attended high school.

He attended Berea College, where he received a degree in agriculture in 1939, and more importantly, where he met Alberta Burgess. With a slight prod from the preacher, Everett and Alberta were married on July 6, 1940, the first couple to be married in the Calvary Presbyterian Church of Big Lick. They remained together as loving husband and wife for 62 years, and to their union, a much beloved daughter, Mary Nina, was born.

He served as a health inspector in Louisville, KY (The stories he could tell would make you want to never eat in a restaurant.) A member of the aptly named "Greatest Generation", he joined the navy during WWII and served as a medical corpsman, as a "skeeter beater," working on malaria control in the South Pacific.

He moved with his family to Cumberland County in 1948, where he first taught in the GI schools set up for veterans after WWII. He started his public-school career at Big Lick in 1952 and spent 30 years as a teacher, principal, and superintendent.

He was a member, Elder, and Sunday School Teacher at Calvary Presbyterian Church of Big Lick, past member of the American Legion, member of the Sons of the American Revolution, and the Retired Teachers Association.

Everett died after a protracted slow decline in his health on December 6, 2007, at the age of 91 years and 4 months.

He is survived by:

[I read a list of survivors, and inserted "numerous former students, fellow teachers, neighbors and friends."]

"...man has been implanted with a small seed of the image of [God], a seed that struggles to survive and flourish in our being from birth to death. The 'tamed' of the earth are those who recognize and work to make this seed do what [God] meant for it to do. The 'untamed' are those who constantly rebel against this force."

So wrote Everett L. Gibson in his book *The Tamed & the Untamed*. No words could constitute a more fitting epithet. He was among the tamed. But it was a lifelong struggle to keep himself there.

It should be no great surprise that every chapter in his book is entitled "Discipline" though many of the stories do not speak of discipline as we ordinarily use the word. Everett understood that discipline comes from the same root as disciple. Sometimes we think we can be disciples without discipline, but Everett knew differently.

Like the Apostle Paul, Everett recognized that the good we intend we often do not do, and the bad we abhor we sometimes do anyway. And like Paul he understood that the dual mechanisms for overcoming this flaw in human nature are faith and self-discipline.

Faith and self-discipline are what made Everett the man that he was and kept him from becoming the person he feared he could be.

Faith and self-discipline helped him to live successfully with diabetes most of his life. Few people who suffer from severe diabetes as Everett did, live as long or suffer as few debilitations from the disease as he did. It was his discipline and his faith that enabled him to be victorious over the disease.

More importantly, his faith and self-discipline enabled him to tame the demons he found lurking in his heart. Perhaps most apparent of those demons was his infamous temper. His temper could flash as quickly and burn as hot as any I have ever seen.

Everett held my father in high regard, as testified to by a chapter in his book. Likewise, my father had high esteem for Everett. Everett recalls in his book how he approached my father with some trepidation when he asked about buying the farm in Big Lick, fearing that the price would be too high. He relates how surprised and relieved he was to learn that the price was only about 1/3 what he had thought it would be. Everett didn't know, but I know the rest of that story. My father had deliberately held on to that particular farm in the hope that someone like Everett and his family would purchase it. I can remember more than one occasion when I overheard my father say, "The Gibsons would be the ideal ones to have that farm." As much as Everett wanted that farm, my father wanted the Gibsons in Big Lick.

However, in spite of this mutual respect, I have witnessed my father and Everett argue with such intensity that everyone in their presence cringed, and I have known Everett to be so mad at my father that he wouldn't speak to him for a week or more. But their friendship and mutual respect remained throughout their lives. Often when leadership was needed, my father turned to Everett.

I mention this not to recall a trait that some found unseemly at times but to note that Everett's taming of his temper is instructive to us all. It may not be our temper, but all of us have demons of the soul, bits of our personality that tempt and goad us toward remaining among the untamed. Everett's victory over his temper can reassure us that through faith and self-discipline we, too, can overcome the demons that threaten to make us less than what God intends.

Everett's was not undone by his temper and his anger did not linger. He was as gracious in offering forgiveness as he was in accepting forgiveness extended to him. He understood the necessity to forgive because he experienced the need to be forgiven. He tamed his anger and channeled its energy into productive work. It is a remarkably clear testimony to the power of faith and self-discipline.

Always a teacher, Everett continues to instruct us even beyond the grave-guiding us in habits of heart and mind and soul that will enable us to live fuller, richer, more useful, loving and forgiving lives.

Everett was loquacious - how he loved to talk. There was nothing wishy-washy about Everett. He was a strict but kind disciplinarian, a firm but not inflexible leader, and he loved to share his opinion on almost any subject. He was so willing to share his point of view and so certain in his opinions, that I was sometimes reminded of the Peanuts cartoon: Linus and Charlie

Linus asks: "In heaven do they grade on a percentage or on a curve."
          "On a curve, of course," Charlie Brown answers.
          "How can you be so certain," Linus inquires.
          "I am always certain," says Charlie Brown, "About things that are a matter of opinion."

Everett was many things - a loving husband, married for 62 years to Alberta, a father and grandfather, a farmer, a quarryman, a storyteller and writer, a Christian and churchman, an intense thinker, self-taught theologian, and sometimes preacher. He was a leader in his community serving 8 years as School Superintendent and 17 years as a Commissioner of the South

Cumberland Utility District, in which position he helped Big Lick and others get public water. But I will remember him most as a teacher.

I always thought Everett made a mistake by leaving the classroom. He did so because his talents as a leader drew him into positions of authority and control. He thought he could do more for education as a leader than in the classroom. But at heart, he was always a teacher. In my 22 years of formal education, I have had many instructors, many counselors, some of whom were reputed to be among the best in the country, but I have never experienced a better teacher than Mr. Gibson.

Some will remember him as a disciplinarian. I am one of the few here that was present on that day when he broke 4 mule shoes as a demonstration of strength to a group of teenage boys at the Big Lick School, some of whom were bigger than he was. As he recounts in his book, he had few discipline problems after that. Little did we know that it was a staged stunt, though we should have guessed that from the fact that he presented us 4 new shoes with which to continue our game of horseshoes.

On one occasion, I experienced his paddling, but I was more impressed by another more spontaneous demonstration of his disciplinary skill. Two of my classmates were cutting up and disrupting class. Suddenly Mr. Gibson exploded at them and among the things he said (the part I remember) was, "I'd come back there and crack your heads together if I wasn't afraid of getting splinters in my hands." He never touched them, but they remained quiet thereafter.

He was always thinking ahead of the curve, and his most successful act as a disciplinarian at the Big Lick School was the introduction of the discipline of organized sports. This, more than anything else, changed attitudes toward school and offered many students a reason to be there. It was a factor in my own life as the skills I learned there and the recommendation I got from him helped me to become an athlete in high school.

For me, above all else, he remains a teacher. Many of the things he did as a teacher years ago would still be considered cutting-edge today. He was creative, imaginative, energetic, enthusiastic, innovative, brilliant, courageous, and contagious. He loved learning and caused others (especially young men) to see it as important. Whether it was in the classroom or in front of his Sunday School Class, he could impart knowledge with exceptional skill and thoroughness.

If Everett were here in this world with us today, perhaps this is what he might say to us:

> *"To Those I Love" by Isla Richardson.*
> *If I should ever leave you whom I love*
> *To go along the Silent Way,*
> *Grieve not,*
>
> *. . .*
>
> *Please do not let the thoughts of me be sad,*
> *For I am loving you just as I always have.*
>
> *. . .*
>
> *We cannot see Beyond,*
> *But this I know:*
> *I loved you so – t'was heaven here with you."* [1]

[I led an Interim Prayer and a hymn was played.]

[The Meditation on Hope and Witness to the Resurrection was presented by another minister.]

[Benediction and dismissal to place of burial for a Committal Service.]

NOTES:

1. In the service, I read the whole poem, but Copyright constraints limit me to printing what I have above. I encourage you to find and read a copy of the whole poem.

POLLY CAMPBELL OBITUARY/EULOGY AND REMARKS – FEBRUARY 6, 2008

I was charged with doing only the Opening and the "Obituary/Eulogy" for this Service, and I wandered not far from that assignment.

"Blessed be the God and Father of our Lord Jesus Christ!"
"By God's great mercy we have been born anew to a living hope through the Resurrection of Jesus Christ from the dead."
"Praise be to God, for we do not grieve as those who have no hope!" Jesus said, "I am the resurrection and the life. Those who believe in me, though they die, yet shall they live."
"Come to me all who are burdened and heavy laden, and I will give you rest."
"Blessed are those who mourn; they shall be comforted."
"Our help is in the name of the Lord who made heaven and earth!"

Funerals are historic occasions. They are one of the ways we mark time. Before calendars came into common use, funerals served as a way of remembering other important events. "I remember," Someone might say, "That happened the year Aunt Amy died."

The year 1913 saw several events that would shape our lives:

Constitutional amendments establishing the Income tax and the popular election of senators were adopted.

The first mass produced Model T rolled off of Henry Ford's assembly line in Highland Park, Michigan.

The first home electric refrigerator was introduced.

The Suffragette movement was gearing up (it would be 7 years before women got the right to vote in U. S. elections).

We were 6 years away from WWI, 28 years from WWII, and 30 years from the first use of penicillin.

None of those events shaped the lives of us in this room more than what happened on July 7 of that year. In Emory, Va. a daughter was born to John Luke and Glenna Senter Hardin. They named her Mary Pauline.

As a young woman, she would drive her father to the local drug store where he would smoke his daily cigar. It was there that she met a Tusculum College freshman who was clerking in the drugstore. It proved to be a happy coincidence, and on Sept. 15, 1942, Mary Pauline Hardin became Polly Campbell, and she and J. T. Shared a life together as loving wife and husband for almost 60 years until his death 5½ years ago.

Polly had opinions, opinions that sometimes ran counter to the popular culture in which she found herself. And she was not afraid of quietly expressing those opinions. I was reminded of her the other day when I heard an interview with one of the African Americans who as a young man had helped to start the civil rights movement as one of the first four persons to sit in at a Woolworth's lunch counter in Greensboro, NC. He was explaining how that day, he learned never to stereotype anyone. At the lunch counter where they sat in, there was an older white-haired white woman who eyed them in what he took to be a suspicious manner. He thought, there sits a died-in-the-wool white racist. But as she left, she placed her hands on the young black men's shoulders and said quietly, "Way to go, boys. I'm so proud of you..." I thought of Polly.

She was strong-willed and disciplined. A lifelong smoker until she decided to stop, she stopped cold turkey and never looked back. Pragmatic and adaptable, she was serene in the face of difficulties and hard choices. As she often advised others, she took one day at a time, did her own thing, and didn't sweat the small stuff.

She took strength from the words of Jesus recorded in the 6th chapter of Matthew:

"...do not be anxious about your life...Look at the birds of the air... Which of you by being anxious can add one minute to her span of life...Consider the lilies of the field, how they grow; they neither toil nor spin. Yet, even Solomon in all his glory was not arrayed like one of these...do not be anxious...seek first God's kingdom and righteousness, and all these thing shall be yours as well...Therefore, do not be anxious about tomorrow, for tomorrow will be anxious for itself. Let the day's own trouble be sufficient for the day."

Polly did not set out to be a doctor's wife. Shortly after she married J.T. he joined the air force and thought he would become a commercial pilot. But a doctor's wife - an old-fashioned country doctor's wife she became, but she did not define herself solely that way. Throughout most of her married life, she had her own career as a Girl Scout professional (or Professional Girl Scout), commuting to Knoxville to work for the Tanasi Council of Girl Scouts.

She did not choose to marry a man who would become obsessed with serving his profession and his patients. But the wife of such a man she became, and she bought into the whole bit. If J. T. was obsessed with service to his patients (to the great benefit of many of us), she was co- dependent with him, enabling him to become who he was. Those of you who remember Dr. Campbell fondly should know that he could not have been who he was without Polly being who she was.

Polly died as she had lived, quietly and serenely, on February 4, 2008, after a long slow decline in her health.

She is survived by: *[I read a list of survivors.]*

Alfred, Lord Tennyson used a seafaring image to express thoughts that Polly wanted remembered at this occasion. He wrote:

> *Sunset and evening star*
> *And one clear call for me!*
> *And may there be no moaning of the bar,*
> *When I put out to sea.*
> *For tho' from out our bourne of Time and Place*
> *The flood may bear me far,*
> *I hope to see my Pilot face to face*
> *When I have crossed the bar.*
> *"Crossing the Bar" By Alford, Lord Tennyson* [1]

However, it's the words of Isla Pascal Richardson that remind me of what Polly might say if she could speak to us today:

> *"If I should ever leave you whom I love*
> *To go along the Silent Way,*
> *Grieve not,*
>
> *. . .*
>
> *Please do not let the thoughts of me be sad,*
> *For I am loving you just as I always have.*
>
> *. . .*
>
> *We cannot see Beyond,*
> *But this I know:*
> *I loved you so – t'was heaven here with you."* [2]
> *"To Those I Love"* by Isla Pascal Richardson

Let Us Pray: *[I led an interim prayer and a hymn was sung.] [The Rev. Pete Ullmann presented a Meditation of Witness to the Resurrection.]*

[Benediction and dismissal to place of burial for a Committal Service.]

NOTES:
1. At the service, I read the whole poem but am constrained here by Copyright regulations to print no more than I have printed here. I encourage you to find and read the whole poem.
2. Ibid. I also read this whole poem at the service but can only print what is here. I also encourage you to find and read the whole poem.

AGNES KNOX HALL OBITUARY/EULOGY - AUGUST 31, 2008

I did only the Obituary/Eulogy

"Blessed be the God and Father of our Lord Jesus Christ! By God's great mercy we have been born anew to a living hope through the Resurrection of Jesus Christ from the dead."

"Praise be to God, for we do not grieve as those who have no hope!" Jesus said, "I am the resurrection and the life. Those who believe in me, though they die, yet shall they live"

"Come to me all who are burdened and heavy laden, and I will give you rest."

"Blessed are those who mourn; they shall be comforted."

"Our help is in the name of the Lord who made heaven and earth!"

We are gathered to take account of change; to pay attention to sorrow; to grieve a loss and celebrate a homecoming; to remember and to thank God for the life of **Agnes Marie Hall**; and to bear witness to the **victory** of eternal life over sin and death which is ours in Christ Jesus.

Her last birthday, August 9, was a happy day for Agnes Hall. It was Saturday of the 2008 Highway 127 Yard Sale and, she had, in her estimation for the first time, made money from that spectacle in which she had participated every year.

She loved yard selling. She liked talking to the browsers and the buyers whether she made money or not. Make no mistake about it; however, she intended to make money. Perhaps it was her own frugality and sense of value, or perhaps it was being married for 53 years to a man who was as tight as the spots on a blue tick hound, but she meant to make money at a yard sale.

She would re-price items she thought Sheila had priced too low. Ob had collected a barn full of antiques and collectibles. Agnes told Sheila, "It is my mission for the rest of my life to clean out that barn, so that you won't give it away."

OBITUARY/EULOGY

Born on the ninth day of August 1929, in the Grassy Cove community, Agnes was the second child and second daughter of the 8 children born to Crockett and Jessie Garrison Knox.

As a young woman, Agnes completed nursing training at Fort Sanders Hospital in Knoxville, serving as Vice-President of her nursing class and being named Most Outstanding in that class. Agnes was a Nurse with a capital N. It was not merely the way in which she made a living. It was not merely her profession. For Agnes, nursing was a way of life. It was the way she related to others. Even after she retired, she continued to take care of others - always serving them, never wanting to be served herself.

For most of her career she was employed by the Cumberland Clinic Foundation. Some of us remember the pioneering doctors from that clinic - Metcalfe, Young, Evans, Seaton, and others who transformed the face of medical care in Cumberland County. Agnes was there by their side for 39 of those years. To my way of thinking, her most masterful feat as a nurse was working for and with Dr. J. T. Campbell during the years he worked at the Clinic. Dr. Campbell had a reputation of being hard on nurses - often reducing some of them to tears. But Agnes saw through his gruffness, deflected his sometimes-harsh demeanor and became his most trusted aide and assistant.

On June 4, 1954, Agnes married Ob Hall, and he, and the children they adopted, Sheila and Greg, and the grandchildren that came later became the center of her life. She adored them and lavished her affection and her time on them. Whether it was in her devotion to her children, the extensive scrapbooks she kept for each of her grandchildren, being the "Nanny Walmart" for her grandson, or in doing the housework and yard work at her daughter's house as well as her own, she constantly demonstrated her care and love for them. She kept up with everything in their lives - making sure that all of them kept their appointments and often reminding her grandchildren to "take care of your teeth and get a good education."

Agnes was a faithful member of Calvary Presbyterian Church of Big Lick, taking great joy in the fact that she was able to return to church over the past year after many years of being unable to attend because of Ob's health.

Agnes loved to work in the garden, saying each year, "This may be the last year I will be able to do this," but then every year, repeating the action. She liked to sew, to cook (especially a special breakfast on Christmas morning), and to do the other chores we associate with being a homemaker. Her children and grandchildren said she could do 40 hours work in one day, often outworking them even though she was twice or three-five times their ages. She was a little old fashioned, being one of the few who still hung her wash out to dry.

Agnes never gave up. Even after returning from the hospital this last time, she would break beans and ask for other chores to do. One of her great fears was that she would become an invalid, requiring others to care for her. It was a thought she could not bear.

Her years of nursing experience told her what was potentially ahead for her. And in the end, she seems to have decided, like her Native American forebears, that it was a good day to die.

Agnes died peacefully on August 29, 2008. She was 20 days past her 79th birthday.

She is survived by

> *[I read a list of survivors including "Wally - the dog she did not want but came to love calling him 'My Baby.'"]*

In June 1954, Agnes moved into the house in Homestead where she spent the rest of her life and where she died. For many years I have passed that house almost every day on my way to town-sometimes seeing Agnes' wash on the line, sometimes seeing Agnes set up for a yard sale. In reflecting on Agnes' life and the location of her house, I am reminded of this poem by Sam Walter Foss. It is entitled "The House by the Side of the Road."

The House by the Side of the Road
By Sam Walter Foss (June 19, 185 - February 26, 1911)

> *I see from my house by the side of the road,*
> * By the side of the highway of life:*
> *The men who press with the ardor of hope;*

> *The men who are faint with the strife.*
> *But I turn not away from their smiles nor their tears,*
>   *Both part of an infinite plan –*
> *Let me live in a house by the side of the road*
>   *And be a friend to man.*

In her later years, Agnes came to love the ocean which she had seen for the first time at age 65. On visits there with her sisters, she would often get up early and take long walks on the beach. And she always loved to watch the hummingbirds outside her window.

If she could speak to you today, she might well say, in the words of Isla Pascal Richardson:

> **"To Those I Love"**
> By Isla Pascal Richardson
>
> *If I should ever leave you whom I love*
> *To go along the Silent Way,*
> *Grieve not,*
>
> *. . .*
> *Please do not let the thoughts of me be sad,*
> *For I am loving you just as I always have.*
>
> *. . .*
> *We cannot see Beyond,*
> *But this I know:*
> *I loved you so – t'was heaven here with you."* [2]

Let Us Pray. *[I led an interim prayer.]*

[The service was completed with a Meditation of hope and witness to the resurrection by the Rev. Pete Ullmann.]

[Dismissal to place of burial for a committal service.]

NOTES:
1. I read more of this poem at the service, but one can get away with more with the spoken word (especially if it is non- commercial) than you can with the written word. According to Copyright regulations, I have reprinted here all that I can of this poem without special

permission – which is virtually impossible to get. I encourage you to find the whole poem and read it. It is easily available at several sources.

2. Again, I read the whole poem at the service. I have printed here all I am permitted to print. Again, I encourage you to find a copy of the whole poem and read it. Try the internet.

RUBY SELBY OBITUARY/ EULOGY – OCTOBER 02, 2009

"Blessed be the God and Father of our Lord Jesus Christ! By God's great mercy we have been born anew to a living hope through the Resurrection of Jesus Christ from the dead."

"Praise be to God, for we do not grieve as those who have no hope!" It is not that we do not grieve, but rather when we grieve, we do so within the hope we have in Christ Jesus.

Jesus said, "I am the resurrection and the life. Those who believe in me, though they die, yet shall they live"

"Come to me all who are burdened and heavy laden, and I will give you rest." "Blessed are those who mourn; they shall be comforted."

"Our help is in the name of the Lord who made heaven and earth!"

We are gathered to take account of change; to pay attention to sorrow; to grieve a loss and celebrate a homecoming; to remember and to thank God for the life of Ruby Selby; to witness to the Resurrection, and to rejoice in the victory of eternal life over sin and death which is ours in Christ Jesus.

OBITUARY/EULOGY

Ruby Selby was born on June 18, 1929, on the banks of Daddy's Creek across the road from the place we know as Sutton's Ford - though none of us can remember when it was a ford. Ruby remembered virtually everything there was to know about Sutton's Ford, but even she could not remember when it was a ford, nor who the Sutton was for whom it was named.

She was the second daughter and the fourth or fifth child of Emmett and Mamie Swafford Selby. Since she and Ray were twins, I don't know her exact birth order.

Ruby died after a long struggle with declining health and was released from the pain and suffering of this world on September 29, 2009, exactly 3 years and 25 days after her twin brother, Ray.

She is survived by: *[I read a list of survivors.]*

In my life, I have come to understand that dependability is more important than ability. If I have my choice for a partner or co-worker or friend between a person of great ability and a person of great dependability, I have learned that is better to choose the latter.

Ruby was the definition of dependability. It is simply enough to say about Ruby's character that other people trusted her with their money. For years she was the bookkeeper for Brewer's Department Store, and she served for over 15 years as the treasurer of Calvary Church of Big Lick (the third longest term of service in that position in the 75-year history of the church).

Ruby was a take-charge person. Though her brothers did the outside work, she ran the Selby farm. Sometimes she took charge in a "Take-no- prisoners" kind of way. Some might even say she was bossy at times. But she had an ability to lead and she was recognized for it in her family and her church.

Yet, in the deeper recesses of her soul, Ruby was satisfied with the simpler thing of life, family, faith, friends.

There is an old hymn that originated with a group of Christians known as the Shakers. We know them mostly today through the simple, practical and sturdy but beautiful furniture that is still called by their name. Called "*Simple Gifts*", the hymn goes, in part:

> *Tis a gift to be simple, tis a gift to be free,*
> *Tis a gift to come down where we ought to be,*
> *And when we find ourselves in the place just right,*
> *It will be in the valley of Love and delight.*
> *When true simplicity is gained*

To bow and to bend, we will not be ashamed.
To turn and to turn will be our delight
Til by turning, turning, we come round right.

Ruby had the gift of simplicity. Most of us are still seeking for things. Ruby was satisfied long ago. I often think that Ruby and others like her are the ones "turned round right" who have discovered the key to the "valley of love and delight."

[I led an interim prayer and a hymn was played.]

[I completed the service with a Meditation, prayer, benediction and dismissal to place of burial for a committal service.]

PAUL DAVID BURGESS OBITUARY/EULOGY – MARCH 12, 2010

I did this funeral service by myself in March, 2010. The deceased was a devout Christian and devoted Churchman. He was 93 at the time of his death. William Sloane Coffin once said, "The trick is to die young as late as possible.F No one I have known came closer to living that maxim than Paul David Burgess.

OPENING

Blessed be the God and Father of our Lord Jesus Christ! By God's great mercy, we have been born anew to a living hope through the Resurrection of Jesus Christ from the dead."

> *"Praise God, we do not grieve as those who have no hope!"*
> *Jesus said, "I am the resurrection and the life. Those who believe in me, though they die, yet shall they live."*
> *"Come to me all who are burdened and heavy laden, and I will give you rest."*
> *"Blessed are those who mourn; they shall be comforted."*
> *"Our help is in the name3 of the Lord who made heaven and earth."*

Paul Burgess - Husband, Father, Grandfather, Brother, soldier, sailor, scholar, professor, Christian, Churchman, farmer, gardener, whittler, hunter, fisherman, beagle hound fancier, and friend is gone from among us. We will grieve his passing and mourn his loss, but we must celebrate his life.

We celebrate because his was a long, full, useful, purpose filled life that demonstrated why today is a **victory celebration**. And friends, it is a victory celebration not only because every Christian funeral is such but particularly because Paul in his life, demonstrated so clearly what the New Testament writers mean when they say that in Christ we can be victorious over the forces of sin and death.

We are gathered to take account of change; to pay attention to sorrow; to grieve a loss; to celebrate a homecoming; to renew the hope that is ours in Christ Jesus; and to remember and to thank God for the life of Paul and for sharing him with us.

OBITUARY/EULOGY

Paul was born in Putnam County on January 17, 1917, the son of David I. and Lela Hicks Burgess. His education was interrupted by a stint in the Navy from 1946-49, during which time he also found time to marry Lois

M. on April 18, 1948. They lived together as loving husband and wife for nearly 62 years, and to their union five children were born.

He graduated from Tenn. Tech., the Univ. of Missouri, and the Univ. of Chicago, the last time with a PhD. He taught at and served in the Extension Service of the Univ. of Missouri until his retirement in 1982. Some people return home to die. Paul returned home to live.

He returned to his roots in Putnam County to live as a farmer, gardener, whittler, hunter, fisherman, and lover, breeder and trainer of beagle hounds. W. C. Fields is reputed to have said: "Never trust a man who likes dogs or children." I say to you, never trust a man who has not been licked by dogs or loved by children. He was past President of the Upper Cumberland Beagle Club, and I never see a beagle anymore but that I think of Paul.

Paul was a Christian and a churchman of the highest order serving for many years as a deacon and Elder in the Presbyterian Church both in Columbia, Missouri and at Union Grove in Putnam County. He also served frequently in the higher governing bodies of the Presbyterian Church.

Having said he was "Ready to go," Paul died peacefully on March 10, 2010.

He is survived by: *[I read the list of survivors.]*

It is enough to say about Paul, that I knew him for many years before I learned that he had a PhD. He never boasted of his achievements or called himself "Dr." He was just Paul, a plain and humble man of immense integrity, insight, vision, wisdom, generosity, dependability and character.

He was the kind of Christian, church member and leader that Pastors dream about and are fortunate to encounter. He was Biblically and theologically informed - a Biblical scholar who kept many study resources in his personal library and used them. He took the training to be a lay pastor just for his own personal edification. He was always seeking a deeper and wider understanding of Scripture and Christian theology. And he shared his faith in his love for his fellow humans and in his service to his Church and community. I spoke with a retired minister tonight who said that Paul was the best Sunday school teacher she had ever had. He was, she said, a better Bible teacher than her seminary professors.

He was a charter member of the Board of Directors of Creative Compassion, Inc. I will never forget some of the looks and comments he got when he came to one of our early volunteer workings on a home for a low-income family and unfurled himself out of his Mercedes dressed in his overalls. In a way that was a good representation of the two sides (or at least two of the several sides) of Paul.

We are not promised any number of days on this earth, and we cannot have permanence in this world. We are all dying, being "given up to death," as the Apostle Paul said, "in order to show that the transcendent power belongs to God, not to us."

The best that we can hope for in this world is to have our lives touched by the Hand of God - and one of the next best things among the best that most of us can ever hope to experience in this life - is to have our lives touched by someone who is straight & true, loving & caring, kind & generous, accepting & forgiving.

To the degree that we have all experienced that through Paul Burgess, we know a little of what it means to be touched by the Hand of God. And our memory of that makes us as richly blessed as it is possible to be blessed in this life.

If Paul could speak with us today, perhaps something like this is what he would say - in the words of Isla Pascal Richardson from a poem entitled "To Those I Love:"

"TO THOSE I LOVE"
By Isla Pascal Richardson

"If I should ever leave you whom I love
To go along the Silent Way,
Grieve not,

. . .

Please do not let the thoughts of me be sad,
For I am loving you just as I always have.

. . .

We cannot see Beyond,
But this I know:
I loved you so – t'was heaven here with you." [1]

[I offered an opportunity for any others to make any remarks they wished to at this time, and one other minister, Paul's present pastor, responded with a few words.]

[I led an interim prayer and a hymn was played.]

[I completed the service with a Meditation on Hope and Healing: A Witness to the Resurrection, a prayer, and a benediction.]

[Dismissal to place of burial for a committal service.]

NOTES:

1. I read the whole poem at the service, but by Copyright regulations can only present this eight-line excerpt here. I encourage you to find and read the whole poem.

SIDNEY HEDGECOTH OBITUARY/EULOGY – JUNE 29, 2010

I did the "Obituary/Eulogy" only for this service

"Blessed be the God and Father of our Lord Jesus Christ! By God's great mercy we have been born anew to a living hope through the Resurrection of Jesus Christ from the dead."

"Praise be to God, for we do not grieve as those who have no hope!"

Jesus said, "I am the resurrection and the life. Those who believe in me, though they die, yet shall they live"

"Come to me all who are burdened and heavy laden, and I will give you rest."

"Blessed are those who mourn; they shall be comforted."

"Our help is in the name of the Lord who made heaven and earth!"

Sidney L. Hedgecoth - Husband, Father, Grandfather, Brother, soldier, farmer, gardener, businessman, entrepreneur, baker, asphalt layer, bus driver, craftsman, care giver, neighbor and friend is gone from among us.

We will grieve his passing and mourn his loss, but we must celebrate his life.

We are gathered to take account of change; to pay attention to sorrow; to grieve a loss; to celebrate a homecoming; to renew the hope that is ours in Christ Jesus; and to remember and to thank God for the life of **Sid Hedgecoth** and for sharing him with us.

OBITUARY/EULOGY

Sid was born in Cumberland County on November 25, 1938, the son of Verden Lewis and Minnie Pugh Hedgecoth. He graduated from high school at Homestead and spent several years in Ohio. He served in the U.S. military where he worked as an ambulance driver. He drove a bus and worked many other jobs during his life, retiring from Flowers Bakery.

He was an entrepreneur and businessman who owned various businesses during his lifetime including a restaurant, and several rental properties which he had developed. He was a craftsman who made clocks, wooden storks to announce the arrival of a baby, and other objects - which he frequently gave away.

He loved to grow things and raised large gardens and vegetable patches. Every time you visited Sid in the summertime, he had vegetables to give you. This was the first year that he had not planted a large garden.

Sid had a wry sense of humor and loved to tease people. Perhaps it was his humor that kept him going so long. He defied death many times - from the time he was almost electrocuted to his many bouts with blood clots and poor circulation. My son called him a "bionic man" for the fact that he had so many synthetic blood vessels installed. Some people thought Sid might give up after he lost a foot to his disease, but it barely slowed him down. He went on doing pretty much what he had always done, though he had to do them a little differently to accommodate his loss of the foot.

With Sid, what you saw was what you got. There was nothing flaky or dishonest about him. He never worried about what he could not do but just went on doing what he could as well as he could.

Though he had served in the military with honor, Sid was more a lover than a fighter. He enjoyed helping others and did so in many ways. He was so quiet and unassuming about it that most people never knew how many people he helped and in how many ways.

You would not call Sid shy, but he was not aggressive or pushy. But he mustered up the courage to march up to Carolyn's front door one day - sort of out of the blue and asked her if she would go out with him. They were married on December 26, 1979. From their union, one child, Matthew, was born. Sid also became a faithful stepfather to Carolyn's other children.

As Carolyn's health failed, Sid became a compassionate care giver. He once said that he was not going to cook. But he did cook and take care of the house and Carolyn. In our marriage vows, we swear to be faithful to our spouse through good times and bad times, through good health and bad. Sid lived up to his word.

He had a gift for friendship and was especially close to the group of pals that met regularly at the Dairy Queen. He will be missed from among their fellowship.

Sid died quietly at home in his sleep on June 26, 2010. He is survived by: *[I read a list of survivors.]*

Sid spent the last 31 years of his life as my neighbor, living just down the road from me in his house by the side of the road. This poem by Sam Walter Foss seems appropriate. It is entitled "The House by the Side of the Road."

> **The House by the Side of the Road**
> By Sam Walter Foss (June 19, 1858 - February 26, 1911)
>
> *"I see from my house by the side of the road,*
> *   By the side of the highway of life:*
> *The men who press with the ardor of hope;*
> *   The men who are faint with the strife.*
> *But I turn not away from their smiles nor their tears,*
> *   Both part of an infinite plan –*
> *Let me live in a house by the side of the road*
> *   And be a friend to man."* [1]

Let us Pray: *[I led an interim prayer.]*

[Another minister offered words of hope and witness to the resurrection.] [Dismissal to place of burial for a committal service.]

NOTES:

1. I read more of poem at the service, but am permitted to print only this one verse.

STAN TOLLETT OBITUARY/EULOGY – JULY 18, 2010

I did this entire service.

"Blessed be the God and Father of our Lord Jesus Christ! By God's great mercy we have been born anew to a living hope through the Resurrection of Jesus Christ from the dead."

"Praise be to God, for we do not grieve as those who have no hope!"

Jesus said, "I am the resurrection and the life. Those who believe in me, though they die, yet shall they live."

"Come to me all who are burdened and heavy laden, and I will give you rest."

"Blessed are those who mourn; they shall be comforted."

"Our help is in the name of the Lord who made heaven and earth!"

We are gathered to take account of change; to pay attention to sorrow; to grieve a loss; to renew the hope that is ours in Christ Jesus; and to remember and to thank God for the life of **Stan Tollett** and for sharing his life with us.

OBITUARY/EULOGY

Stan was born on June 1, 1957, the second son of Creed and Louise Henry Tollett. He lived out his life in Big Lick and never ventured far from home. He was kind and courteous, loyal, faithful and truthful. There was no guile or deceit in him. He was a plain and simple man, never accounted great as the world measures such things but great in the hearts of those who loved him.

He was an avid reader especially of western novels and the annual Almanac and enjoyed gaining new knowledge. To bolster his knowledge about animals and folklore, he often consulted with his friend Pete Bradley, saying, "If I don't know it, Pete will." He enjoyed collecting coins and guns.

He was a carpenter by trade and engaged in it as long as his health permitted. He liked Country music and listening to the Grand Ole Opry - especially the old time Opry, before contemporary country changed the sound of the music.

I remember Stan as a young man. He helped us build our house starting when he was in high school. That was where he was first introduced to carpentry. He was an enormous help, smart and capable with great physical skills and a mind that was as quick as a whip. You only had to show him how to do something once and he had it down pat. You did not have to tell him what to do again. He was personable, easy to work with, and worked well with others. Over the course of the past 20 years at Creative Compassion, I have worked with several novice carpenters. Only one other of them has been as quick a study or has caught on to things as quickly as Stan did.

I also was a teammate of Stan's, playing softball with him over several summers. He was as skilled an infielder as I ever played with. I remember him as one of, if not the best softball second baseman in Cumberland County. My son reminded me at lunch that one of the first time's Lynn hit a home run it cracked Stan's windshield. I think we took up a collection to help him pay for it.

Stan may not have been born to play baseball, but he was apparently named to do so. According to legend at least, his father named him partially after the great baseball player Stan "The Man" Musial who was the National League MVP the year Stan was born.

Stan overcame many medical problems and struggled with many demons during the latter part of his life. I don't mean mythical demons but the real kind that accompanies, are brought on by or result from the overuse of certain substances.

One of the great regrets of my life is that I could not find the power to free Stan of his demons. It may appear that in the end, the demons won. But that is not the end of the story. Stan is at a place now where there is someone with the power to free him from his demons. He will suffer from them no more. Today, he is at comfort and at peace.

Stan died after a long illness and many years of declining health on July 16, 2010.

He is survived by: *[I read a list of survivors.]*

Stan loved you all even if he did have a peculiar way of showing it sometimes. Perhaps if he were to speak to us today, Stan might say this, in the words of Isla Pascal Richardson:

> **"To Those I Love"**
> By Isla Pascal Richardson
>
> *"If I should ever leave you whom I love*
> *To go along the silent way, grieve not*
> *. . .*
> *And when you hear a song or see a thing*
> *That reminds you of me*
> *Please do not let the thought of me be sad*
> *For I am loving you, just as I always have.*
> *You were so good to me!*
> *. . .*
> *I loved you so - 'twas heaven here with you."* [1]

Let us Pray: *[I led an interim prayer and a hymn was played.]*

[I completed the service with a Meditation of Hope and Healing: A Witness to the Resurrection, a prayer, and a benediction.]

[Dismissal to place of burial for a committal service.]

NOTES:

1. I read the whole poem at the service but am constrained by Copyright regulations to limit the printed version to no more than eight lines. I encourage you to find the whole poem and read it.

AARON H. KONSTAM MEMORIAL SERVICE REMARKS – JANUARY 24, 2015

[As delivered]

> *I was the primary one of several who offered Eulogies at this service.*

Baruch atta, Adonai Elohenu, melech ha'olom.

Blessed are You, O Lord our God, King of the Universe. That's about all the Hebrew I know, but I would add: Blessed are You, O Lord our God, who has redeemed us and Your people Israel.

Some of us have asked or been asked to speak today. Others of you will have to treat this as a Friends meeting and speak later when and if the Spirit moves you.

Aaron is not the first of my brothers-in-law to die. But he is the first with whom I felt a kindred spirit. I found in him a compatriot in the never- ending quest for social justice.

A word about witnesses. Aaron was big on witnesses. He believed in them. Before there were death certificates or funeral records, there were witnesses. As witnesses, you are more than spectators, you are participants who can later say, regardless of the written record, "Yes, Aaron Konstam lived and died in his 79th year on January 20, 2015. I know because I was at his funeral service."

We are gathered here to pay attention to sorrow, to take account of change, and to give thanks for the life of Aharon ben Moshe, better known to us as Aaron Konstam.

I first encountered Aaron in a letter from my sister in 1960. We were both young then and somewhat given to satire. But it wasn't Pat's satirical observations about Aaron ("he walks like a duck" and so forth) that struck me. What I noticed was that my sister was in love. She had been in love before or thought she was, but she had never written of others with the intimacy she wrote about Aaron.

I next encountered Aaron in a family conference at which neither he nor I were present. I knew what Pat and my parents were talking about in my absence. And knowing my sister, I had already guessed the outcome of the conference. From then on, it was a great joy to get to know Aaron and to watch my mother go from reluctant acceptance to enthusiastic support of their marriage.

For at least 43 years (and much longer for some of us), the wit and wisdom, the kindness and compassion, the thirst for justice of Aaron Konstam has brightened and enlightened bits of our world. As of January 20, 2015, that has changed. Life moves on. Death remains.

"No one can step in the same river twice because both the person and the river have changed." [Heraclitus] Only eternity remains unchanged. We should rejoice and give thanks for the past, but we cannot go back there to live.

But wherever you go, you will not go alone. As it is written in the 43rd Chapter of Isaiah:

> *". . . Fear not, for I have redeemed you; I have called you by name, you are mine. When you pass through the waters, I will be with you, and when you pass through the floods, they shall not overwhelm you; when you walk through the fire you shall not be burned. The flame shall not consume you, for I am the Lord your God, the Holy One of Israel, your Savior."*

We are not promised any number of days on this earth, and we cannot have permanence in this world. We are all dying, being "given up to death" as one scribe has described it.

The best that we can hope for in this world is to have our lives touched by the Hand of God - and one of the next best things - among the best that most of us can ever hope to experience in this life - is to have our lives touched by someone who is straight & true, loving & caring, kind & generous, accepting & forgiving.

To the degree that we all experienced that through Aaron, we know a little of what it means to be touched by the hand of God. And our memory of that makes us as richly blessed as it is possible to be blessed in this life.

Could he speak to us today perhaps Aaron might say this, in the words of Isla Pascal Richardson:

> ***"TO THOSE I LOVE"***
> By Isla Pascal Richardson
>
> *"If I should ever leave you whom I love*
> *To go along the Silent Way,*
> *Grieve not,*
> *. . .*
> *Please do not let the thoughts of me be sad,*
> *For I am loving you just as I always have.*
> *. . .*
> *We cannot see Beyond, But this I know:*
> *I loved you so – t'was heaven here with you."* [1]

A Jewish Rabbi who lived many centuries ago, like many other Rabbi's down through the ages, had disciples who preserved and wrote down some of his teachings. Among those were these:

> *"Blessed are the merciful, for they shall obtain mercy.*
> *"Blessed are the peacemakers, for they shall be called sons of God.*
> *"Blessed are those who hunger and thirst for righteousness, for they shall be satisfied."*

Perhaps that is all that needs to be said about Aaron Konstam, but I have more.

Aaron gave up what could have been his claim to fame - research, writing, perhaps an invention or innovation that would have made him famous. He gave them up to teach, advise, and befriend undergraduates. It was his life's work, and one of his life's loves.

He cared about individuals and knew that the genuine substance of life is not defined by technological advances, political or military conquests, or cultural innovations, but by what happens to individuals.

Aaron Konstam, the Jewish Mensch, he of the beautiful, brilliant, expansive, eclectic, astute, acute, agile mind, the astounding memory, the acerbic wit, the good humor, the thirst for justice; husband, father, brother, brother-in-law, scholar, teacher, advisor, Mensa member, Xena the Warrior Princess aficionado, Dolly Parton devotee, book lover, library advocate, companion, compatriot, colleague, friend, and bootleg Rabbi, whose smile could brighten the darkest room or the dullest discussion: is gone. We will mourn his death but we must celebrate his life.

We celebrate because his was a productive life lived well with purpose and meaning and integrity.

The one sure obligation that the living have to their loved ones who have died is to live life to its fullest just as they would have wanted us to do. That is what they would want us to do. Thanks be to God for giving him life and for sharing him with us. Indeed, how blest we are to mourn today, for it means that we had the rare privilege of loving and being loved by one of God's unique individuals - so loquacious, as has been said, that he could not sit through a single faculty meeting without speaking up, and who always had an explanation, even if it was incomplete, for the most baffling or most mundane issues known to humankind.

"Life is eternal, love is immortal, and death is only a horizon, and a horizon is nothing but the limit of our sight." [2]

Aaron prepared the whole service for his son's Bar Mitzvah. Among the readings was a poem, a Psalm really, that tells us all we need to know about Aaron Konstam. It is entitled "If You Look at the Stars and Yawn." It's meant to be read responsively, but since we are not set up to do that today, I will read all parts of it.

> "Praise me, says God, and I will know that you love me. Curse me, says God, and I will know that you love me. Praise me or curse me,
> And I will know that you love me.

"Sing out my graces, says God.
Raise your fist against me and revile, says God.
Sing out graces or revile,
Reviling is also a kind of praise, says God.
"But if you sit fenced off in your apathy, says God,
If you sit entrenched in: 'I don't give a hang,' says God
If you look at the stars and yawn;
If you see suffering and don't cry out;
If you don't praise and you don't revile,
Then I created you in vain, says God.

"As seekers after the truth, O God, we confess the hesitancy and
inconstancy which hinder us in our search. That which we find is
often unwelcome and uncomfortable; we evade the truth and
reassure ourselves by self-deception, clinging to old familiar
errors or cherishing the lie in the soul. The problems of our time
are bewildering; we take refuge in evasion and indifference.
Speak then, O God, to our fugitive souls, to renew both our
candor and our courage."

What else is there to say? If there are indeed 36 righteous ones for whose sake the world is spared, Aaron was among them. Who will replace him?

Amen and Amen.

NOTES:

1. I read the whole poem at the service, but am constrained here by Copyright regulations to limit what I print to no more than eight lines of text.
2. Penn, et al., Op. Cit. For more information, see **Appendix A** at the end of this Collection.
3. Though I had the following things in my notes I did not use them in the Eulogy as I delivered it: The Shema ("Shema' Yisrael Adonai Elohenu Adonai echad" [Hear, O Israel, the Lord our God, the Lord is one]; "observant, devout Jew;" "humorous" (Susan's suggestion); "full of life and laughter; "who believed in the eternal care of the God of Abraham, Isaac, and Jacob."

JIM MILAM OBITUARY/ EULOGY AND REMARKS – MAY 1, 2015

I was charged with doing only an Obituary/Eulogy for this funeral of one of my best friends. Three other ministers participated in the service.

I told someone last night that Jim must have been awfully good or awfully ornery since it takes four preachers to get him sent off to the next world. You are witnessing a rare occasion: Both Jim and I in a suit and tie at the same time. The last time that happened was probably at Jim and Linda's wedding 45 years ago.

I was bush hogging Monday and had to remind myself not to go too close to my pond because Jim was no longer available to pull me out if I got stuck. I almost got stuck anyway.

In response to another posting on Facebook about Jim, our daughter Susan posted: "Jim was a good friend to our family. I have known Jim since I was 6 years old. He was always someone we could rely on."

Perhaps that is all that needs to be said about Jim, but being a country preacher, I have more to say.

OBITUARY/EULOGY

Jim Milam - Teacher, Farmer, Shorthorn Breeder, Mechanic, Welder, Car Restorer, always available Helper, Dinner Companion, Bootleg taxi and ambulance driver, Sudoku puzzle solver, Lady Vols fan, Son, Brother, Brother-in-law, Uncle, Neighbor, Friend, the precise, meticulous persevering perfectionist, the one with the beautiful, omnipresent smile on his face, is gone from among us.

For 41 years I have lived as his neighbor and friend. I will miss him; Lord, how I will miss him.

We will weep for his loss, we will mourn his passing, but we must celebrate his life. We celebrate because his was a full, useful, purpose filled life that demonstrated why today is a victory celebration. And we celebrate because this is a victory celebration in which we remember one who, with God's help, was victorious over the forces of sin and death.

We are gathered to take account of change; to pay attention to sorrow; to grieve a loss and celebrate a homecoming; to renew the hope that is ours in Christ Jesus; and to remember and thank God for the life of Jim Milam and for sharing that life with us.

Jim was born 69 years and 4 months ago in Oak Ridge, the first child of Ruel and Sue Bates Milam. After Oak Ridge High School, he graduated from Tennessee Tech University where he was a member of the Pershing Rifles Elite Drill Team. After service as an Army investigator, he taught in the Cumberland County school system for 25 years before retiring to pursue his lifelong ambition - to live and work on his own 100-acre farm. In doing so, he did not need a field hand or a hired hand for he had Linda. *[The congregation, knowing how he depended upon Linda to help him with all kinds of chores, roared with laughter.]*

He had a keen, alert, active mind and was a lifetime learner. Known for his dependability, he was a man of his word and a storehouse of information which he shared freely. He loved to talk and eat and was an enjoyable dinner companion. He maintained an active interest in the world around him, and must have been something of a mathematical genius for he solved Sudoku puzzles in his spare time.

I know of no one who ever asked Jim for help and was refused. He would stop what he was doing, no matter how important it was to him, to help you with whatever you asked. He was a skilled mechanic and a master welder. He has pulled my rear end out of the fire more than once. But my, was he particular. I admit there were projects I did not take to Jim for his help. I knew exactly how I wanted to do the project. I knew if I took it to Jim, he would have another way. I knew no matter how much I argued, we would end up doing it Jim's way.

Though not much of a churchman, he was a devout Christian who was prepared to meet his maker.

Jim died quietly and peacefully in the early morning hours of April 27, 2015, after a short but severe illness.

He is survived by: *[I read a list of survivors.]*

I first encountered Jim on a hot July 4th in 1970, at his and Linda's wedding. We were all young then, and he was brash, confident and sure of himself. What he did not seem to realize was that he was marrying a woman that was, in every way, his equal.

I used to think it was evidence of the unfairness of nature that Jim and Linda, who would have been perfect parents, had no children. But I finally decided it was so they could lavish their love on all those other children - those they taught in school, those in Linda's Sunday school classes, their nieces and nephews, the foster children Butch and Vickie took in, and the children of friends. I saw a picture of Jim on Facebook Monday night. He was holding Nathaniel Ullmann shortly after Nathaniel's birth. Jim's face was beaming. He could not have looked more pleased or proud if he had been the father himself.

Shortly after Jim was diagnosed with brain cancer, I sat and talked with him for some time. We talked of death and dying. Jim was not afraid of death, though he did not relish the possible pain that sometimes accompanies the process of dying. Thankfully he experienced little of that. He told me that he thought the tumor was inoperable (though it had not yet been diagnosed as such). I told him that he could not yet possibly know whether that were true or not. As it often did, it turned out that Jim was right. He said that when God decided it was time for him to go, he would go. I encouraged him to fight the tumor since we could never know when it was time for us to die. We talked of Dylan Thomas' poem that begins *"Do not go gentle into that good night; But rage, rage against the dying of the light."*

Glioblastoma. Even the name sounds ominous. The disease is worse. It is one of the most aggressive, fastest growing, most difficult to treat, and deadliest of all cancers. Average time from diagnosis to death is 4 - 6 months. Jim took it to the outer edges of that time frame. Jim did not rage but continued to greet visitors with a warm smile. But neither did he go gentle into that good night; he fought the cancer with all the tools available to modern medicine.

I hoped and prayed that Jim would be an exception, but, alas, that was not to be.

We are not promised any number of days on this earth, and we cannot have permanence in this world. We are all dying, being "given up to death," as the Apostle Paul said, "in order to show that the transcendent power belongs to God, not to us."

The best that we can hope for in this world is to have our lives touched by the Hand of God - and one of the next best things - among the best that most of us can ever hope to experience in this life - is to have our lives touched by someone who is straightforward & true, loving & caring, kind & generous, accepting & forgiving, honest, honorable, & dependable.

To the degree that we have all experienced that through Jim Milam, then we know a little of what it means to be touched by the Hand of God. And our memory of that makes us as richly blessed as it is possible to be blessed in this life.

He could be stubborn, even bullheaded, and liked to do things his way. But everyone who ever met him liked him. Perhaps it was because he had the mark of true humility - he could laugh at himself.

Most of you are unfamiliar with the term "mensch." It is a Yiddish word used mostly by urban Jews of European descent. It means a person of integrity and honor. It is reserved for the most respected members of the community. If ever there were a goyim (gentile) who deserves the term "mensch," surely it is Jim Milam.

There is one thing you can still do for Jim. That is to go on living life as fully, as joyfully, and as meaningfully as possible just as he would want you to do. It will be hard at first and there will never be any final closure to the wound you have suffered for a giant rip has been torn in the fabric of your lives and a part of the fabric is gone. But it is the one sure obligation that the living have to their loved ones who have died, and with God's help it will get easier over time.

Thanks be to God for giving him life and for sharing him with us. Indeed, how blest we are to mourn today, for it means that we had the rare privilege of knowing, loving and being loved by one of God's unique individuals.

For at least 45 years (much longer for some) the wit and wisdom, the kindness and compassion, the bright smile, the honesty, integrity, and dependability of Jim Milam has brightened and enlightened bits of our world. As of April 27, 2015, that has changed. Life moves on. Death remains. *"There seems a shadow on the day, His smile no longer cheers; A dimness on the stars at night; Like eyes that look through tears."* [1]

But *"death is only a horizon and a horizon is nothing but the limit of our sight."* [2] I know not what the future holds, but I know who holds the future. And the resurrected Christ is enough to comfort those who trust in him.

"No one can step in the same river twice because both the person and the river have changed." 3 Only eternity remains unchanged. We should rejoice and give thanks for the past, but we cannot go back there to live.

But wherever you go, you will not go alone. As it is written in the 43rd Chapter of Isaiah:

> *". . . Fear not, for I have redeemed you; I have called you by name, you are mine. When you pass through the waters, I will be with you, and when you pass through the floods, they shall not overwhelm you; when you walk through the fire you shall not be burned. The flame shall not consume you, for I am the Lord your God, the Holy One of Israel, your Savior."*
>
> *[Isaiah 43: 1b – 3] Amen.*

Let us Pray. *[I led an interim prayer and a hymn was played.]*

[The service was continued and completed by other ministers.]

NOTES:
1. From John Greenleaf Whittier's poem, "Gone." See **Appendix A** at the end of this Collection for a longer excerpt.
2. Penn, et al., Op. Cit. For more information, see **Appendix A** at the end of this Collection.
3. Heraclitus of Ephesus (Greek Philosopher 540-480 B.C.) This quote is also often attributed to certain unnamed Native Americans.

MEDITATIONS AND REMARKS

GENERIC FUNERAL MEDITATION A

[I opened this message by reading a small selection of scripture passages from among those listed in Appendix B at the end of this collection.]

We gather today in joy and in sorrow to celebrate a homecoming and to grieve a loss. For it is our faith that _ (who so strongly desired to be at home) has now truly arrived at home, beyond the frailties and pain of mortal flesh. Believing that our loss is her gain, we commit her into the hands of the Eternal Father whose creative love and power once gave her life and shared that life with us. That same love and redeeming power transforms the darkness of death into the light of eternal day, causing life to spring forth even from the grave.

When he was about 9 years old, our son began to collect moths and butterflies. He kept it up for a year or so and even won a prize for his collection one year at the Fair. His cousin is a year younger and has recently begun his own collection of moths and butterflies. His mother told us of an incident that happened several months ago. David (the cousin) brought a dried, curled up leaf into the house and convinced her to keep it around. After several weeks his mother insisted that it had to be thrown out. David put up a screaming fit and told her she was destroying a beautiful moth. She told him he could keep it in the garage. He put the leaf in a box and carefully covered the box opening with screen wire. When several more weeks passed with nothing happening, she decided it was nothing but a dead leaf. She waited for him to forget about it so she could throw it out. But he checked it every day. Then one day, everything changed. He brought her to look in the box. The curled-up leaf was still there, but it had a hole in one end of it. Inside the box a beautiful little moth flitted about, full of life.

It is with that kind of conviction that we commit our loved ones to God's care. Perhaps that is part of what Jesus meant when he said "Unless you become like a little child you shall not enter the Kingdom of God."

To be sure there is sorrow here today. One purpose of a funeral is to pay attention to sorrow. Sorrow is inevitable when we stand beside the grave of one whom death has taken from among us. At other times we may get so caught up in the struggle for success or so entangled in the material things of life that we forget that the sub-structure of life is shot through and through with sorrow.

Sorrow is a basic ingredient of every life. Jesus, the perfect human being is called "a man of sorrows, acquainted with grief." Mixed with every happiness is the potential for sorrow. This universal experience of suffering and sorrow is one of the deepest wells in the unity of life. It comes to all alike. It is a revelation of our common humanity. To live and to love is invariably and inevitably to know sorrow.

There is no shame in your sorrow. It is a mark of your humanity. The only shame (if any) is our failure to allow sorrow to knit our hearts together with all our suffering brothers and sisters. What a different world it would be, how different our lives would be, if we would only recognize and accept this fellowship of sorrow.

Death takes away our loved ones and that causes changes in our lives. A second purpose of a funeral is to take account of change. But for the Christian neither the separation nor the change is final. The Christian knows whether here or there we are never separated from the love of God. That gives us strength in living and peace in dying.

Perhaps the greatest burden of the change is the loneliness. "I, I only am left" we may think. There may be many people around, but they seem distant. They may not have felt what I am feeling. A great wall seems to rise between our broken heart and other people, no matter how sympathetic they are.

The way out of this well of loneliness, the path back to fellowship with others is through Christ. Jesus demonstrated this from the cross when he spoke to his mother and his beloved disciple John. They were among the small circle of brokenhearted souls who gathered around the cross. Each felt alone, isolated in grief, cut off from all others. Jesus speaks first to Mary saying, *"Woman, behold your son."* Then he says to John, *"Behold your mother."* And it is written that *"from that hour the disciple took her into his own home."* (John 19: 26-27) Alone in their grief, they had found each other through Christ.

"Home" is one of the best-loved words in our language. The child wants to be home at night. The elderly, too, wants to be in a well-known and well- loved place. But home is more than a roof and walls or carpet on the floor, or even the sound of dearly loved voices. Home is a sense of security. It is feeling safe behind eternal battlements that keep pain and suffering at bay. It is the faith that love will heal the final hurt and speak the last word.

And when you get right down to it, love is also part of what a funeral is about. It is love that gives us grief. If we knew no love, we would have no sorrow. And it is love that can cure our pain. The kind of love that Jesus gave to Mary and John. The kind of love that shined through _____s life all these years. The kind of love which the Apostle Paul referred to when he said:

> *"Love is patient and kind; love is not jealous or boastful; it is not arrogant or rude. Love does not insist on its own way. It is not irritable or resentful. It does not rejoice in wrong, but rejoices in what is right."* (1 Corinthians 13: 4-6)

The kind of love George Matheson had in mind when he wrote:

> *"O love that wilt not let me go*
> *I rest my weary soul in Thee.*
>
> *O joy that seekest me through pain*
> *I cannot close my heart to Thee.*
>
> *I trace the rainbow through the rain*
> *And feel the promise is not vain*
> *That morn shall tearless be."*

There is a big void - an emptiness - a big hole in our lives right now - a giant rip that cannot be made like new because part of the fabric is gone. Only God can mend it, and He will if we give him a chance over time. There has been a change in our lives and we can never return to a former time to live, but in God's time, the grave is no more final than the delivery room. If we will allow God to work in us, He will renew the purpose of our lives. We shall mount up with wings like eagles, and we shall dwell in the house of the Lord forever. You will walk through pain and sadness and travail in the days ahead. But wherever you walk, you will not walk alone.

> *"Fear not," God says through Isaiah, "for I am with you. Be not dismayed, for I am your God. I will strengthen you; I will help you; I will uphold you. . . When you pass through the waters I will be with you; and [when you pass through] the rivers, they shall not overwhelm you. When you walk through fire you shall not be burned, and the flame shall not consume you. For I am the Lord your God, the Holy One of Israel, your Savior."* (Isaiah 41:10; 43: 3-3)

Sorrow, change and loneliness are powerful emotions and frightful experiences. They can overwhelm and defeat us unless they are faced in light of the greater strength of God's abidingness. So we pay attention to sorrow; we take account of change; we walk through loneliness, but we do so with the abiding love of God seen in the life, death, and resurrection of His Son, Jesus Christ.

> *"Abide with me: fast falls the eventide:*
> *The darkness deepens; Lord with me abide!*
> *When other helpers fail, and comforts flee,*
> *Help of the helpless, O abide with me.*
>
> *"I fear no foe with Thee at hand to bless;*
> *Ills have no weight, and tears no bitterness.*
> *Where's death's sting? Where, grave, thy victory?*
> *I triumph still, if Thou abide with me."*
>
> - Henry Francis Lyte

> *"What then shall we say to this," the Apostle Paul writes, "if God is for us, who is against us? He who did not spare his own Son but gave Him up for us all, will he not give us all things with Him? . . . Who shall separate us from the love of Christ? Shall tribulation or distress [sorrow or change or loneliness]? . . . NO! In all these things we are more than conquerors through Him who loved us. For I am CERTAIN that neither death nor life . . .*

nor things present, nor things to come . . . nor anything else in
all creation will be able to separate us from the love of God in
Christ Jesus our Lord." (Romans 8: 31- 32; 35; 37-39)

_____ has passed along the hallway of death. We cannot know what
is at the other end of that hallway, but we know who is there, and the Risen
Christ is enough to comfort and reassure those who trust in him.

Let Us Pray.   *[I led a closing prayer and benediction, then directed*
removal to the place of burial for a committal service.].

GENERIC FUNERAL MEDITATION B

Some variation of this Meditation was used on numerous occasions. You will find parts or all of this Meditations used in many of the Meditations I have included in this Collection.

Death intrudes on us all. We walk again today through the valley of its shadow. Its reality cannot be long avoided or denied. Sooner or later, it stalks out our hiding places and calls upon us at the most inopportune times.

No respecter of persons, it comes to all: to some it comes as a thief in the night; to others it comes as a long-awaited friend, but it comes to all. We never know when it may come to us or to one we love. It is never fully expected, and we are never completely prepared for it. It always brings sorrow and pain and loss. Its intrusion into our lives dulls life's brightness and casts a shadow of heartbreak on our souls.

But in Christ Jesus that is not the end of the story. While the outward reality is substantially the same, the inner experience is vastly different for those who trust in Jesus Christ. In Christ, death assumes a different face. It is no longer a frightening enemy robbing us of all we hold dear but merely the door into another room of the Father's house. It is no longer the darkness that empties life of its meaning; it is rather the gladness of going home.

> *"What then shall we say to this?" the Apostle Paul wrote to the Romans, "If God is for us, who is against us? He who did not spare his own Son, but gave him up for us all, will he not give us all things with him? . . . Who shall separate us from the love of Christ? Shall tribulation, or distress, or persecution, or famine . . . or peril? . . . No, in all these thing we are more than conquerors through him who loved us. For I am certain that neither death,*

nor life, . . . nor things present, nor things to come, . . . nor anything else in all creation, will be able to separate us from the love of God in Christ Jesus our Lord." (Rom. 8:31-32, 35, 37-39)

It is good to remember the past, but we cannot go back there to live. The one sure obligation the living have to their dead loved ones is to go on living life as fully, as joyfully, and as meaningfully as possible. But wherever you go in the future, you will not go alone.

Through Isaiah, God2 speaks to us:

"Fear not, for I am with you, be not dismayed, for I am your God. I will strengthen you, I will help you, I will uphold you...Fear not, for I have redeemed you; I have called you by name, you are mine. When you pass through the rivers, they shall not overwhelm you. When you walk through fire you shall not be burned, and the flames shall not consume you. For I am the Lord your God, the Holy One of Israel, your Savior." (Isaiah 41:10; 43:1b-3)

"Death, you see, is only a horizon, and a horizon is nothing - nothing but the limit of our sight."[1] We cannot know what is beyond that horizon, but we know who is there, and the Resurrected Christ is enough to comfort and reassure those who trust in Him.

Let us Pray. *[I led a closing prayer, a hymn is played or sung, the benediction and removal to place of burial for a committal service.]*

NOTES:

1. Penn, et al., Op. Cit. For more detail see **Appendix A** at the end of this collection.

RALPH HAMILTON 12/20/1974 MEDITATION

MEDITATION ON HOPE and HEALING:
WITNESS TO THE RESURRECTION

[I read a selection from among the Scripture passages printed in Appendix I do not remember which passages I read.]

Death is hard at this time of year. You are preparing for Christmas and along comes a Good Friday that seem unfair, unjust, cruel – a Good Friday when death seems triumphant, God seems distant or dead, when even the brightness of the noonday sun is dimmed by the shadow of your sorrow.

But the dark and death and dreariness of Good Friday must give way to the bright and beauty of Easter Morn. So it is for you also:

> The dimness which appears to be the dusk ushering in a never-ending night;
> May turn out to be the early morning light which precedes a new day bright.

> The strife is over, the battle done
> The victory of life is won
> The song of triumph has begun – Alleluia.

Christian faith, whatever else it may be, is a religion of hope and resurrection – constantly nervous with newness. That what the Apostle Paul is saying in the 15th Chapter of I Corinthians where he writes: ". . . in fact Christ has been raised from the dead, the first fruits of those who have fallen asleep. For as by a man came death, by a man has come also the resurrection of the dead. For as in Adam all die, so also in Christ shall all be made alive . . . The last enemy to be destroyed is death. 'For God has put all things in subjection under his feet . . ." [I Corinthians 15:20-37a). Our hope is built not on the frail vessel of human health, nor on modern medical miracles, but purely and simply upon the promises of God.

And on our own personal Good Fridays, when we are faced with the reality of death and the structures of despair, we must speak of the Resurrection – that decisive event of the empty cross and the empty tomb. For in the cosmic drama of God's search for man, it is the lonely cross and the unsealed empty tomb which finally reveal the full power of God's everlasting love. The victory of powerless love over loveless power.

That love, of course, cannot be explained for love is personal and only the impersonal things in this world are susceptible to explanation. The more personal a thing is the more limited is our ability to describe and explain it. For instance, can any of you fully explain your love for another human being?

Just as with human love, God's love can be known and trusted, but it cannot be explained. The Christian faith is not so much believing without proof as it is trusting without reservation. And it is trust in the love of God that is our hope – the hope that is born on Easter morn.

The angels word to the shepherds at the birth of Christ is God's word to you today, "Fear not!" Fear not the grave; fear not the parting; fear not the uncertain future. The grave is no barrier to God and should be no barrier to us. In God's time the tomb is no more final than the womb.

"Life is eternal, love is immortal, and death is only a horizon, and a horizon is nothing but the limit of our sight."1 Your husband, father, brother, loved one, and friend has passed beyond that horizon. We do not know what awaits him there, but we know who awaits him, and the Babe of Bethlehem who lived and died and rose again is sufficient.

As the Apostle Paul sees it, if we have spiritually died and been raised anew in Christ, there is nothing to fear in physical death. The fear of the unknown, the fear of some final condemnation are no longer ahead of us, but in Christ, they are already behind us. The sting of death has been drawn, the grave robbed of its victory.

> "O death where is your victory?
> O death where is your sting? . . .

Thanks be to God who gives us the victory through our Lord Jesus Christ."

(I Corinthians 15: 55; 57)

We know that Ralph is freed from all the pain and suffering and distress, the fright, the fear, the frustrations of this life. We know that he is freed from all the shackles of this life to share the joy which God has prepared.

As we all hope one day to do, he can now sing with the saints throughout the ages, in the words of that magnificent old spiritual: "Free at last, free at last; Great God Almighty, I am free at last."

Amen.

Let us pray: *[I led a closing prayer.]*

   [The hymn form of Crossing the Bar was played.]

   [Benediction and Dismissal to place of burial for a Committal Service.]

NOTES:

1.   Penn et al., Op Cit. For a full explanation of the phrase see **Appendix A** at the end of this Collection.

FANNY HALE
01-22-1979
MEDITATION

MEDITATION ON HOPE and HEALING:
WITNESS TO THE RESURRECTION

But regardless of all the good there is to say about her, funerals are for mourning. And there is inevitably a sadness here today that no amount of talking will take away. William Wordsworth wrote of "Lucy" "who dwelt among the untrodden ways. . .a violet by a mossy stone, half hidden from the eye. . .

> *She lived unknown, and few could know*
> *When Lucy ceased to be;*
> *But she is in her grave, and oh,*
> *The difference to me!"*

"And oh, the difference to me." That's the sadness we share today. It is not for Mrs. Hale who has passed beyond the pain and suffering, the cares and burdens of life here – indeed we know that there is rejoicing in heaven today because one of God's true servants is home.

No, let us not mourn for her but for those of us who remain. We are poorer now. Part of the richness of our lives has passed beyond our grasp. There is a big void – a big hole – in our lives, a giant rip in the fabric of our lives that can never be made like new for part of the fabric is gone. Only God can mend it, and he will if we give him a chance over time.

Mrs. Hale has passed through the hallway of death. We cannot know what is at the other end of that hallway. But we know who is there, and the risen Christ is enough. Whittier wrote:

> I know not what the future hath   [1st Verse]
> Of marvel or surprise;
> Assured alone that life and death
> God's mercy underlies.
>
> . . .
>
> I know not where His islands lift   [5th Verse]
> Their fronded palms in air;
> I only know I (we) cannot drift
> Beyond His love and care.

"I do not know what the future holds, but I know who holds the future" [Homer]. Perhaps Whittier expressed it best for us when he wrote in another poem entitled "Gone."

> There seems a shadow on the day,
> Her smile no longer cheers;
> A dimness on the stars of night,
> Like eyes that look through tears.
>
> Alone unto our Father's will
> One thought hath reconciled;
> That He whose love exceedeth ours
> Hath taken home his child.

All praise be to God who gives us the victory through Jesus Christ. Amen.

[Dismissal to place of burial for a committal service.]

BILL/OSCAR REED 05/05/1979 MEDITATION

MEDITATION OF HOPE and HEALING: WITNESS TO THE RESURRECTION[1]

"He Heals the Brokenhearted"

When Jesus came back to his home synagogue in Nazareth and was asked to read the scripture lesson, he turned to a passage in Isaiah which, better than any other, described the purpose of his life and ministry. One of the reasons he had come he read was "to heal the brokenhearted." [Luke 4: 18; KJV]. He was the ambassador of God's comfort. He had come to walk with us and help us through just such sadness as is ours today.

Healing is always an important part of His task. So today, as the living Christ, as the One who promised, "Lo, I am with you always to the close of the age." [Matthew 28: 20b]. He is here offering to heal the broken heart, to strengthen the feeble, shaking knee, to comfort and soothe the aching breast, to bring the love and consolation of God.

Through experiences in His own life, Jesus became able to understand and to help others. He who stood beside the grave of a friend and wept stands with us today and shares our tears. He understands and because He understands, He can heal our broken hearts. One of the ways he does this is to help us keep sorrow in its proper place. Sorrow has its place, but unless it is kept in proper perspective, it can blot out everything else so that nothing seems real except the bitter pain and awful loss.

But Christ reminds us to see our loss within the totality of life. We are to remember the good gifts which God has provided. We are to recall the days of blessed fellowship we have had with the one now gone. He bids us to put our sorrows, our moments like this, in the setting of our faith in God.

Death takes away our loved ones, but it cannot separate them or us from the love of God in Jesus Christ. Isn't that the message of the cross? Isn't that the meaning of the Resurrection? Death, the one final enemy that everyone must face, does not terrify the Christian. We know that whether here or there we are never separated from the love of God. Neither the trials nor temptations of this life nor the inevitability of death, can separate us from God's love.

Jesus said, "In my Father's house are many rooms . . . I go to prepare a place for you." [John 14: 2] So death becomes only part of a great journey within our Father's house. We find peace when we realize that the sorrows of life are only a part of the whole of life in which God is ever present and ever strong.

Christ bids us to be thankful. But you ask, "Preacher how can we be thankful in the midst of such great sorrow? What do I have to be thankful for today?" Thankfulness and gratitude are not always the product of sunny skies and prosperous seasons. Often the grace of gratitude is born in the darkest hour. If you will allow Christ to touch your tear-blinded eyes, he can show you much for which to be thankful even in the midst of loneliness and loss. He will enable you to give thanks for the years you shared fellowship with your husband, father, loved one and friend. How blest you are to grieve today, for it means that you had the privilege of knowing, loving and being loved by Bill/ Oscar Reed.

Beneath the loneliness of this hour, there may be an abiding gratitude: Gratitude to God for the one we mourn today and gratitude for the hope of resurrection which faith in Christ renews within us.

The Father's house has many rooms,
Our Father's house has mansions fair
And some are reached through gathered gloom,
Some are reached by silent stair.
But He keeps house and makes it home,
Whichever way his children come.
                    Marianne Farningham

Another way that Christ helps heal the brokenhearted is by showing us that we are not alone. Part of the burden that comes with grief is the burden of loneliness. "I am left alone" is the natural feeling. The way out of this loneliness, the path back to fellowship with others is by way of Christ. Around the cross of Christ is gathered a small group of mourners. One is Mary, mother of Jesus. Another is John, the disciple Jesus especially loved. From the cross, Christ says to Mary, "Woman behold your son." And to John he says, "Behold your mother." And it is recorded that "And from that hour the disciple took her into his own home." [John 19:26-27]. Alone in their grief, they found one another through Christ.

So today, Christ would keep you who seem so alone in your hour of sorrow aware of the fellowship of your family, friends and neighbors. He would take your hand and put it into the hands of others, binding you closer together and thereby helping to heal your broken heart.

Let us pray.   *[Here I led a closing prayer.]*

[A hymn was played.]

[Dismissal to place of burial for a committal service.]

NOTES:

1. This Meditation/Message was shortened and adapted from a Funeral Message first preached by Eugene Smathers, on November 25, 1954.

JIM FINLEY 03/03/1980 MEDITATION

MEDITATION ON HOPE and HEALING: WITNESS TO THE RESURRECTION

Beyond paying attention to sorrow and giving gratitude for the one whose life we remember, a funeral is for listening. It's for listening to the Word of God as it comes to us through scripture, and it's for listening to the Word of God spoken through the life of the one now gone. Sometimes there is no Word there because the person refused to allow himself/herself to be a channel for God's Word. At other times the Word that comes to us through the life of the one remembered is garbled.

We live in a world where darkness often seems to blot out the light and death seems triumphant over life. We look for some assurance more powerful than the fullness of the sun or the brightness of spring flowers that this is not the case. We seek things that demonstrate the light will overcome the darkness and life is more powerful than death. I suggest to you that we have that in the life of Jim Finley.

In Jim's case, the Word is clear and it echoes Jesus' teaching in Matthew 5:13:

> "You are the salt of the earth, but if a mineral has the appearance of salt but lacks the taste and characteristics of salt how can it be used to cook or preserve food? It is good for nothing but to be thrown out and trampled underfoot."

Jesus is here emphasizing the importance of substance (what we do) over form (how we do it). We are diseased today with a preference of form over substance. One is less likely to get in trouble for cheating on his/her tax than he/she is for filling out the form incorrectly. A foolish example of how we sometimes stress form over substance.

So much in Jim Finley's life reflects this teaching of Jesus. Jim cared little for form but much for substance. The other night his family was discussing why he started wearing what they called "outrageous" ties. Some of them thought it was simply because his children gave them to him. That is fully believable. But what some of the others thought is even more believable. That it was a silent protest over the pressure he was getting to dress more flashily to better conform to his company's self-perceived "image."

I have no idea why Jim took to wearing gaudy ties but knowing him, it is entirely possible that he did it as a subtle protest against the meaningless form of dress which had nothing to do with the substance or quality of his work.

Perhaps the most obvious example of his preference for substance over form is this funeral itself. Some of you have undoubtedly noticed and may think it odd that there is no casket here and that the casket was not opened for viewing and will not be opened. These were Jim's express wishes. And I think it was because he knew that the substance of a life is not contained in its bodily form but in the content of one's character and the strength of one's soul.

I think Jim would consider the embalmed, prepared, and preserved body to be mere form - much like the shell of a nut after the nut has been removed. He would not want any fascination with the mere form of who he was to detract from the rich and hearty flavor of his substance. Indeed, it is a time for listening.

So for those of us left behind, a funeral is a time for sorrow, for gratitude, and a time to listen. But in God's eyes a funeral is no more final than a delivery room. Those who, like Jim Finley, walk with God know that there is a source of power and meaning that is deathless, that cannot be killed, and will not die. That power can be trusted to nurture, care for, and preserve all that is good.

We have lost a good man, but the promise is still ours. So with the Apostle Paul we can say:

> "I am sure that neither death, nor life, nor angels, nor principalities, nor things present, nor things to come, nor

powers, nor height, nor depth, nor anything else in all creation will be able to separate you from the love of God in Christ Jesus our Lord."

[Romans 8: 38-39]

In the final analysis, for the Christian, "death" and "deceased" are meaningless words. Perhaps "moved" would be more appropriate. "Transferred" is a good word to use for occasions like this. In 1951, Jim Finley transferred his membership from somewhere else to Calvary Presbyterian Church of Big Lick and from there to another church and then back again. Now, in 1980, it becomes our responsibility and privilege to announce the transfer of our beloved brother, with the highest recommendations of his brothers and sisters in Christ, from the church in Big Lick to the church triumphant and eternal, "which has foundations whose builder and maker is God." [2]

All praise be to Christ who gives us the victory. Let Us Pray. *[I led a closing prayer.]*

Benediction and dismissal to place of burial for a committal service.

NOTES:
1. Sadly, as of 2015, the Big Pine no longer stands, having finally succumbed to the woodman's chainsaw.
2. This ending was adapted from an ending to a funeral message that was first delivered by my father, Eugene Smathers in 1962.

IDA RHEA PARHAM 10-03-1980 MEDITATION

MESSAGE OF HOPE AND HEALING:
WITNESS TO THE RESURRECTION

We are nearing the season of Thanksgiving and this is a day of thanksgiving. "But Preacher," you say, "thanksgiving is so hard at a time like this." That is understandable. Death has torn a gap in the fabric of our lives. A giant piece of the mosaic that made our lives rich and full and meaningful is now gone.

It is bewildering sometimes how our heart tries to shield us from a reality that the mind recognizes is true. Wednesday morning, I went to see Ida in the middle of the morning. Her door was still locked. There was no answer when I knocked. There was no sign of life. All evidence pointed to the reality that lay inside. But my heart said, "deny, deny, maybe it is not so."

I drove to Jake's; no one was home. I drove to the cemetery, thinking I might find Jake there to no avail, and then I drove home to call the Combs and the Halls to see if they knew anything. All the time my head was telling me the reality that Ida was dead. But my heart was driving me to try to find something that would make that awful reality not so. I went back to Ida's with my wife and boosted her through a loose window in Ida's bedroom to confirm the dreaded reality.

Death intrudes on us all, and its reality cannot be long denied. No respecter of persons, to some it comes as a long-awaited friend; to others as a thief in the night, but it comes to all. We never know when it will come - in youth - in the prime of life; its certainty may become clearer as we grow older, but it is never fully expected. It always comes as a dreadful surprise, and it always brings with it sorrow and pain and loss. We are never completely prepared for it, and its intrusion into our lives (the second time in a week for some of us) dulls life's brightness and casts a shadow of heartbreak on our souls.

Yes, thanksgiving is hard at a time like this, yet it shouldn't be so for Christians. While the outward reality is substantially the same for everyone, the inner experience is vastly different for those who trust in Jesus Christ. Christ came into the world to redeem us from the forces of sin and death. Through his death and resurrection, he has banished the fear of death by the more powerful love of God.

In Christ, death assumes a different face. It is no longer a frightening enemy, robbing us of all we hold dear. It is merely the door into another room in the Father's house. It is no longer the darkness that empties life of its joy and meaning. It is rather the gladness of going home.

The Apostle Paul wrote to the Corinthians: "So we do not lose heart. Though our outer nature is wasting away, our inner nature is being renewed every day." (2 Corinthians 4:16) The grave is no barrier to God, and thus should be no barrier to us. "Life is eternal and love is immortal, and death is only a horizon and a horizon is nothing but the limit of our sight."[1] We cannot see what is beyond that horizon, but we know who is there, and the resurrected Christ is enough to comfort, console, and renew those who trust in him.

Let us pray.   *[I led a closing prayer and a hymn was played.]*

    [Benediction and removal to place of burial for a committal service.]

NOTES:
1. Penn, et al., Op. Cit. For a full explanation, see **Appendix A** at the end of this Collection.

CREED TOLLETT 01-24-1982 MEDITATION

MEDITATION ON HOPE and HEALING:
WITNESS TO THE RESURRECTION

Writing to the Galatians, the Apostle Paul said, "The fruits of the spirit are love, joy, peace, patience, kindness, goodness, faithfulness, gentleness, self-control." [Galatians 5:22-23a]. Praise be to God who by his Grace brought those fruits to such abundant harvest in the life of Creed Tollett.

There is an old, generally unfamiliar, Shaker hymn, entitled "Simple Gifts," which goes:

"SIMPLE GIFTS"
A Shaker Hymn
By Elder Joseph Brackett, Jr.

"Tis the gift to be simple, tis the gift to be free
Tis the gift to come down where we ought to be.
And when we find ourselves in the place just right
It will be in the valley of love and delight.

When true simplicity is gained
To bow and to bend, we will not be ashamed
To turn and to turn will be our delight
Til by turning, turning we come round right."

Creed had the gift of simplicity. Never greedy or grasping, he was satisfied with what he had. What a different world this might be if more of us had this gift - no more greed or envy or jealousy that turns husband against wife, brother against sister, nation against nation. I cannot help but think that Creed was the one "turned round right;" the one who had discovered the key to "the valley of love and delight." How glorious it would be if more of us would allow ourselves to be "turned, turned, til we come round right."

The Psalmist wrote:

> *O Lord, who shall sojourn in your house?*
> *Who shall dwell on your holy hill?*
>
> *He who walks blamelessly, and does what is right,*
> *and speaks truth from his heart;*
> *Who does not slander with his tongue,*
> *and does no evil to his friend,*
> *nor finds fault with or blames his neighbor. . .*
> *Who swears to the truth even if it hurts him. . .*
> *Who does not take a bribe against the innocent.*
> *He who does these things shall never be moved.*
>
> [Psalms 15:1-3; 4b; 5b]

That Psalmist must have known someone a lot like Creed.

In truth, we have so much to be thankful for today and so little to be sad about. Yesterday, Mrs. Jane Tollett, Creed's stepmother, told me that once she learned of Creed's condition and of the fact that there was no reasonable hope that he would ever be returned to good health, she no longer prayed for God to keep Creed alive. She prayed instead that God would give Creed victory in death - that Creed would be allowed to die in dignity and be enabled to overcome the spiritually disabling power of death. That prayer was answered, and it was so.

Creed's patient humility, his essential dignity, and his polite kindness shined through to the end. The manner in which Creed, Louise and their family have faced and overcome the terrible ordeal of the last few weeks has been a moving testimony to the power of the Resurrection.

We have so much for which to be thankful, but thanksgiving at time like this is oh so hard. Death has torn a gap in the fabric of our lives, a giant piece of the mosaic which made our life rich and full and meaningful is now gone.

And nothing I can say today and nothing that any of us can do tomorrow will make that awful reality go away.

There is no shame in our pain, hurt and sorrow we feel or the tears we shed today. They are a mark of our common humanity and the flip side of love. How much richer we are to have had the opportunity to love and be loved by Creed Tollett. How much richer we are than we would be if we had never known him. How blessed we are to grieve today.

Death intrudes on us all and its reality cannot be long denied. No respecter of persons, it comes to all. To some, it may come as a thief in the night, to others who have suffered long, as Creed did, it comes as a long-awaited friend. We never know when it may come - perhaps in youth or in the prime of life. Its certainty may become clearer as we grow older, but it is never fully expected. It is always a dreadful surprise and it always brings sorrow, pain, and loss. Its intrusion into our lives dulls life's brightness and casts a shadow of heartbreak on our souls.

Thanksgiving is indeed hard at a time like this, but it shouldn't be. While the outward reality is substantially the same for everyone, the inner experience is vastly different for those who trust in Jesus Christ, who through His resurrection has banished the fear of death through God's yet more powerful love.

In Christ, death assumes a different face. It is no longer a frightening enemy, robbing us of all we hold dear, but merely the door through which we must pass to enter another room in the Father's house. It is no longer the darkness that robs life of its meaning. It is rather the joy of going home.

So the Apostle Paul writes to us: "Though our outer nature is wasting away, our inner nature is being renewed every day." [II Corinthians 4:16b] "Death is swallowed up in victory! O death where is your victory. O death where is your sting." [I Corinthians 15:55]

God has pulled death's stinger. The grave is no barrier to God and, thus, should be no barrier to us. "Life is eternal and love is immortal. And death is only a horizon, and a horizon is nothing, nothing but the limit of our sight."1 We cannot see what is beyond that horizon, but we know who is there, and the resurrected Christ is enough!

All praise to God who has given Creed victory.

Let us Pray: *[Closing prayer, Benediction and dismissal to place of burial for a committal service.]*

NOTES

1. Penn, et al., Op. Cit. For a fuller explanation see **Appendix A** at the end of this Collection.

FRED HASSLER FEBRUARY 1, 1983 MEDITATION

MEDITATION/REMARKS on HOPE and HEALING:
WITNESS TO THE RESURRECTION

A good man is gone from among us. We walk again through the valley of shadows – when the ties that have bound together family and friends have been broken by death. In moments like these, we feel battered and beaten by disappointment and grief.

When Jesus came back to his home synagogue in Nazareth and was asked to read the scripture lesson, he turned to a passage in Isaiah which, better than any other, described the purpose of his life and ministry. One of the reasons he had come he read was "to heal the brokenhearted." [Luke 4: 18; KJV]. He was the ambassador of God's comfort. He had come to walk with us and help us through just such sadness as is ours today.

Healing is always an important part of His task. So today, as the living Christ, as the One who promised, "Lo, I am with you always to the close of the age." [Matthew 28: 20b]. He is here offering to heal the broken heart, to strengthen the feeble, shaking knee, to comfort and soothe the aching breast, to bring the love and consolation of God.

Through experiences in His own life, Jesus became able to understand and to help others. He who stood beside the grave of a friend and wept stands with us today and shares our tears. He understands and because He understands, He can heal our broken hearts. One of the ways he does this is to help us keep sorrow in its proper place. Sorrow has its place, but unless it is kept in proper perspective in can blot out everything else so that nothing seems real except the bitter pain and awful loss.

But Christ reminds us to see our loss within the totality of life. We are to remember the good gifts which God has provided. We are to recall the days of blessed fellowship we have had with the one now gone. He bids us to put our sorrows, our moments like this, in the setting of our faith in God.

Death takes away our loved ones, but it cannot separate them or us from the love of God in Jesus Christ. Isn't that the message of the cross? Isn't that the meaning of the Resurrection? Death, the one final enemy that everyone must face, does not terrify the Christian. We know that whether here or there, we are never separated from the love of God. Neither the trials and temptations of this life nor the inevitability of death, can separate us from God's love.

Jesus said, "In my Father's house are many rooms . . . I go to prepare a place for you." [John 14: 2] So death becomes only part of a great journey within our Father's house. We find peace when we realize that the sorrows of life are only a part of the whole of life in which God is ever present and ever strong.

Christ bids us to be thankful. But you ask, "Preacher how can we be thankful in the midst of such great sorrow? What do I have to be thankful for today?" Thankfulness and gratitude are not always the product of sunny skies and prosperous seasons. Often the grace of gratitude is born in the darkest hour. If you will allow Christ to touch your tear-blinded eyes, he can show you much for which to be thankful even in the midst of loneliness and loss. He will enable you to give thanks for the years you shared fellowship with your husband, father, loved one and friend.

Beneath the loneliness of this hour, there may be an abiding gratitude: Gratitude to God for the one we mourn today and gratitude for the hope of resurrection which faith in Christ renews within us.

> *The Father's house has many rooms,*
> *Our Father's house has mansions fair*
> *And some are reached through gathered gloom,*
> *Some are reached by silent stair.*
> *But He keeps house and makes it home,*
> *Whichever way his children come.*
> Marianne Farningham

Another way that Christ helps heal the brokenhearted is by showing us that we are not alone. Part of the burden that comes with grief is the burden of loneliness. "I am left alone" is the natural feeling. The way out of this loneliness, the path back to fellowship with others is by way of Christ. Around the cross of Christ is gathered a small group of mourners. One is Mary, mother of Jesus. Another is John, the disciple Jesus especially loved. From the cross, Christ says to Mary, "Woman behold your son." And to John he says, "Behold your mother." And it is recorded that "And from that hour the disciple took her into his own home." [John 19:26-27]. Alone in their grief, they found one another through Christ.

So today, Christ would keep you who seem so alone in your hour of sorrow aware of the fellowship of your family, friends and neighbors. He would take your hand and put it into the hands of others, binding you closer together, and thereby helping to heal your broken heart.

> "Abide with me: fast falls the eventide;
> The darkness deepens; Lord, with me abide!
> When other helpers fail, and comforts flee,
> Help of the helpless, O abide with me.
>
> I fear no foe, with Thee at hand to bless,
> Ills have no weight, and tears no bitterness;
> Where is death's sting? Where, grave, thy victory?
> I triumph still, if Thou abide with me!"
>   "Abide with Me" by Henry F. Lyte

There is a big void, a big hole in our lives – a giant rip in the fabric of our lives that can never be made like new again, for a part of the fabric is gone. Only God can mend it. And He will if we give Him a chance over time. "I know not what the future holds, but I know who holds the future." [Homer] Fred has passed along the hallway of death. We cannot know what is at the other end of that hallway, but we know who is there, and the risen Christ is enough.

John Greenleaf Whittier wrote:

> "I know not what the future hath
> Of marvel or surprise;
> Assured alone that life and death
> God's mercy underlies.
>
> . . .
>
> I know not where His islands lift

Their fronded palms in air;
I only know [we] cannot drift
Beyond His love and care."
--Excerpt from "The Eternal Goodness," John Greenleaf Whittier.

On another occasion Whittier wrote:

"There seems a shadow on the day,
[His] smile no longer cheers;
A dimness on the stars of night,
Like eyes that look through tears.

Alone unto our Father's will
One thought hath reconciled;
That He whose love exceedeth ours
Hath taken home his child."
--Excerpt from "Gone," John Greenleaf Whittier.

Underneath our lives with all their sorrow and change are "everlasting arms." Sorrow and change, suffering and death have been conquered in Christ's cross and Resurrection. And we, in the very midst of sorrow and change, can share in that victory through faith. "Lord we believe, help Thou our unbelief."

"What then shall we say to this? If God is for us who is against us? He who did not spare his own Son, but gave him up for us all, will he not also give us all things with him? Who shall bring any charge against God's elect? It is God who justifies; who is to condemn? Is it Christ Jesus, who died, yes, who was raised from the dead, who is at the right hand of God, who indeed intercedes for us? Who shall separate us from the love of Christ? Shall tribulation, or distress, or persecution, of famine, or nakedness, or peril, or sword? [Shall sorrow or change?] NO! In all these things we are more than conquerors through him who loved us. For I am sure that neither death, nor life, nor angels, nor principalities, nor things present, nor things to come, nor powers, norheight, nor depth, nor anything else in all creation, will be able to separate us from the love of God in Christ Jesus our Lord." [Romans 8: 31-35; 37-39]

All praise be to God who gives us the victory through Jesus Christ. Amen.

Let us Pray: ***[I led a closing prayer and a hymn was played]***

[Benediction and dismissal to place of burial for a committal service.]

NOTES:
1. Parts of this Meditation/Remarks were shortened and adapted from a Funeral Message first preached by Eugene Smathers, on November 25, 1954.

AARON H. WOOD
08/02/1983
MEDITATION

MEDITATION ON HOPE and HEALING:
WITNESS TO THE RESURRECTION

We gather today in joy and sorrow to celebrate a homecoming and to grieve a loss. For it is our faith that Aaron, who so strongly desired to be home, has now truly arrived at home beyond the frailties and pain of mortal flesh. Believing that our loss is his gain, we commit him into the hands of the Eternal Father whose creative love and power once gave him life and shared that life with us, and whose same love and redeeming power transform the darkness of death into the light of eternal day, causing life to spring forth even from the grave.

Death intrudes upon us all. No respecter of persons, it comes to great and small alike – to some it comes as a long-awaited friend, to others as a thief in the night, but to all it comes. We never know when it will come – to us or to one we love. To some, it comes in youth, in the prime of life. To others at the end of a long and useful life. Its certainty may become clearer as we grow older, but it is never a welcomed guest, never fully expected, and we are never completely prepared for it. It always comes as a dreadful surprise, and it brings sorrow and pain and loss. Its intrusion into our lives dulls life's brightness and casts a shadow of heartbreak on our souls.

However, while the outward reality is substantially the same for everyone, the inner experience is vastly different for those who trust in Jesus Christ – who came into the world to redeem us from the forces of sin and death.

Through His death and resurrection, He has banished the fear of death by the yet more powerful love of God.

In Christ, death assumes a different face. It is no longer a frightening enemy robbing us of all we hold dear but merely the door into another room of the Father's house. It is no longer the darkness that empties life of its meaning but rather the gladness of going home. So as the Apostle Paul wrote, "though our outer nature is wasting away, our inner nature is being renewed every day."

Nevertheless, today is filled with sorrow. Jesus, too, stood by the grave of a friend and wept. Tears carry no shame – they are the mark of our common humanity. Sorrow and grief are unavoidable as we stand by the grave of one whom death has taken from among us. Sorrow is a basic ingredient of life – to live is to grieve. Jesus, the complete man, was called "a man of sorrows, acquainted with grief." Mixed with every happiness is the possibility of sorrow. One of the deepest unities of life is this universal experience of suffering and sorrow – it comes to all alike. To live and to love is invariably and inevitably to know sorrow.

Thus there is no shame in our sorrow. The only shame is our failure to allow sorrow to knit our hearts with the hearts of all our brothers and sisters in the one great family of God. What great transformations could take place in our personal lives and in our troubled world if all would only recognize and accept this fellowship of suffering.

Yes, sorrow and grief are legitimate and unavoidable parts of any funeral, but so is love. Christians are not terrified by death because we know that whether here or there our loved one cannot be separated from the love of God in Jesus Christ.

Perhaps the greatest burden of grief is loneliness. The way out of this, the path back to fellowship with others, is by way of the love of Christ. In a simple but beautiful act from the cross, Jesus revealed this truth. At the foot of the Cross, two figures huddled together with the little circle of the brokenhearted. One is a woman, the mother of Jesus. The other is the beloved disciple, John. To Mary, Jesus says, "Woman behold thy son." To John He says, "Behold thy mother." And it is recorded that thereafter John "took her into his own home."

Yes, loneliness is part of a funeral, but so is love. It is love that gives us grief. If we knew no love, we would know no grief. This is the kind of love that Paul wrote about when he said, "Love is patient and kind; love is not jealous or boastful; it is not arrogant of rude. Love does not insist on its own way; it is not irritable or resentful; it does not rejoice at wrong but rejoices in the right."

The kind of love George Matheson had in mind when he wrote:

> "O love that wilt not let me go,
> I rest my weary soul in thee
>
> O joy that seekest me through pain
> I cannot close my heart to thee.
>
> I trace the rainbow through the rain
> And feel the promise is not vain
> That morn shall tearless be."

It is this abiding love of God which gave Aaron life and which shined in his life that will finally overcome our sorrow and wipe away our loneliness. As Isaiah wrote:

> "Fear not, for I am with you; be not dismayed, for I am your God. I will strengthen you, I will help you, I will uphold you . . . When you pass through the waters I will be with you, and through the rivers, they shall not overwhelm you; when you walk through the fire, you shall not be burned and the flame shall not consume you, For I am the Lord your God, the Holy One of Israel, your Savior." [Isaiah 1b – 3].

> To quote and paraphrase the Apostle Paul, "What then shall we say to this, if God is for us [what can it matter if other things are against us?] He who did not spare his own Son but gave him up for us all, will He not give us all things with Him. . .What shall separate us from the love of Christ? Shall tribulations or distress, [grief or loneliness] . . . NO, in all these things we are more than conquerors through Him who loved us. For I am SURE that neither death, nor life . . . nor things present, nor things to come . . . nor anything else in all creation will be able to separate us from the love of God in Christ Jesus our Lord." [Rom. 8: 31-32, 35, 37-39].

There is a great void – an emptiness- a big hole in our lives right now – a giant rip that cannot be made whole again, for a part of the fabric is gone. Only God can mend that rip, and He will if we give Him a chance over time. There has been a change in our lives, and we can never return to a former time to live, but in God's time, the grave is no more final than the delivery room. And if we will allow Him, he will renew the purpose of our lives and we will mount up with wings of eagles and we shall dwell in the house of the Lord forever.

Aaron has passed along the hallway of death, but the grave is no barrier to god and should be no barrier to us. "Life is eternal and love is immortal, and death is only a horizon, and a horizon is nothing but the limit of our sight."1 We cannot see what is beyond that horizon, but we know who is there and the resurrected Christ is enough.

Perhaps John Greenleaf Whittier said all I have tried to say in two verses of his poem, God's Love and Care:

> *"I know not what the future hath*
> *Of marvel or surprise*
> *Assured alone that life and death*
> *His mercy underlies.*
>
> *. . .*
> *I know not where his islands lift*
> *Their fronded palms in air,*
> *I only know we cannot drift*
> *Beyond his love and care."*

NOTES:
1. Penn, et al., Op. Cit. For a fuller explanation, see **Appendix A** at the end of this Collection.

GLADYS WOOD SELBY 09/06/1983 MEDITATION

MEDITATION OF HEALING AND HOPE:
WITNESS TO THE RESURRECTION[1]

Shortly before He was to die on the cross, Jesus said to His disciples:

> *"Let not your hearts be troubled; believe in God, believe also in me. In my Father's house are many rooms. If it were not so, would I have told you that I go to prepare a place for you? And if I go and prepare a place for you, I will come again and take you to myself, that where I am you may be also."* (John 14: 1-3)

These words of comfort and hope have soothed the bereaved breasts of countless persons in their dark hour of grief and loss. They can likewise be a source of healing and strength for us in the sadness of this day. As we walk through the valley of the shadow cast by the death of our loved one, we can have the agony of defeat transformed into the assurance of victory if only we trust in God.

The Christian life consists not so much of believing without doubt as it does of trusting without reservation. There is no balm to sooth the darkness of this shadow if death is the end of it all. The way to smooth over this rough spot is trust in God. If we understand that the one we love has merely passed beyond our physical sight and touch into another and richer realm of existence where she can await us, then this dark shadow can be transformed into the bright joy of victory. This is what trust in God brings.

When our world seems to be collapsing around us, Jesus says: "Let not your hearts be troubled: believe in God; believe also in me. . ." [John 14: 1]. At a time like this, in our darkest hours, Jesus invites us to trust that God is stronger than death so that even the seemingly unbearable becomes bearable. And even in the darkness, we can see a glimmer of light that can lead us on. Jesus asks us to look to Him as a window through which we can see into the very heart of God. He implores us to see his death on the cross as evidence of how far the love of God will go for us. And to see His Resurrection as the first fruit of that which awaits all of those who trust in Him.

"Let not your hearts be troubled. . ." would be nothing less than cruel unless He who speaks them has the power to relieve us of our troubles. Paul goes on to say: "He that spared not His own Son, but gave Him up for us all . . . will he not also give us all things with Him?" [Romans 8:32]. That is Christ's legacy of hope.

More vast than our eyes can see, or our hands can touch, or our minds can imagine is the Father's house. When we pass beyond the pleasures and veil of tears that this world holds, we go into other rooms, other dimensions of living. If we have prayed for our loved one's health and wholeness, and we have trusted God to answer that prayer, we can be assured that He has answered our full petition either within or beyond the bounds of our vision. That, too, is Christ's legacy of hope.

A little boy's face brightened when he was told that his friend's father who had died was with God. "Oh, then," the little boy said, "He's still real." That is the assurance of the Risen Christ. Those whom we have loved and lost awhile have not ceased to be, though we see them no more with our physical eyes. They are still real.

Jesus asks those who trust Him to believe him. "If it were not so, would I have told you?" [John 14: 2]. Those words enable us to surrender our loved ones with a sense of peace and assurance. Christ has loved them all their lives. He died for them. The same love that gave them life and gave them to us in the first place will continue to love them as they pass through doors to other rooms. The same words comfort us in our grief and redeem our lives from futility.

There is an old prayer which says: "as thou hast given them this new tie to bind them to the world unseen, so grant unto them that where their treasure is, there may their hearts be also." You are her treasures.

When we speak of the "communion of saints," we are not talking only about the living. Among this communion are those who have passed on to the world unseen. This makes the world unseen a home unto our hearts. So our journey through this world of joy and pain has not become meaningless. It is a movement toward a destination; it is a movement toward going home.

Let Us Pray.   *[I led a closing prayer, and a hymn was played.]*

[Benediction and removal to the place of burial for a committal service.]

NOTES:
1. This Message was adapted in large part from Funeral Remarks delivered by Eugene Smathers, 1932-1968.

VERDIE CROFT HALL 11/29/1983 MEDITATION

MEDITATION ON HOPE AND HEALING: WITNESS TO THE RESURRECTION

Death intrudes on us all and its reality cannot long be denied. It is no respecter of persons. To some, it may come as a thief in the night. To others, it comes as a long-awaited friend. But it comes to all. And we never know when it will come. Its certainty may become clearer as one grows older, but for those left behind it is never fully expected. It always comes as a dreadful surprise. We are never prepared for it. It's intrusion into our lives always brings sorrow, pain, and loss. It dulls life's brightness and casts a shadow of heartbreak on our souls.

However, while the outward reality is substantially the same for everyone, the inward experience is vastly different for us who trust in God through Jesus Christ. In Christ, death assumes a different face. It is no longer a frightening enemy robbing us of all we hold dear but merely the door into another room in the Father's house. It is no longer the darkness that empties life of all meaning. It is rather the joy of going home.

So the Apostle Paul wrote: *"Though our outer nature is wasting away, our inner nature is being renewed every day."* [2 Corinthians 4: 16B].

The grave is no barrier to God and, thus, should be no barrier to us. In God's time, the grave is no more final than the delivery room. "Life is eternal and love is immortal and death is only a horizon and a horizon is nothing but the limit of our sight." 1 We cannot see beyond that horizon, but we know who is there. And the resurrected Christ is enough.

Paul wrote: *"We know that if this earthly shack we live in is destroyed, we have a house built by God, not made with human hands, eternal and spiritual. Here, indeed, we groan and can hardly wait to get into our spiritual dwelling, so that we will not be standing out naked [in the rain]. For as long as we remain in this earthly shack, we have many worries and anxieties. It is not that we want to be without a house, but we want a better dwelling – so that our dying may be swallowed up by life [in Christ Jesus]. God himself is preparing us for this very thing and has given us the Holy Spirit as a guarantee."*

[II Corinthians 5: 1-5]

In 1954 Stewart Hamblin wrote what became the top country songs of that year. I dare to quote parts of it now not only because my father thought it appropriate for a Christian funeral, but because it is related to the scripture from II Corinthians I just quoted, and because I think Mrs. Hall, who passed on to her offspring not only a love for all types of music but also the genes to play and sing them; I think that she would appreciate the spirit and message of the chorus from the top country hit of 1954, This Old House:

"Ain't goin'need this house no longer;
Ain't goin' need this house no more
* Ain't got time to fix the shingles; Ain't got time to fix the floor;*
Ain't got time to oil no hinges;
Nor mend the broken window panes.
Ain't goin' need this house no longer,
I'm gettin' ready to meet the saints."

We will soon take the house Mrs. Hall lived in home for the last time, but she's not there anymore. She's gettin' ready to meet the saints.

And in the church we have a term far more fitting than "deceased" to describe this occasion. When a Christian moves from one church to another, we say she has "transferred" her membership. In 1921, Verdie Hall transferred her membership from the Methodist Episcopal Church to Calvary Presbyterian Church of Big Lick. And now it becomes my responsibility and privilege to announce the transfer of our beloved sister, with the highest recommendation, from the Church temporal and temporary to the Church eternal and triumphant located in that *". . .city which has foundations, whose architect and builder is God."* [Hebrews 11: 10b] 2

Let us pray. ***[I offered a closing prayer here.]***

[Benediction and dismissal to place of burial for a committal service.]

NOTES:
1. Penn, et al., Op. Cit. For a fuller explanation, see **Appendix A** at the end of this Collection. The rest of the paragraph is all mine.
2. This closing adapted from a funeral closing by Eugene Smathers 1932-1968.

EUCLE BURGESS 07/07/1986 MEDITATION

MEDITATION ON HOPE AND HEALING:
WITNESS TO THE RESURRECTION

But for right now, there is sorrow – an inevitable emotion whenever we meet to give thanks for one that death has taken from us. There is no shame in our tears. They water the eternal rose of love. For sorrow and grief are but the flip side of love. To love and be loved means inevitably to suffer sorrow and grief.

Death intrudes on us all and its reality cannot be long denied. No respecter of persons, it comes to all. To some it comes as a thief in the night; to others as a welcome friend. To Eucle it came with sudden abruptness, though he had anticipated it. But to those of us left behind, it is never a welcomed guest. It always brings sorrow, pain, and loss. Its intrusion into our lives dulls life's brightness and casts a shadow of heartbreak on our souls. Indeed, there is sadness here today.

But there must also be rejoicing: Joyful thanksgiving for the life of Eucle Burgess so graciously shared with us, and rejoicing over the fact of the Resurrection and the victory over sin and death so eloquently witnessed in Eucle's life.

For those who are in Christ, death takes on another face. It is no longer merely the pain and longing of separation but the joy and comfort of going home. It is no longer the end of all that makes life worth living, but merely another stage in our trip to our Father's house. The passage from John 14: 2a, generally translated "in my Father's house are many rooms," may also be translated "On the way to my Father's house are many resting places." With

Eucle's death, both he and we have arrived at a new resting place. We cannot go back to the old place to live; for us, things have changed forever. There will be a certain sadness in our days, a kind of void that cannot be filled. But life goes on for us, and in Christ, we know that the joy and fullness and meaning of life does not end with the death of a loved one.

In the fourth chapter of II Corinthians, the Apostle Paul writes, "Death is overtaking us [himself and his fellow workers], but you [the Corinthian Christians] must go on living." [2 Corinthians 4: 12; MFS translation]

Part of the hope of the dying rests with the living. The one sure obligation that we have to our loved ones who have died is to go on living life to its fullest.

A victory celebration is always a time for rejoicing. But how do we rejoice with broken hearts? How do we laugh with eyes that see through tears? I rejoice because through the Grace of God, Eucle Burgess became a part of my life.

My life is richer and fuller for having known, loved and been loved by Eucle. Indeed, all our lives are so much fuller, richer, and happier because he was a part of them. So much so that a day of sorrow is turned into a day for rejoicing – a time to praise God for giving Eucle life, for making him into the uniquely marvelous person that he was, and for graciously sharing him with us.

The same graciousness of God that gave Eucle life, that inspired him to goodness and brought him into our lives can now sustain our souls and renew our spirits in this time of grief. The Grace of God is like the sunlight. It is always there, even if sometimes covered by clouds, but we must walk out into it.

The very first Psalm begins: "Blessed is the man who walks not in the counsel of the wicked, nor stands in the way of sinners, nor sits in the seat of scoffer. . ." and ends that thought with the words "He is like a tree planted by streams of water, that yields its fruit in its season, and its leaf does not wither. . ." [Psalm 1: 1; 3a).

That psalm reminds me of the huge white pine that sits on Daddy's Creek behind Emmett Selby's. Four feet in diameter, 12 feet around, 160 feet tall, it towers above the lesser trees around it. Foresters estimate that it was a seedling when the pilgrims landed at Plymouth Rock. Somehow through all these years, it alone has withstood the ravages of wind and wildfire and the woodmen's ax, each year dropping its seeds to begin new life.

And that tree reminds me of Eucle – steadfast, straight, strong, abiding, productive, dependable. Rooted in the rich soil of traditional values, nourished by streams of living faith, he, too, stood amidst the storms of life with quiet strength, dignity, and steadfastness, unpretentiously giving of himself, dropping seeds of kindness and good cheer of neighborliness and friendship.

Eucle was so full of love for others that it literally showed on his face. I seldom notice the face in a coffin part of the shell that someone leaves behind. But I could not help but notice the lines Eucle left etched on his earthly face. They were what are sometimes called "smile lines." They speak of warmth and friendliness, of graciousness, gentleness, and good cheer.

Though in life, he was known as a worrier who was frequently agitated over the possibility of some sort of obscure calamity, he will be remembered for the content of his character and the quality of his friendship. If you were ever the recipient of his grace and generosity, as I was, or if you ever lived near him or worked with him or been close to him in any other way, you know an easy definition for the word "neighbor." It is "Eucle Burgess."

Anyone who knew Eucle well knows that to know him was sometimes to disagree with him. You seldom had to guess what Eucle thought or where he stood. He did not go out of his way to be superficially agreeable and could at times, be infuriatingly contentious. But to have been his friend and to have disagreed with him was to experience the very essence of brotherly love - warmth, affection, acceptance, and support that transcended all the differences which might have caused enmity between him and you.

It is revealing that although he was a lifelong, staunch, dedicated, devoted, and active Republican, two of his closest friends were equally committed Democrats. His friendship knew no bounds, and you could not be excluded from it by any earthly condition or circumstance. To know Eucle's friendship was to experience something boundless, unfettered by the sin of selfishness.

The 15th psalm is attributed to David. In it he writes:

> *O Lord, who shall you invite into your house?*
> *Who shall come to live on your Holy Hill?*

He who walks blamelessly;
who does what is right;
who seeks truth from his heart;
who can be trusted to say honestly what he thinks;
whose word can be trusted;
who does not slander with his tongue;
who does no evil to a friend,
nor repeats a derogatory report against his neighbor;

who sticks by his word and promise even if it causes him injury;
who is dependable, trustworthy and not two-faced;
who will not cheat nor injure the innocent for any amount of money.

[Psalm 15; MFS translation]

David would have liked Eucle . . . liked him a lot!

Sam Walter Foss could have been writing of Eucle when he penned this verse inspired by a line from Homer:

"I see from my house by the side of the road,
By the side of the highway of life:
The men who press with the ardor of hope;
The men who are faint with the strife.
But I turn not away from their smiles nor their tears,
Both part of an infinite plan –
Let me live in a house by the side of the road
And be a friend to man." [1]

I am reminded of the 5th Chapter of Genesis. Hidden away among the list of "begats" and "begones" we find this remarkable and beautiful commentary on one of them: "Enoch walked with God and then he was not, for God took him. [Genesis 5: 24] A child explained this passage by saying: "Enoch and God used to take long walks together. And one day they walked further than usual, and God said, 'Enoch, you must be tired; come into my house and rest.'" Because of the kind of man he was, Enoch's friends knew that his life led not to a grave but to God. Eucle Burgess and God used to take long walks together, and - well, you know the rest of the story. . .

Eucle was never one to make a lot of changes. Though he traveled in his work, home was always Big Lick in the house under the hill where he had been born. He lived in the same house for 70 years, belonged to the one church for 57 years, was married to one woman for 48 years.

Today Eucle makes the one final move that we all must make, and in the church, have a word far more fitting than "deceased" for this occasion. When a Christian moves his or her membership from one church to another, we say that he/she has "transferred" his/her membership.

So it becomes our privilege and responsibility today to announce the transfer of our beloved brother, Eucle, with the highest recommendations of his pastor and fellow Elders from the church temporal and militant to the church triumphant and eternal, located in that city which has foundations whose builder and maker is God.

Praise be to God. Amen and Amen.

Let us pray: *[I led a closing prayer and benediction and dismissed to the place of burial for a committal service.]*

NOTES:
　　1.　In the service, I read the whole five-verse poem but am limited by law to the eight lines printed above.

LAWRENCE S. CARPENTER 04/04/1986 MEDITATION

The deceased in this case was my father-in-law. This service was done in small town Ohio, and the expectations were different than they are in Southern Appalachia. Therefore, I did no Obituary for this service, only a Eulogy. The Eulogy and the Meditation are somewhat scrambled together. There is not a really clean break between them. But it was the Eulogy part that was most remembered by those who were there and which gave them the most comfort. And that helped convinced me that an Obituary/ Eulogy, something I had always done, was an important part of a funeral. The Meditation was done first in this service, also a departure for me.

MEDITATION OF HOPE AND HEALING: WITNESS TO THE RESURRECTION

Standing in this spot five days after Easter, I have memories of what joy this church gave Larry when it was first completed. The pride he displayed as he first showed it to me was almost sinful. He was especially moved by the window behind me. At the time, it was the only stained- glass window that was complete. He explained in detail how it was constructed and what had gone into its planning. The stained-glass windows in the church, now complete, depict the life of Christ. And this is, of course, the Resurrection window.

I remember, too, the witness of those who ministered to Larry during the season of Lent and Holy Week as his body succumbed to the ravages of cancer – how it was that he faced death with determination, dedication, and devotion, without any regret or remorse or recrimination. What a remarkable testimony to the power of the Resurrection – the victory of love over sin and of life over death. Friends, this is a **Victory Celebration!**

As we drove up here Wednesday, through Tennessee and Kentucky, the redbuds – that tree which in our region signals the advent of spring – were in full bloom. When we return home, the dogwoods will likely be out. Even here – 500 miles closed to the North Pole – I have seen scrubs in bloom and maple and elm trees in full bud. Right here, were we gather to share our sorrow and grieve a death, right here in this same sanctuary, later today, there will be a wedding. The signs of life are all around us.

But for now, there is sorrow – an inevitable emotion whenever we meet to give thanks for one that death has taken from among us. There is no shame in our tears; they water the eternal rose of love. Sorrow and grief are but the flip side of love. To love and be loved means inevitably to suffer sorrow and grief.

Death intrudes on us all and its reality cannot long be denied. No respecter of persons it comes to all. To some, it comes as a thief in the night. To Larry, it came as a welcome friend, as it does to many who have lived a long and useful life only to be racked with pain near the end. But to those of us left behind, it is never a really welcomed guest. It always brings sorrow and pain and loss. Its intrusion into our lives dulls life's brightness and casts a shadow of heartbreak on our souls. Indeed, there is sadness here today.

But there must also be rejoicing. Joyful thanksgiving for the life of Larry Carpenter so graciously shared with us. And rejoicing over that to which Larry so triumphantly testified during the last weeks and days of his illness – the Resurrection.

For those who are in Christ, death takes on another face. It is no longer merely the pain and longing of separation but the joy and comfort of going home. It is no longer the end of all that makes life worth living, but merely another stage in our trip to our Father's house. The passage from John 14 (read earlier) and generally translated, "In my Father's house are many rooms," may also be translated "On the way to my Father's house are many resting places." With Larry's death, both he and we have arrived at a new resting place. We cannot go back to the old place to rest; for us things have changed forever. There will be a certain sadness in our days, a kind of void that cannot be filled. But life goes on for us and in Christ, we know that the joy and fullness and meaning of like does not end with the death of a loved one.

A victory celebration always carries with it joy and sorrow. Someone is often lost on the way to victory. And how do we rejoice with broken hearts? How do we laugh with eyes that see through tears? I rejoice because by the Grace of God Larry Carpenter became a part of my life. I know how that happened. His daughter and I fell in love and got married.

My life is fuller and richer for having known, loved and been loved by Larry. Indeed, all our lives are so much fuller, richer, and happier because he was a part of our lives. So even though today is a day of sorrow, it is also a day to rejoice – a time to praise God for Larry's life and for making him the unique person he was and who graciously shared him with us. The same graciousness of God which gave Larry life and inspired the goodness in him, and brought him into our lives that can now sustain our souls and renew our spirits in this time of grief. That graciousness is always there, but we must walk out into it.

JAMES ALLEN TINCH 09-02-1987 MEDITATION

MEDITATION ON HOPE and HEALING:
WITNESS TO THE RESURRECTION

Death intrudes upon us all. No respecter of persons, it awaits us all and its reality intrudes upon us every time we lose someone we love. Its reality cannot be wished away. The pain and emptiness it leaves behind cannot be whisked away by any words I may say. Christians are not excused from this experience. And no matter how deep our faith, how confident our convictions, how firm our hope is, we can never be completely prepared for the pain and despair it brings into our lives. Death's intrusion into our lives dulls life's brightness and casts a shadow of heartbreak over our souls.

Death is a powerful intruder and neither its reality nor its pain can be long denied. Though it may come as a welcome friend to one who has suffered long and hard, it is never a fully welcome guest to those of us left behind.

And yet, while the outward reality is substantially the same for everyone, the inward experience may be vastly different for those who trust in Christ. For those in Christ, death takes on another face. It is no longer merely the pain and longing of separation but also the joy and comfort of going home. It is no longer the end of all that makes life worth living, but merely another stage in the trip to our Father's house.

"Though our outer nature is rotting away," wrote the Apostle Paul, "our inner nature is being renewed every day." [2 Corinthians 16b].

The grave is no barrier to God - a casket no more a final resting place than a baby's cradle. "Life is eternal and love is immortal and death is only a horizon and a horizon is nothing - nothing but the limit of our sight." 1 We cannot know what is beyond that horizon, but we know who is there and the resurrected Christ is enough.

In the fifteenth chapter of I Corinthians, the Apostle Paul writes, *"When the perishable puts on the imperishable, and the mortal puts on immortality, then shall come to pass that which is written: Death is swallowed up in victory. O death, where is thy victory? O death, where is thy sting?"* [1 Corinthians 15: 54-56].

And so the sorrow and loss we experience today must be mingled with the gratitude and joy of victory, for we are gathered to pay our respects to one of God's good men. A man who lived a quiet, simple life. A plain, humble man never accounted "great" of "important" as the world measures such things, but great in those qualities of character which truly endure. Never the possessor of a multitude of goods, James nevertheless lived a good life, faithful to the place and people and worked to which God called him.

There are those who would suggest that because he accomplished nothing "worthwhile" as the world sees things that his life counted for nothing. After all, he never wrote a book, never composed a song, never invented a great machine, never made a million dollars, never traveled far beyond the small community where he was reared. I would remind those people that Jesus never did any of those things, either. Moreover, I would point out that the substance of our lives is shaped and defined not by scientific advance nor worldly achievement but by the content of the character and the strength of soul of those whom we count as loved ones and friends.

Some will say he "Never had much." But he had all that really matters. He was reared in a loving family who taught him love and faith, which he embodied and passed on to others. He had a place to call home, a loving family, useful work to do, people to love who loved him in return. When all the teachings of the great prophets of the Bible are boiled down, they can be expressed in three verses from the sixth chapter of Micah: "What does the Lord require of you, except to act justly, practice kindness, and walk humbly with your God." [Micah 6: 8]. We can thank God that in James we had one among us who, insofar as it was within his power, practiced these traits.

In the second chapter of Philippians, Christ is shown to be the example to follow in humility, and Christians are counseled to "Do nothing from selfishness or conceit, but in humility count others better than yourselves. Let each of you look not only after his own interests but also after the interests of others." [Philippians 2: 3-4]. We can thank God that in James we had one among us who lived up to this teaching.

The fifth chapter of Galatians contains a list of the "fruits of the Spirit" - those things that result from a life lived in obedience to Christ and the Holy Spirit. They are: "love, joy, peace, patience, kindness, goodness, faithfulness, gentleness, self-control." [Galatians 5: 22-23]. We can thank God that in James we had one among us who produced such "fruits of the Spirit."

The fifth chapter of Genesis is a genealogy of humankind from Adam to Noah. For all of the people listed it says "so-and-so" lived so many years and he died, with one exception. Only Enoch is singled out for a special notation. Of Enoch it is written, "Enoch walked with God, and he was not, for God took him." [Genesis 5: 24]. The recorders of the genealogy knew that Enoch's life led not to a grave, but to God.

How much more sure can we be who put our trust in Jesus Christ, of whom it is written: "God raised him up, having loosed the pangs of death because it was not possible for him to be held by them" [Acts 2:24]. Those who are bound to Christ are held in a relationship which the grave cannot destroy.

Christ's victory over death was evident in James' life and in the way he faced his final illness with quiet serenity, calm certitude, and patient perseverance.

But you may say, if this is a victory celebration, why do we feel so bad, so defeated? Because, like at many victory celebrations, there was a casualty, so today is also shrouded in sadness. There is an expected sense of loss, recollections of things there was no time to do - which there will never be time to do. Recollections of things we would like to have said that we never got around to saying; perhaps of things said which we wish had never been said.

But more significantly, there is sadness here today because of love. There is no shame in your tears. They water the eternal rose of love. Sorrow and grief are but the flip side of love. To love and be loved means that we will inevitably suffer sorrow and grief. We cannot have a life with love without grief. Perhaps grief is God's way of reminding us of what is really important in life - the relationships in which we learn to love one another. How much richer, how much fuller your lives are today for having loved and been loved by James.

"What then shall we say to this? If God is for us, who is against us? He who did not spare his own Son, but gave him up for us all, will he not also give us all things with him? . . . Who shall separate us from the love of Christ? Shall tribulation or distress [affliction or hardship, sorrow or change]? NO, in all these things we are more than conquerors through him who loved us. For I am certain that neither death nor life . .. nor things present, nor things to come . . . nor anything else in all creation will be able to separate us from the love of God in Christ Jesus our Lord." [Romans 8: 31- 32; 35; 37-39 altered slightly by MFS]. 2

There is a big void - an emptiness - a big hole in our lives now - a giant rip that cannot be made like new for a part of the fabric is gone. Only the Lord can mend that rip, and God will if we give God a chance over time. There has been a change in our lives, but in God's time, the grave is no more final, no more an end to anything than is the delivery room. And if we will allow God, the Lord will renew the purpose of our lives. And we will mount up with the wings of eagles; we shall dwell in the house of the Lord forever.

All praise be to God who gave James Tinch life and gave him to us. Amen. Let us Pray: [I led a closing prayer.]

[Benediction and dismissal to place of burial for an internment service.]

NOTES:
1. Penn, et al., Op. Cit. For more information, see **Appendix A** at the end of this Collection.
2. This is my most often quoted passage of Scripture. You will find it laced among the Obituaries/Eulogy and Meditations in this Collection, sometimes straight from the RSV and sometimes altered slightly by myself. In fact, you have already encountered it several times above.

GEORGE W. COOKE, JR. 06/22/1988 MEDITATION

MEDITATION on HOPE and HEALING:
WITNESS TO THE RESURRECTION

Death intrudes upon us all. Its reality cannot long be denied. No respecter of persons, it comes to all – to old and young, to rich and poor, to well- known and unknown, to Christian and pagan. To some, it comes as a welcome friend. To others, as to George, it comes as a thief in the night. It seldom waits until we are prepared, coming to us on its own time-table. And to those left behind, it never comes as a welcome guest. It comes as a great disrupter of our plans and hopes. As it passes by us, it takes with it one we love and leaves in its wake sorrow and pain and loss. Its intrusion into our lives dulls life's brightness and casts a shadow of heartbreak over our souls. Today (June 22) may be one of the longest days of the year, filled with the longest period of light, but for us, it is a day of gloom when darkness casts its pale upon us.

"There is a time," says the Preacher of Ecclesiastes, "for every matter under heaven – a time to be born and a time to die; a time to laugh and a time to weep; a time to dance and a time to mourn." (A portion of Ecclesiastes 3: 1-12) Today is a time to weep; a time to mourn. There is no shame in our tears. They water the eternal rose of love. Sorrow and grief are but the flip side of love. To live and love and be loved means inevitably to suffer sorrow and grief. Today is a time for sorrow.

Yet, the sorrow and loss we experience today must make way for gratitude and joy, for we are here to give thanks to Almighty God for the life of one of God's special people. A man who may never have been accounted great or powerful as the world measures such things but who possessed those qualities of character and strength of spirit which marked him as one of God's special messengers.

While the outward experience of death is essentially the same for everyone, the inward reality is vastly different for those who trust in Christ. In Christ, death takes on another face. It is no longer merely the pain and longing of separation but the joy of going home. It is no longer the end of all that makes life worth living but merely another stage in our journey to the Father's house.

The passage from chapter 14 of the Gospel of John normally translated "In my Father's house are many rooms," may also be translated, "On the way to my Father's house there are many resting places." With George's death, both he and we have arrived at a new resting place. We cannot go back to the old place to live; for us things have changed forever. There will be a certain sadness in our days, a kind of void that George once filled that can no longer be filled; an abiding loneliness. But life goes on and in Christ, we know that the joy and meaning of life does not end with the death of a loved one. The one sure obligation we have to our loved ones who have died is to go on living life to its fullest.

But how do we rejoice with broken hearts? How do we laugh with eyes that see through tears? We rejoice because through the Grace of God George Cooke became a part of our lives. The sudden, unexpected and unexplainable nature of George's death reveals to us the capriciousness of life; the fact that ion this world there are no certainties, no guarantees, no final security. But that downside of life's uncertainties is balanced by the wonder and wisdom of God's Grace revealed to us through George's life.

None of us have any guarantee that someone like George will be a part of our lives. Many people never have such an experience. Indeed, what a rare privilege is ours today to have known, loved, and been loved by George Cooke. We grieve today because of a blessing not because of a curse.

We grieve because by the Grace of God, George Cooke became a part of our lives. How much poorer we would be today, how infinitely sadder it would be if we had never known him as husband, father, brother, loved one, neighbor and friend.

The very first Psalm begins: "Blessed is the man who walks not in the counsel of the wicked, nor stands in the way of sinners, not sits in the seat of scoffers.

He is like a tree planted ty streams of water that yields it fruit in its season, and its leaf does not wither."

Every time I read that Psalm, I am reminded of a massive white pine tree that stands on the banks of Daddy's Creek near where I live. Most of us call it simply "the big pine." It is over 4 feet in diameter, over 12 feet around and towers over the lesser trees which surround it. It is considered the largest pine tree in Tennessee. It was, according to foresters, a seedling when the Pilgrims landed at Plymouth Rock. Somehow through all these years, it alone has withstood the ravages of wind and wildfire and the woodman's ax, each year dropping its seeds to begin new life.

Perhaps those of you who knew him best, sense, as I do, a connection between that pine and George Cooke. Steadfast, straight, strong, abiding, productive, dependable, George stood amid the storms of life with quiet strength and dignity, with steadfastness of purpose, with trustfulness, dropping seeds of kindness and good cheer, of quality workmanship, dependability, and neighborliness year after year after year.

"I have taught you these things," Jesus says to his disciples in John 15:11, "so that my joy may be in you, and that your joy may be full. "In Galatians 5: 22-23 the Apostle Paul lists the fruits of the Spirit. Among these, second only to love he lists joy.

George had the gift of joy. It is a remarkable gift to be so full of joy that it rubs off on others whenever you are around them. George had this gift, which is even more remarkable when you consider that life had dealt George some devastating blows, including disabling injuries and long periods of convalescence, first to himself and later to his son.

Are we to believe that this fullness of joy was an accident? Or was it evidence of Christ working in and through George's life. If you believe, as I do, the latter, then you must know that his joy is even fuller today than it was on Sunday when he last shared it with family and friends.

In Ephesians 2: 11-18, the Apostle Paul said (and I paraphrase), "Christ is our peace. He has broken down the dividing wall of hostility – reconciling hostile groups on both sides of the wall to God in one Body through the Cross, thereby bringing the hostility to an end."

One of God's gifts to George was the ability to make the truth of this passage come alive by transcending stereotypes and overcoming prejudices. Folks, I am a hillbilly, a native of the hills and hollows and ridges that make up the Cumberland Plateau and the Head of the Valley. I know how hard it is for an outsider to become accepted in the community as a native. George was a northerner, a native of and a life- long 4th generation New Yorker, an Irish-Norwegian descendant of vaudeville performers. Moving into the Head of the Sequatchie Valley in Bledsoe County, he was about as much of an outsider as one could be. All the conventional wisdom, the stereotypes, the prejudices suggest that he would not be readily accepted; that he would have a hard time working his way into the life of the community.

But on the strength of his personality, his love and care, his compassion and commitment, his eagerness to share of himself and his substance, in four short years, he had captured the hearts of his new neighbors and found himself not only accepted but enthusiastically endorsed as a member of his new community.

The ability to understand and to act on the understanding that those things we have in common as children of God is greater than all those things we use to divide ourselves into insider and outsider, suspicious and hostile groups was a mark of who George was and one of the things that God would have us learn through his life.

In the first letter of John (1: 5b;6; 2:10) it is written: "God is light and in him is no darkness at all. . . if we walk in the light, as he is in the light, we have fellowship with one another and the blood of Jesus his son cleanses us from all sin. . . He who loves his brother abides in the light and in it there is no cause for stumbling. . ."

He was married on the longest day of the year. He died and will be buried during that time of year when the daylight is the longest. Perhaps it is symbolic. George loved the light. When he and Ellen built their dream house on a ridge overlooking the head of the Sequatchie Valley, they built in a massive front window, extending the whole height of the house, facing east toward the rising sun, the rising light. George was a man of light, and while it cannot be said of any of us that we are completely filled with the light. It can be said of George Cooke that there was not much darkness in him.

George did not live a long life by contemporary standards. He died much too soon - too soon for us really to comprehend. It is impossible to explain why a heart so large, so expansive would give out so quickly. Yet it cannot be said that he lived anything other than a full life. He experienced more, lived more, loved more, contributed more than many who live far longer lives. Longevity has its place, but it has little to do with the mark of a person's life. It is sad when all that can be said at the end of a life is that so and so lived for many years and he died. This is all that is said of Methuselah in the Bible. But in that same chapter (Genesis 5) one person is singled out for special notation.

Of Enoch it is written, "Enoch walked with God and he was not, for God took him." [Genesis 5: 4]. Enoch's friends knew that his life led not to the grave but to God. A child once explained this verse by saying, "Enoch and God used to take long walks together. One day they walked further than usual, and God said, 'Enoch you must be tired, come into my house and rest.'" Perhaps George, too, took long walks with God, and (as Paul Harvey says), you know the rest of the story.

If George could speak to us today, perhaps he would know exactly what to say to soothe the ache in our hearts. In your recollections, you have told me that he always seemed to know the right thing to say. Perhaps he would say something like this from a poem entitled "To Those I Love" by Isla Pascal Richardson:

TO THOSE I LOVE"
By Isla Pascal Richardson

"If I should ever leave you whom I love
To go along the Silent Way,
Grieve not,

. . .
Please do not let the thoughts of me be sad,
For I am loving you just as I always have.

. . .
We cannot see Beyond,
But this I know:
I loved you so – t'was heaven here with you." [1]

The grave is no barrier to God. It need be no permanent barrier to us, "Life is eternal, love is immortal, and death is only a horizon and a horizon is nothing but the limit of our sight." [2]

> *"What then shall we say to this?" Paul wrote to the Romans. "If*
> *God is for us who is against us?*
> *. . . Who shall separate us from the love of Christ? Shall tribulation*
> *or distress, or persecution, or famine, or nakedness, or peril, or*
> *sword? . . . NO, in all these things we are more than conquerors*

through him who loved us. For I am sure that neither death, nor
life, . . . nor things present, not things to come, . . . nor anything
else in all creation, will be able to separate us from the love of
God in Christ Jesus our Lord." (Romans 8: 31-39, shortened)

Praise be to God, Amen.

Let Us Pray.   *[I led a closing prayer, and a hymn, "How Great Thou Art"*
was played.]

    [Benediction and dismissal to place of burial for a committal service.]

NOTES:
1. This is my most used piece of poetry. In the service I read the whole poem, but the legal constraints of Copyright law restrict me here to no more than these eight lines.
2. Penn, et al., Op. Cit. For a fuller explanation see **Appendix A** at the end of this Collection.

ANNA MARY BRADLEY 06/30/1989 MEDITATION

MEDITATION ON HOPE AND HEALING:
WITNESS TO THE RESURRECTION

***[This Meditation is partly a continuation of the Eulogy printed in
Part One of this Collection.]***

In the 23rd Psalm, which Anna Mary liked so well and which I read moments ago, it is written:

> *"He shall lead me in paths of righteousness (or right paths) for
> the sake of His name."*

Those whom God chooses are led in right paths in order to witness to the name of God, to show what God is like, to demonstrate His power. Anna Mary was surely so led.

The 15th psalm is attributed to David. In it he writes:

> *O Lord, who shall you invite into your house?*
> *Who shall come to live on your Holy Hill?*
>
> *She who walks blamelessly;*
> *who does what is right;*
> *who seeks truth from his heart;*
> *who can be trusted to say honestly what he thinks;*
> *whose word can be trusted;*

who does not slander with his tongue;
who does no evil to a friend,
nor repeats a derogatory report against his neighbor;
who sticks by his word and promise even if it causes him injury;
who is dependable, trustworthy and not two-faced;
who will not cheat nor injure the innocent for any amount of
money.

[Psalm 15; MFS translation]

Perhaps David knew someone a lot like Anna Mary. In Genesis 12: 1-2 it is written:

"Now the Lord said to Abram, 'Go from your country and your
kindred and your father's house to the land I will show you. And
I will make of you a great nation, and I will bless you, and make
your name great, so that you will be a blessing.'"

Anna Mary, like Abram and Sarai, was one of those who were called from the homeland of their parents and led to a land they had never seen before there to become a blessing. Between 1917 and 1940, four remarkable people were led by God to leave the land of their parents and travel to a land where they had never been before - a land called Big Lick and Cumberland County, Tennessee. There they remained for the rest of their lives and became a blessing to three generations of people.

Anna Mary is the last of these four to pass beyond the tangled web of this world into a wider kingdom. And with Anna Mary's passing, we can look back and see two generations that have grown up in Big Lick and Cumberland County whose lives have been blessed and enriched by this sojourner who came and stayed. Indeed, how blessed we are today because God has so richly rewarded us by allowing us to have loved and been loved by this remarkable woman - as wife, mother, grandmother, mother-in-law, neighbor and friend.

Anna Mary often quoted this passage of Scripture from the Gospel of Matthew, and it is appropriate that we remember it now as we remember her:

"Happy are the humble, for theirs is the kingdom of heaven.
"Happy are those who mourn, for they shall be comforted.
"Happy are those who are not arrogant, for they shall inherit
the earth.

"Happy are those who hunger and thirst for righteousness, for they shall be satisfied.
"Happy are the merciful, for they shall obtain mercy.
"Happy are the pure in heart, for they shall see God.
"Happy are the peacemakers, for they shall be called sons and daughters of God. . ."

Matthew 5: 3-9 (MFS translation)

Anna Mary's life was a witness to the presence, power, and purpose of God. She was led in right paths for the sake of His name. Don't waste this witness. Take heed so that your life may be similarly blessed.

But no matter how ardent the words of praise, no matter how rich our memories, they cannot mask, they cannot eliminate the sorrow and grief we share today. Death intrudes on us all. None of us are immune from it. Sooner or later it tracks down our footsteps and discovers our hiding places. To some, it comes as a long-awaited friend. To others, it comes as a thief in the night. And even though we may know it is coming, we are never fully prepared for it. To those left behind, it always comes as a dreadful surprise and brings with it the pain and suffering of sorrow and loss. Its intrusion into our lives dulls life's brightness and casts a shadow of heartbreak on our souls.

Yet, while the outward reality may appear to be substantially the same for everyone, the inward experience is vastly different for those that are in Christ. In Christ, death assumes a different face. It is no longer a frightening enemy, robbing us of all we hold dear, but merely the door into another room of the Father's house. It is no longer a darkness that empties life of its meaning, but rather the gladness of going home.

The grave is no barrier to God and thus, should be no barrier to us. In God's time the tomb is no more final than the womb. "Life is eternal, love is immortal, and death is only a horizon, and a horizon is nothing but the limit of our sight." 1 We cannot know what is beyond that horizon, but we know who is there. We cannot know what the future holds, but we know who holds the future, and the Resurrected Christ is sufficient to comfort and reassure those who trust in Him.

In 1940, Anna Mary Everman transferred her church membership from a church elsewhere to the Calvary Presbyterian Church of Big Lick. Since then she has been a loyal, faithful, and beloved member of that church. But today, she makes the one last move that we all must make. And so it becomes our duty and privilege to announce the transfer of our beloved sister, Anna Mary

Bradley, from the church temporal to the church triumphant and eternal located in that "city which has foundations whose maker and builder is God." 2 [Hebrews 11: 10]

Amen. Let us Pray: *[I led a closing prayer, and a hymn was played.]*

   [Benediction and dismissal to place of burial for a committal service.]

NOTES
   1. Penn, et al., Op. Cit. For more information, see **Appendix A** at the end of this Collection.
   2. Adapted from a funeral closing by Eugene Smathers 1932- 1968.

BELLE BLAYLOCK KERLEY 08-17-1989 MEDITATION

MEDITATION OF HOPE AND HEALING:
WITNESS TO THE RESURRECTION

In the third chapter of Colossians, the Apostle Paul writes of the new life in Christ:

> *"Put on then, as God's chosen ones, holy and beloved, compassion, kindness, lowliness, meekness, and patience, forbearing one another and, if one has a complaint against another, forgiving each other. . . And above all these put on love, which binds everything together in perfect harmony."*
>
> (Colossians 3: 12-15)

And in the 12th chapter of the Letter to the Romans, he again describes the life of a Christian in Christ:

> *"Let love be genuine; hate what is evil, hold fast to what is good; love one another with brotherly affection; outdo one another in showing honor. Be aglow with the Spirit, serve the Lord. Never flag in zeal, be aglow with the Spirit, serve the Lord. Rejoice in your hope, be patient in tribulation, be constant in prayer . . . practice hospitality . . . Rejoice with those who rejoice, weep with those who weep. Live in harmony with one another; do not be haughty, but associate with the lowly; never be conceited. Repay no one evil for evil . . . If possible, so far*

as it depends upon you, live peaceably with all . . . Do not be overcome by evil, but overcome evil with good."

What a testimony; what a witness to the power of the Gospel was the life of Belle Kerley. She was a living example proving that these are not merely words and impossible to achieve in real life, but are the living truth that can be incarnate in the life of one willing to devote her life to them.

Funerals are a time for remembering and for rejoicing over God's good gifts shared with us through the life of the loved one now gone beyond this world. But also funerals are a time to grieve, because death intrudes upon us all. And no matter how well we think we have prepared for it, it always comes as a dreadful surprise. Its intrusion into our lives bring sorrow and pain and loss. It dulls life's bright ness and casts a shadow of heartbreak on our souls.

Yet you must know that your grief today is but the flip side of love. You grieve because you loved and were loved. The only way to be spared grief in this world is to do without love. Moreover, above all else a funeral is to remind us of the victory over sin and death that is ours in Jesus Christ and shined forth in the life of Belle Kerley. We grieve but we do not grieve as those who have no hope.

In Christ, death assumes a different face. It is no longer a frightening enemy robbing us of all we hold dear; no longer the darkness that brings emptiness into our lives. It is merely the door we pass through to arrive at another room in the Father's house; it is the joy of going home.

As I prepared for this service, I went outside last night to watch the full eclipse of the moon. As the shadow of the earth crept slowly between the sun and the moon, the night got darker and darker until it was pitch black. But as the eclipse subsided, the moon emerged from the earth's shadow. Only you could not see the moon for the clouds. But you could tell it was there because there was light coming through the clouds and the night was noticeably brighter. It was then that what I needed to say today came to me.

I thought of Belle. Over the past few months, her life on earth slipped away much as the moon slipped behind the earth's shadow. And just as the moon emerged on the other side of the eclipse, Belle's life will emerge on the other side of death's veil. We cannot see Belle just as I could not see the moon. But we know she is there by the light of her countenance which continues to radiate among us.

330 | MIKE SMATHERS

She can say with the Apostle Paul:

> *"I have fought the good fight. I have finished the race; I have kept the faith. Henceforth there is laid up for me the crown of righteousness, which the Lord, the righteous judge, will award to me on that Day, and not only to me but also to all who have loved his appearing."* [2 Timothy 4: 8]

Let Us Prayer. *[I led a closing prayer and a hymn was played.]*

[Benediction and removal to place of burial for an internment and committal service.]

JACK TOLLETT
MARCH 3, 1990,
MEDITATION

MEDITATION OF HEALING AND HOPE:
WITNESS TO THE RESURRECTION

We are gathered here, first of all, to pay attention to sorrow. This is inevitable and unavoidable as we bid a final farewell to a respected and beloved family and community member. Sorrow and grief are marks of our common humanity. Even Jesus was said to be "a man of sorrows, acquainted with grief." (Isaiah 53: 3b). Sorrow and grief are a part of every person's experience.

Do not hide your tears. There is nothing shameful in them. They are but the flip side of love. To do without grief would require that we do without love. If there be any shame, it is only in our failure to allow our tears to remind us of our kinship with all other persons. Our grief reveals that under the surface of all our differences, we are brothers and sisters with all others.

The second purpose for a funeral is to help us take account of change. Life in this world is a pilgrimage, a journey toward an assured but unseen future. We will never arrive at our final destination in this world, although we sometimes mistakenly think that we have. And then along comes a death and with it the realization that life moves on, only eternity remains unchanged. As life moves along in brings changes into our lives and will leave us behind mired in self-pity and bitterness unless we adjust to its movement and changes.

The one sure duty that the living have to their loved ones who have died is to go on living life as full, as joyfully, as meaningfully as possible. That is what they would want us to do. We must not withdraw or forsake life but go into the future with courage and hope. To live life well we have to adjust our lives to change.

Those words of Jesus: "In my Father's house are many rooms. . . "(John 14: 2) may also be translated "on the road to my Father's house are many resting places." Life here on earth is like climbing a high mountain and along the trail are many stopping places where we can rest awhile. But the journey must soon be resumed if we are to reach the summit.

It has been said, "No man can step into the same river twice, for both the man and the river have changed."1 Life does not stand still. It is never today what it was yesterday and will not be tomorrow what it is today. Death is one of those events that brings this clearly into focus. After a death nothing will ever be the same again. This does not mean that life has lost all meaning and purpose, all hope and joy. But it does mean that we must face the reality of death and not try to go back to a former time to live. We must move forward into a new situation, knowing that on this earth we have no final abiding place.

We should remember the past with gratitude and appreciation, but we cannot go back there to live. There is no final closure to a death. It leaves a wound. A wound will heal with time if we trust God, but it will remain as a reminder, and it will flare up and ache from time to time. But to survive in wholeness and joy we must take account of the change that has happened in our life, and go forward from here (as the Navaho say) with beauty before us, beauty behind us and beauty beside us.

The third purpose of a Christian funeral is to remember the sustaining certainty of God's abidingness. So we pay attention to sorrow and we take account of change in light of God's abiding presence through the Resurrection of Jesus Christ from the dead and the gift of the Holy Spirit.

We walk again through the valley of shadows where death has broken the ties that bound together family and friends. In times like these sorrow, fear, loss, grief, loneliness, distrust, and perhaps selfishness, guilt and rebellion stir with in us. We are broken within and our brokenness cries out for wholeness and healing.

In Jesus Christ, his cross and resurrection, we have God's healing for our brokenness. Life as we experience it on earth is not as God intends it to be. God's purpose is health and wholeness, life abundant and eternal. God does not abandon us in our brokenness, but comes to us in Jesus Christ and is broken for our healing. "This is my body broken for you," (1 Corinthians 11:24; Luke 22:19) Jesus tells his disciples and us. Christ bring healing for our brokenness by showing us the steadfast love and trustworthiness of God. Any who do not know the peace and assurance that comes from knowing of God's abiding love and faithfulness might find it by taking into their life Jesus Christ as Lord and Savior.

Jack never traveled much in his life. He died across the road from where he was born. He and Anna Lou lived in only two places during their 45 years of marriage. Today Jack makes the one last journey that we must all make. He has journeyed to that realm beyond our touch and sight. We cannot know what is in that realm, but we know who is there, and it is the resurrected Christ who greets Jack today.

There are some who might suggest that this meeting will not be a happen one for Jack. But I have read the Gospels, and I do not believe that. I invite any of you to read them for yourselves, and then decide what the Christ whom Jack will meet is like. Is it the Christ who taught his disciples to forgive 70 times 7 (that is, infinitely)? Or is it a Christ of wrath and vengeance who mercilessly exacts punishment upon those who have failed to pass all the tests of faith and doubt, belief and disbelief, integrity and hypocrisy that this world sets before us?

The Bible has several beautiful and a few scary visions of what life is like beyond the grave. I do not claim certainty of what awaits any of us there. I think we have enough to worry about in this life and can best leave worrying about life beyond to God. But I do believe the words of the Psalmist when he wrote:

> "Where shall I go from your Spirit? Or where shall I flee from your presence?
> If I ascend to heaven, you are there! If I make my bed in Hell you are there!
> If I take the wings of the morning and dwell in the farthest most parts of the sea,
> Even there you had shall find me, and your right hand shall hold me. If I hide myself in the darkness and there be no light around me, Even the darkness is not dark to you, the night is as bright as the day For the darkness is as light to you." (Psalm 139: 7-12)

The promise to Jack and to all of us is that there is no place we can go that is beyond God's love and care.

Let Us Pray.   *[I offered a closing prayer and a hymn was played.]*

[Benediction and removal to place of burial for a committal service.]

NOTES:
1. Heraclitus (Greek Philosopher). Also attributed to certain unknown Native Americans.

RED BRADLEY
05/01/1990
MEDITATION

MEDITATION on HOPE and HEALING:
WITNESS TO THE RESURRECTION

ELMO and THE GOSPEL

Death intrudes upon us all, and it reality cannot long be denied. No respecter of persons, it comes to all. To some, it comes as a thief in the night; to others as a long-awaited friend, but to those left behind it is never a welcomed guest. It always brings sorrow, pain, and loss. Its intrusion into our lives dulls life's brightness and casts a shadow of heartbreak on our souls. Indeed, there is sadness here today.

We are sad because our lives will never be the same. Some of the richness has gone out of the world. Red's voice, laughter, stories will never again be heard among us. His insights, his wisdom, his wit will no longer sparkle, enliven, and enlighten our deliberations. BUT HIS SPIRIT.

AH, HIS SPIRIT - that is something else. It does not disappear as quickly as the physical, the body. As long as there are any among us, inspired by Elmo's spirit, by Elmo's example who remain more concerned for the common good than private gain;

1. As long as any of us remain willing to sacrifice self for the good of a neighbor;

2. As long as any remain compassionately committed to making life better for the whole community than we are to make it more comfortable for ourselves;
3. As long as any among us are willing to try an unconventional approach, to keep trying, to never give up even in the face of seemingly insurmountable odds;
4. As long as any of us are willing to see the humor even in the most difficult situations, to retain a sense of humor, an ability to laugh at ourselves, even under the most trying circumstances;
5. As long as there are those among us who remain unflinchingly loyal to the promises we make, to every commitment we undertake, regardless of the reasons for forsaking them;
6. As long as we continue to believe that love and forgiveness are sweeter than hate and revenge;
7. As long as any of us continue to resonate to the rhythms of Elmo's symphony; as long as any of us respond in kind to the quality of his character; as long as any of us continue to be inspired by his example;
8. As long as any of this remains alive in us and as long as we pass it along to our children and our children's children, then Elmo's spirit will not disappear from among us.

Wait a minute, someone may say, you are just praising the human spirit. I don't think so. That is the whole point. The spirit that shined in Elmo's life was not his alone. It was not something he produced by his will or his effort alone. It was given to him by God. It was given to him by Jesus because he had given himself to Jesus. And that is why today is a victory celebration.

The victory we celebrate today is not really Elmo's - though it was through his faith that we saw it. It is Christ's victory - a victory not only for the world beyond but one which can be appropriated in this life. A fact so clearly illustrated by the life of Elmo Bradley. It is a victory not only over death but also over sin. It is a victory -

1. of all that makes life beautiful over that which makes it ugly;
2. of all that makes life worthwhile over that which makes it meaningless;
3. of all that is honorable over the dishonorable;
4. of the spirit of adventure over the spirit of defeat;
5. of giving over greed;
6. of dedication and dependability over deceit and deception;
7. of sacrifice over selfishness;

8. of love and forgiveness over hate and vengefulness.

I believe God had a purpose in Elmo's life, and that purpose did not disappear when Elmo departed this world. If you want to be like him, then give your life to Jesus the way he gave his. Elmo was blessed, and if anyone ever demonstrated what the Bible means when it says "you are blessed in order that you may be a blessing to others," it was Red Bradley. So let's celebrate the victory in Jesus so clearly demonstrated in the life of this remarkable man we lay to rest today.

Among the disciples, the one who was most dependable, the one that could be counted on to be there when he said he would, the one that was most constant in purpose and most trustworthy in action was Peter. In my mind's eye Peter has always and will always look a lot like Elmo Bradley.

But preacher, you may say, how do we celebrate with broken hearts? How do we rejoice with eyes that see through tears? I rejoice today because by the Grace of God Elmo Bradley became a part of my life. Our lives are so much richer for having known, loved and been loved by Elmo Bradley. The same Grace of God that animated Elmo's life can now sustain our souls and renew our spirits in this time of grief.

> In the very first Psalm, the Psalmist writes, "Blessed is the man who walks not in the counsel of the wicked, nor stands in the way of sinners, nor sits in the seat of scoffers, but his delight is in the law of the Lord He is like a tree planted by streams of water, that yields its fruit in its season, and its leaf does not wither. . ." (Psalms 1:1-2a, 3)

God always keeps the future open while closing doors of the past. We can put the past behind us. Whatever guilt we may have; whatever regrets we may harbor; all the things we wish we had said but didn't; all the things we said but shouldn't have; all the things left undone which we wish we had done; all the things done that we wish hadn't been - those doors are all closed and will remain so unless we insist on prying them open. Yes, we can put the past behind us, but we cannot go there to live.

In the fourth chapter of II Corinthians, Paul writes, "Death is overtaking us [himself and his fellow workers], but you [the Corinthian Christians] must go on living." The hope of the dying rests with the living. The one sure obligation that the living have to our loved ones who have died is to go on living life to its fullest as they would have wanted us to do.

Elmo was never one to make a lot of changes. He lived and died on the same farm, in the same house where he was born. He has been a member of the same church for 61 years, married to the same woman for 47 years. But today Elmo makes the one final move that we must all make. And in the church, we have a far more fitting word than deceased to describe this occasion. When a Christian moves his membership from one church to another, we say that he/she has "transferred" his/her membership.

So it becomes our responsibility and privilege today to announce the transfer of our beloved brother, Elmo "Red" Bradley, from the church temporal and temporary to the church triumphant and eternal located in that "city which has foundations whose builder and maker is God." (Hebrews 11: 10)

> *"What then shall we Say to this," the Apostle Paul writes, "If God is for us, who is against us? He who did not spare his own Son but gave him up for us all, will He not also give us all things with him. . . Who shall separate us from the Love of Christ? Shall tribulation; or distress; or persecution; or famine; or nakedness; of peril; or sword. . . NO! In all these things we are more than conquerors through Him who loved us. For I am SURE that neither death, nor life, nor angels, nor principalities, nor things present, nor things to come, nor powers, nor height, nor depth, nor anything else in all creation, will be able to separate us from the Love of God in Christ Jesus our Lord." [Roman 8: 31-39]*

Praise be to God. Amen and Amen.

Let us Pray. *[I led a closing prayer and a hymn was played.]*

[Benediction and dismissal to place of burial for a committal service.]

MYRTLE MAE DYE 01-22-1997 ME DITATION

MEDITATION on HOPE and HEALING:
WITNESS TO THE RESURRECTION

It seems appropriate that a sliver of spring has slipped through winter's darkness just at the time Mrs. Dye has slipped beyond our sight and touch. It is almost as if nature itself paused to recognize the kind of person she was. Yesterday, when the sky filled with the thunder of the sun, and its warm rays, made it comfortable to be outdoors in shirt sleeves, one could scarcely remember the cold and ice and snow of last week, but you could not fail to feel inexorably the inevitability of spring.

On this wintry day in our spirits, we, too, should not fail to feel the inevitability of spring because this is a victory celebration. It is so not only because we have been born anew to a living hope through the Resurrection of Jesus Christ from the grave. But beyond that, it is so because Mrs. Dye gave such eloquent testimony in her life to the power of the Resurrection - the power of life and love and faith and grace to triumph over the forces of darkness, death, and despair.

The Psalmists might have had her in mind when they wrote the following (slightly revised):

> "Blessed is the [woman] who walks not in the counsel of the wicked, nor stands in the way of sinners, not sits in the seat of those who sneer;

But [her] delight is in the law of the Lord, and on his law [she] meditates day and night. [She] is like a tree planted by streams of water and yields its fruit in its season, and its leaf does not wither. In all that [she] does [she] prospers . . ."

(Psalm 1: 1-3)

"O Lord, who shall dwell in your house? Who shall rec line on your holy hill?
[She} who walks blamelessly and does what is right; and speaks truth from [her] heart; who does not slander with his tongue and does no evil to [her] friend; nor condemns her neighbor."

(Psalm 15: 1-3)

Why then Preacher, you may ask, if this is a victory celebration, why then, are our hearts so heavy? They are heavy because a funeral is a time for mourning, a time to pay attention to sorrow, to remember that the real substance of life is laced together with the dual threads of sweetness and sorrow.

A funeral is a time to pay attention to sorrow and to take account of change. For almost 85 years, God has blessed and brightened bits of His world and all of our lives through the life of Myrtle Mae Roberts Dye. As of January 19, 1997, that has changed, and that change has brought sorrow and grief and loneliness into our lives.

Yet, you must know that your grief today is but the flip side of love. You grieve because you loved and were loved by Myrtle Dye. The only way to be spared grief would be to go without love. Indeed, how fortunate you are to grieve today, because it means that you had the rare privilege of knowing, loving, and being loved by Myrtle Dye. That is a privilege reserved to you and only a few others.

Yes, funerals are for mourning, and there is sadness here today that no amount of talking will take away. William Wordsworth wrote of "Lucy," a girl "who dwelt among the untrodden ways. . . A violet by a mossy stone, half hidden from the eye. She lived unknown, and few could know when Lucy ceased to be, but she is in her grave, and, oh, the difference to me."

"And, oh, the difference to me." That is the sadness we share today – not for Mrs. Dye who has passed beyond the pain and suffering - the cares and burdens of this life - indeed, we know that there is rejoicing in heaven today because one of God' great servants is home.

So, let us mourn not for her but for us who remain. We are poorer now. Part of the richness of our lives has passed beyond our grasp. There is a big void - an enormous hole - a giant rip in the fabric of our lives that can never be made whole again, for a part of the fabric is gone.

Only God can mend the hole, and He will if we give Him a chance over time. For you see, while death intrudes on us all - while its outward reality is substantially the same for everyone, the inner experience is vastly different for those who are in Jesus Christ. By His death and Resurrection, He has banished the fear of death by the yet more powerful Love of God.

In Christ, death assumes a different face. It is no longer a frightening enemy, robbing us of all we hold dear, but merely the door into another room of the Father's house. It is no longer the darkness that empties life of its meaning but rather the gladness of going home.

So the Apostle Paul wrote: "Though our outer nature is wasting away, our inner nature is being renewed every day." [2 Corinthians 4: 16]. The grave is no barrier to God and should be no barrier to us. "In life and in death, we belong to God," and in God's time, the tomb is no more final than the womb.

"Life is eternal and love is immortal, and death is only a horizon, and a horizon is nothing but the limit of our sight." 1 We cannot see what is beyond that horizon, but we know who is there, and the Resurrected Christ is enough.

For the past 20 years, all the time I have known her, Mrs. Dye's body has been in the grasp of the forces of death. But her spirit never gave in to despair or bitterness or hopelessness or remorse or recrimination.

Paul's words to Timothy are right for her today: "I have fought the good fight. I have finished the race. I have kept the faith. Henceforth, there awaits me the crown of victory which the Lord, the righteous judge, will award me on that Day - and not only me but to all who have loved his appearing."

Let Us Pray.

NOTES:
1. Penn, et al., Op. Cit. For more information, **Appendix A** at the end of this Collection.

WANDA HALL
09/28/1998
MEDITATION

MEDITATION on HOPE and HEALING:
WITNESS TO THE RESURRECTION

Seventy-three years is a long time. Fifty years married is a long time. But not long enough. It is never long enough. It is a hard thing to have preparation for a joyous celebration turned to dust. But we are not promised any number of days on this earth, and we cannot have permanence in this world.

The best that we can hope for is to have our lives touched by the Hand of God. And next to that - the best that most of us ever experience in this life - is to have our lives touched by someone who is truly loving and caring and forgiving. To the degree that you had that with Wanda - as wife, mother, grandmother, mother-in-law, sister, sister-in-law, loved one, co-worker, or friend - then you know a little of what it is to be touched by the Hand of God. And your memory of that makes you as richly blessed as it is possible to be blessed in this life.

Indeed, how blest you are to grieve today, for you grieve because it has been your privilege - for nearly 50 years, more for some of you and for those under 50 for all of your lives - to have loved and been loved by Wanda Rose Brewer Hall.

Wanda was a "singer of life." I am reminded of the following passage from the naturalist, Loren Eiseley. Eiseley wrote it after arising from a brief nap in a forest glade. He told how he awoke one day in a glad in the wood to see a raven devour a nestling song sparrow. He tells the story at some length and then he writes: "It was then that I saw the judgment. It was the judgement of life against death. I will never again see it in notes so tragically prolonged. . . the crystal note of a song sparrow lifted hesitantly in the hush; then another joined in and then another. . .They sang because life is sweet and sunlight beautiful. They sang under the brooding shadow of the raven. In simple truth they had forgotten the raven, for they were the singers of life, and not of death."

Similarly, with Wanda we can say "though I walk through the valley of the shadow of death, I fear no evil, for Thou are with me, Thy rod and Thy staff they comfort me. Surely goodness and mercy will follow me all the days of my life, and I shall dwell in the House of the Lord forever." [Psalm 23: 4; 6]

Perhaps if she could bridge the gap of time and eternity, Wanda might say this to you in the words of Isla Paschal Richardson:

"TO THOSE I LOVE"
By Isla Pascal Richardson

"If I should ever leave you whom I love
To go along the Silent Way,
Grieve not,

. . .
Please do not let the thoughts of me be sad
For I am loving you just as I always have.

. . .
We cannot see Beyond,
But this I know:
I loved you so – t'was heaven here with you." [1]

One final word. As a young man, George Matheson was engaged to a beautiful and talented young woman. Then he went blind, and the young woman decided she did not want a life with a blind preacher. In the face of that double tragedy - losing his sight and losing the love of his life - Matheson wrote one of our great hymns, a portion of which is printed here:

"O Love that wilt not let me go,
I rest my weary soul in Thee;
I give Thee back the life I owe,

. . .
I trace the rainbow through the rain,
And feel the promise is not vain That morn shall tearless be.
. . ."* [2]

Let Us Pray.   *[I led a closing prayer, and a hymn was played.]*

[Dismissal to place of burial for a committal service.]

NOTES:
1. In the service I read the whole poem, but Copyright restrictions permit no more than eight lines to be printed here.
2. Ibid. Again in the service, I read the whole hymn, but am restricted in what I can print here.

LAURA BRADLEY KERLEY 12/08/1998 MEDITATION

MEDITATION on HOPE and HEALING:
WITNESS TO THE RESURRECTION

Today is a victory celebration - not only because every Christian funeral is so, but also because Laura in her life and in the courage and dignity of her dying gave witness to the victory of joy over despair, of kindness over meanness, of love over hate, of acceptance over ridicule, of faith over sin and the forces of life over the forces of death which is ours in Jesus Christ.

Funerals are historic occasions because for most of us, they are one of the ways we mark the passing of time and the changes in our lives. For 89 years, God has blessed and brightened little bits of the world, including every one of us here through the life of Laura Bradley Kerley. As of this past Sunday (Dec 6, 1998) that has changed. History passes on – only eternity remains unchanged.

Eighty-nine years is a long time. Sobering to realize that Laura's birth took place closer to the end of the Civil War than her death did to the end of WW II. She was born 45 years after the end of the Civil War; she died 57 years (almost to the day) after Pearl Harbor and 53 years after WW II ended. A few days before her death, the space shuttle lifted off yet again, but Laura's first trip into Cumberland County was by mule drawn wagon. She was 10 when the very first radio broadcast emanated from station KDKA in Pittsburgh, Pa. Twenty-nine when TV was first introduced at the 1939 World's Fair; in her 40's when it was first seen in Cumberland County; 31 when penicillin was discovered. When I graduated from Seminary and began my life's work, Laura was already the age I am today. She was married as many years as I have lived.

But it is not the sheer magnitude of her years but the content of her character and the strength of her spirit that make today not so much a low point in our own journey from the cradle to the grave as it is a day of rare privilege. Today in another Tennessee town, another family is gathered to lay to rest their loved one who was well-known, famous, influential and powerful. [Reference to Albert Gore, Sr.] Laura was none of those things, but she was rich in those qualities of character which truly endure - those things which the Apostle Paul called the fruits of the Spirit: "Joy, Peace, Patience, Kindness, Goodness, Faithfulness, Gentleness, Self-Control;" [Galatians 5: 22-23) and that other family will be truly blessed today if their memories are as full of meaning and as rich in love as yours are. Indeed, how fortunate we are to grieve today - because our grief means that we had the rare privilege of knowing - and loving - and being loved by Laura Bradley Kerley.

Eighty-nine years is a long time. But not long enough. It is never long enough. It is a hard thing to lose someone who has been a part of our lives for so long. But we are not promised any number of days on this earth, and we cannot have permanence in this world. The best we can hope for here is to have our lives touched by the Hand of God - and next to that - the best that most of us ever experience in this life - is to have our lives touched by someone who is truly loving and caring, kind and generous, accepting and forgiving. To the degree that you had that with Laura -as mother, grandmother, mother-in-law, sister, loved one, neighbor or friend - then you know a little of what it is to be touched by the Hand of God. And your memory of that means that you are as richly blessed as it is possible to be blessed in this life.

But this is also a time to pay attention to sorrow. Death intrudes into our lives. Though it may come as a welcomed guest to one who has lived a long and useful life only to become enfeebled by age and illness, it is never a welcome guest to those of us left behind. It is never fully expected. It always comes as a dreadful surprise. We are never completely prepared for it. It always brings sorrow, pain and loss, and its intrusion into our lives dulls life's brightness and casts a shadow of heartbreak on our souls.

However, while the outward reality is substantially the same, the inner experience is vastly different for those who are in Christ. In Christ, death assumes another face. It is no longer a frightening enemy, robbing us of all we hold dear, but merely the door into another room of the Father's house. It is no longer the darkness that empties life of its joy and meaning. It is rather the gladness of going home.

"Life is eternal and love is immortal, and death is only a horizon - and a horizon is nothing but the limit of our sight." 1 We cannot know what is beyond that horizon, but those who live by faith know who is there, and the Risen Christ is enough.

So the Apostle Paul wrote to the Corinthians (stealing some of Pete's scripture):

> *"We know that if this earthly shack we live in is destroyed, we have a house built by God - not made with human hands, but eternal and spiritual. Here, indeed, we groan and can hardly wait to get into our spiritual dwelling so that we will not be found naked. For as long as we remain in this earthly shack, we have many worries and anxieties. It is not that we wish to be without a house, but we want a better dwelling - so that our dying may be swallowed up by life in Christ Jesus. God himself is preparing us for this very thing and has given us the Holy Spirit as a guarantee."* (2 Corinthians 5:1-5)

In 1954 Stewart Hamblin wrote what became one of the top country songs of that year, based in part upon St. Paul's image of our body as a ramshackle house in which our spirit dwells here on earth and which is to be replaced by a more splendid dwelling upon our departure from this world. My father once said that he wanted this song sung at his funeral. For whatever reason, we failed to get that done. But my father was right. Though hardly the kind of music normally heard at funerals, this song has a message appropriate for a Christian funeral. Some of you may remember this song and if you do, you may also recall that it has a rousing, uplifting, joyous tune - appropriate for a victory celebration such as a Christian funeral. It is entitled "This Old House," and the chorus goes:

> **"THIS OLD HOUSE"** *(Also "This Ole House")*
> *By Stuart (or Stewart) Hamblen (October 20, 1908 – March 8, 1989)*

> *"Ain't goin'need this house no longer;*
> *Ain't goin' need this house no more;*
> *Ain't got time to fix the shingles;*
> *Ain't got time to fix the floor;*
> *Ain't got time to oil no hinges;*

Nor mend the broken window panes.
Ain't goin' need this house no longer,
I'm gettin' ready to meet the saints."

We will soon take the house that Laura lived in here on earth to its final resting place, but she's not there anymore - she's gettin' ready to meet the saints.

Some naturalists say that quail are hatched running. Well, Laura was not born running, but she did start moving from place to place early in life, moving with her family from White to Cumberland County when she was a babe in arms, and she did move around a good bit during her life - from Stringtown to Big Lick; from the banks of Lick Creek to Daddy's Creek; from Big Lick to Harriman and Detroit and back to Big Lick and finally to the little house on Huckleberry Lane where she spent the last 46 years of her life.

Today she makes the one final move that we all must make. In the church, we have a term far more fitting than "deceased" to describe this event. When a Christian moves from one church to another, we say she has "transferred" her membership. So now it becomes our responsibility and privilege to announce the transfer of our beloved sister, Laura, with the highest recommendations of her friends and neighbors and fellow church members, from the church temporal to the church eternal and triumphant, located in "that city which has foundations, whose builder and maker is God." [Hebrews 11:10]

LET US PRAY   *[I led a closing prayer, and a hymn was played.]*

[Benediction and dismissal to place of burial for a committal service.]

NOTES:
1. Penn, et al., Op. Cit. For more information, see **Appendix A** at the end of this Collection.

LENA MAE TOLLETT MEDITATION AND REMARKS FEBRUARY 19, 2003

MEDITATION AND REMARKS OF HOPE and HEALING: WITNESS TO THE RESURRECTION

A funeral is a time to take account of change. Life changes and we can be left behind mired in bitterness if we do not adjust to those changes. It is also a time to pay attention to sorrow. At other times we may get so wrapped-up in the hectic pace of our everyday lives that we forget that sorrow is a part of every person's life. Our grief is but the flip side of love. To truly live, we must love, and if we love, we will experience sorrow. We need not be ashamed of our tears today for they water the eternal rose of love. They are a sign of our common humanity and may be the pathway to a fuller faith. Even Jesus, the complete person, was called a man of sorrows, acquainted with grief. Jesus said, "Blessed are those who mourn; they shall be comforted."

Sorrow is no fun, but accepted in the context of God's comfort, it can be the pathway to a fuller, more mature faith and thus, to a fuller, more complete life - one in which true joy and blessedness may be found. Rightly accepted, sorrow can expand our capacity to care for others, help us to see more deeply into the heart of all who suffer, and equip us for ministry to them.

A funeral is also a time of remembrance and of thanksgiving - thanksgiving for the life of the loved one now departed beyond our sight and touch, and thanksgiving for the gift of eternal life in Jesus Christ.

Thanksgiving is hard at a time like this. Death has ripped the fabric of our lives. A great piece of the mosaic that made our lives rich and full and meaningful is now gone. But a Christian funeral must be a victory celebration, and this one is made all the more meaningful by Lena Mae's own witness to the victory of faith over despair in her life and especially in the courage with which she confronted her final illness - knowing full well that she could not be victorious over it in this life. In so doing, she bore testimony to those words from Paul to Timothy when he wrote: ". . . I am already on the point of [death] . . . I have fought the good fight, I have finished the race, I have kept the faith. Henceforth there is laid up for me the crown of righteousness, which the Lord...will award me...and not only to me but also to all who have loved his appearing." (2 Tim. 4:6-8).

Death intrudes on us all. Its reality cannot be long denied. No respecter of persons: to some it comes as a thief in the night; to others, it comes as a long-awaited friend, but it comes to all. We never know when it may come to us or to one we love.

Its certainty may become clearer as we grow older -and to one beset by a debilitating illness, it may be experienced as release from a life of pain. But to those left behind, it is never fully expected, and we are never completely prepared for it. It always brings sorrow and pain and loss. It intrusion into our lives dulls life's brightness and casts a shadow on heartbreak on our souls.

But in Jesus that is not the end of the story. While the outward reality is substantially the same the inner experience is vastly different for those who trust in Jesus Christ. In Christ, death assumes a different face. It is no longer a frightening enemy robbing us of all we hold dear but merely the door into another room in the Father's house. It is no longer the darkness that empties life of its meaning; it is rather the gladness of going home.

> *"What then shall we say to this?" the Apostle Paul wrote to the Romans, "If God is for us, who is against us? He who did not spare his own Son, but gave him up for us all, will he not give us all things with him? ...Who shall separate us from the love of Christ? Shall tribulation, or distress, or persecution, or famine .. . or peril? . . . No, in all these thing we are more than conquerors through him who loved us. For I am sure that neither death, nor life . . . nor things present, nor things to come . . . nor anything else in all creation, will be able to separate us from the love of God in Christ Jesus our Lord."*
>
> [Roman 8:31-32, 35, 37-39]

Lena Mae never traveled much during her life. She was born and reared in the upper end of the valley, moved about 20 miles when she married and lived the rest of her life in Big Lick. After she was married, she lived in only three houses - and those all on essentially the same piece of property. She lived in the house where she died for the last 56 of her 81 years. Today, however, Lena Mae makes the one last great journey we must all take - she moves from this world of time, tribulation and tears to that holy city eternal in the heavens "which has foundations whose builder and maker is God," [Hebrews 11: 10] where "death shall be no more, neither shall there be mourning nor crying nor pain anymore for the former things have passed away" [Revelation 21:4).

In God's time, the tomb is no more final than the delivery room. "Death, you see, is only a horizon, and a horizon is nothing - nothing but the limit of our sight."1 We cannot see what is beyond that horizon, but we know who is there, and the Resurrected Christ is sufficient to comfort and reassure those who trust in Him.

Let us Pray.   *[I led a closing prayer, and a hymn was played.]*

[Benediction and dismissal to place of burial for a committal service.]

NOTES:
1.   Penn, et al., Op. Cit. For more information, see **Appendix A** at the end of this Collection.

VICKEY KERLEY DAVIDSON
APRIL 14, 2007
MEDITATION

MEDITATION on HOPE and HEALING:
WITNESS TO THE RESURRECTION

In the 11th chapter of his Gospel, John recalls what happened when Jesus went to the tomb of His friend Lazarus:

> "Then Mary, when she came where Jesus was and saw him, fell at His feet, saying to Him, 'Lord, if you had been here, my brother would not have died.' When Jesus saw her and the others who came with her weeping, He was deeply moved in spirit and troubled; and he said, 'Where have you laid him?' They said to Him, 'Lord, come and see.' Jesus wept. So they said, 'See how He loved him!'. . . Then Jesus, deeply moved again, came to the tomb; it was a cave, and a stone lay over it. Jesus said, 'Remove the stone!'. . . So they took away the stone . . . [After he prayed] Jesus cried with a loud voice, 'Lazarus, come out!' The dead man came out, his hands and feet bound with body wrap, and his face wrapped in a cloth. Jesus said, 'Unbind him, and let him go!'"
>
> [John 11: 32 – 44; MFS Translation]

Perhaps Vickey, too, has heard those words from the liberating Christ. Bound by the tentacles of a disease that racked her body and sapped her strength; bound in a body that no longer functioned in this world; perhaps she, too, has heard those words, "Unbind her and let her go!" If so, she can rejoice with the angels that rejoice in the words of that grand old spiritual, "Free at last, Free at last, Great God, Almighty, I am free at last."

But for us, today is a day to pay attention to sorrow. Death intrudes on us all. No respecter of persons, it comes to all, rich and poor, famous and unknown, Christian and non-believer. Though it may be welcomed by one who has lived a full life only to become enfeebled by illness or infirmity, it is never a welcome guest at the table of those of us left behind. It is never fully expected, always coming as a dreadful surprise. We are never completely prepared for it, and it brings sorrow, pain, loss, and loneliness into our lives. It dulls life's brightness and casts a shadow of heartbreak on our souls.

But there is a difference for those who trust in Christ. Although the outward experience is substantially the same, the inward reality is vastly different. In Christ, death assumes another face. It is no longer a frightening enemy, robbing us of all we hold dear, but merely the door into another room in the Father's house. It is no longer the darkness that emptied life of joy and meaning. It is, rather, the gladness of going home.

> The Lord spoke to Isaiah: "Fear not," He said, "For I am with you, be not dismayed, for I am your God. I will strengthen you, I will help you, I will uphold you...Fear not, for I have redeemed you; I have called you by name, you are mine. When you pass through the rivers, they shall not overwhelm you. When you walk through fire you shall not be burned, and the flames shall not consume you. For I am the Lord your God, the Holy One of Israel, your Savior." (Isaiah 41:10; 43:1b-3)

> "What then shall we say to this?" the Apostle Paul writes to the Romans and to us, "If God is for us, who is against us? He who did not spare his own Son, but gave him up for us all, will he not give us all things with him? ...Who shall separate us from the love of Christ? Shall tribulation, or distress, or persecution, or famine . . . or peril . . . No, in all these thing we are more than conquerors through him who loved us. For I am sure that neither death, nor life . . . nor things present, nor things to come . . . nor anything else in all creation, will be able to separate us from the love of God in Christ Jesus our Lord." (Rom. 8:31-32, 35, 37-39)

"Life is eternal and love is immortal, and death is only a horizon - and a horizon is nothing but the limit of our sight." 1 We cannot see what is beyond that horizon, but we know who is there, and the Risen Christ is enough.

Let us Pray: *[I led a closing prayer, and a hymn was played.]*

[Benediction and dismissal to place of burial for a committal service.]

NOTES:
1. Penn, et al., Op. Cit. For more information, see **Appendix A** at the end of this Collection.

OLIVER H. HALL
08-22-2007
MEDITATION

MEDITATION on HOPE and HEALING:
WITNESS TO THE RESURRECTION

The Apostle Paul wrote to the Corinthians: "We know that if this earthly shack we live in is destroyed, we have a house built by God - not made with human hands, but eternal and spiritual. Here, indeed, we groan and can hardly wait to get into our spiritual dwelling so that we will not be found naked. For as long as we remain in this earthly shack, we have many worries and anxieties. It is not that we wish to be without a house, but we want a better dwelling - so that our dying may be swallowed up by life in Christ Jesus. God himself is preparing us for this very thing and has given us the Holy Spirit as a guarantee."

[2 Corinthians 5:1-5; MFS Adaptation].

In the year that Ob and Agnes were married, 1954, Stewart Hamblin had a major hit on the Grand Ole Opry which draws in part on Paul's imagery in that passage from 2nd Corinthians.

It is entitled "This Old House," and the chorus goes:

"THIS OLD HOUSE" *(Also "This Ole House")*
By Stuart (or Stewart) Hamblen (October 20, 1908 – March 8, 1989)

"Ain't goin'need this house no longer;
Ain't goin' need this house no more;

Ain't got time to fix the shingles; Ain't got time to fix the floor;
Ain't got time to oil no hinges;
Nor mend the broken window panes.
Ain't goin' need this house no longer,
I'm gettin' ready to meet the saints."

Tomorrow you will take the house that Ob lived in here on earth to its final resting place, but he's not there anymore - he's gettin' ready to meet the saints.

In the 11th chapter of his Gospel, John recalls what happened when Jesus went to the tomb of his friend Lazarus:

> *"Then Mary, when she came where Jesus was and saw him, fell at His feet, saying to Him, 'Lord, if you had been here, my brother would not have died.' When Jesus saw her and the others who came with her weeping, He was deeply moved in spirit and troubled; and he said, 'Where have you laid him?' They said to Him, 'Lord, come and see.' Jesus wept. So they said, 'See how He loved him!'. . . Then Jesus, deeply moved again, came to the tomb; it was a cave, and a stone lay over it. Jesus said, 'Remove the stone!'. . . So they took away the stone . . . [After he prayed] Jesus cried with a loud voice, 'Lazarus, come out!' The dead man came out, his hands and feet bound with body wrap, and his face wrapped in a cloth. Jesus said, 'Unbind him, and let him go!'"*
>
> [John 11: 32 – 44; MFS Translation]

Ob, trapped in a tree from which there was no escape. Bound by the tentacles of a disease that racked his body and sapped his strength. Bound in a body that no longer served him in this world, Ob, too, has now heard those words from the liberating Christ, "Unbind him and let him go." So those of us around him can say, "See how He loved him." Ob can now rejoice in the words of a grand old spiritual, "Free at last, Free at last, Great God, Almighty, I am free at last."

One of the things Ob learned from traipsing all over the face of Europe during WW II was that he never wanted to travel again. He had seen a lot of the world, and a bloody part it was. He was thereafter satisfied to stay at home. However, today he takes the one last journey that we must all take. And in the tradition of Christ's Church of which Ob and I are a part, we have a far more appropriate word than deceased, or departed, or passed on to describe this occasion. When a Christian moves his membership from one church to another, we say that person has "transferred" his membership. So it becomes my duty and my honor to announce today that our brother Ob has transferred his membership from the Church temporal and temporary to the Church eternal and triumphant located in that *"city not made with human hands whose architect and builder is God."* [Hebrews 11: 10; MFS Translation].

Let us Pray: *[I led an interim prayer, and a hymn was played.]*

[Benediction and dismissal to place of burial for an internment/ committal service.]

RUBY SELBY
OCTOBER 02, 2009
MEDITATION

MEDITATION/REMARKS on HOPE and HEALING:
WITNESS TO THE RESURRECTION

In the 11th Chapter of John's Gospel, the story of Jesus and Lazarus is told this way:

> *"Then Mary, when she came where Jesus was and saw him, fell at His feet, saying to Him, 'Lord, if you had been here, my brother would not have died.' When Jesus saw her and the others who came with her weeping, He was deeply moved in spirit and troubled; and he said, 'Where have you laid him?' They said to Him, 'Lord, come and see.' Jesus wept. So they said, 'See how He loved him!'. . . Then Jesus, deeply moved again, came to the tomb; it was a cave, and a stone lay over it. Jesus said, 'Remove the stone!'. . . So they took away the stone . . . [After he prayed] Jesus cried with a loud voice, 'Lazarus, come out!' The dead man came out, his hands and feet bound with body wrap, and his face wrapped in a cloth. Jesus said, 'Unbind him, and let him go!'"*
>
> [John 11: 32 – 44; MFS Translation]

Like Lazarus, Ruby too was bound. Bound by a body that had betrayed her and was no longer of any real benefit to her in this world. Bound by tentacles of disease and ill health that stole her spirit and sapped her strength. She, too, now has heard the blessing that Lazarus heard: "Unbind her and let her go." And so we, her friends, may observe of her what Lazarus' friends said of him, "See how [Jesus] loves her."

Death intrudes on us all. No respecter of persons, it comes to all, rich and poor, famous and unknown, Christian and non-believer. Though it may come as a welcomed guest to one who has lived a useful life only to become enfeebled by illness and infirmity, it is never a welcome guest to those of us left behind. It is never fully expected. It always comes as a dreadful surprise. We are never completely prepared for it. It always brings sorrow & pain & loss, and its intrusion into our lives dulls life's brightness and casts a shadow of heartbreak on our souls.

However, while the outward reality is substantially the same, the inner experience is vastly different for those who are in Christ. In Christ, death assumes another face. It is no longer a frightening enemy, robbing us of all we hold dear, but merely the door into another room of the Father's house. It is no longer the darkness that empties life of its joy and meaning. It is rather the gladness of going home.

For many months Ruby has struggled with declining health and the limitations of medical procedures. She fought a long battle, but at the end, she could say with the Apostle Paul (who wrote to Timothy, saying)

> "...I am already on the point of [death]...I have fought the good fight, I have finished the race, I have kept the faith. Henceforth there is laid up for me the crown of righteousness, which the Lord... will award me...and not only to me but also to all who have loved his appearing." (2 Timothy 4:6-8).

When Ruby and Ray were 9 years old, they moved with their family two miles south of Sutton's Ford to a little farm house on top of a hill overlooking the top of the mountain (as she and other old timers call the place where Highway 28 begins its descent into the valley). Until today, it was the last move Ruby ever made.

She loved that old house and the farm on which it sits. When I think of Ruby and the house, I am reminded of Stewart Hamblin's top country song of 1954. Though it is hardly the type of music, we usually hear at funerals, my father once said he wanted it played at his funeral. The chorus goes:

> **"THIS OLD HOUSE"** *(Also "This Ole House")*
> *By Stuart (or Stewart) Hamblen (October 20, 1908 – March 8, 1989)*
>
> *"Ain't goin'need this house no longer;*
> *Ain't goin' need this house no more;*

Ain't got time to fix the shingles;
Ain't got time to fix the floor;
Ain't got time to oil no hinges;
Nor mend the broken window panes.
Ain't goin' need this house no longer,
I'm gettin' ready to meet the saints."

We will soon take the house that Ruby lived in her on earth to its final resting place, but she's not there anymore - she's gettin' ready to meet the saints.

Before I was 30, I had lived in a dozen different places. Ruby moved to her place of residence only once in her life. Today she makes the one last move that we must all make. In the Christian tradition of which Ruby and I are a part, we have a far better word than deceased to describe this event. When a church member moves from one church to another, we say she has transferred her membership. So it becomes my privilege today to announce the transfer of our beloved sister, Ruby, with the full and enthusiastic recommendations of her fellow church members, from the church temporal and temporary to the church triumphant and eternal, located in "that city whose builder and maker is God." [Hebrews 11: 10]

Let us Pray: *[I led a closing prayer, and a hymn was played.]*

   [Benediction and dismissal to place of burial for a committal service.]

C. STAN TOLLETT
07-18-2010
MEDITATION

MEDITATION/REMARKS on HOPE AND HEALING: WITNESS TO THE RESURRECTION

When Jesus returned to his home synagogue in Nazareth after his temptation and was asked to read the scriptures, he turned to a passage from the 61 chapter of Isaiah, where it is written:

"The Spirit of the Lord God is upon me . . .he has sent me to heal the brokenhearted. . ." [Luke 4: 18 KJV] That is not all it says, but that is the part that is relevant to our gathering today. Part of Jesus' purpose is to be the ambassador of God's comfort. He came, in part, to walk with us and help us through just such sadness as is yours today.

I cannot speak with any confidence about Stan's standing with his God. But I do believe that neither we nor Stan can venture beyond God's love and care. God's love transcends this life, transcends this death, transcends the difficulties and mistakes of Stan's life. Events such as that which we confront today are not the will and purpose of God. God's purposes as revealed in the life and teaching of Jesus, are health, healing, and wholeness. He is always at work to ease the burden of a broken heart, to bind up the wounds which the world and this imperfect life inflict upon us.

Stan never traveled far in his life. When he died, he still lived on the same place where he took his first steps. Today he makes the one last journey that we all must take. We can rest assured that neither Stan nor we are alone in that journey.

The Bible and the Christian faith do not run from events such as that we confront today. They do not seek to hide from them or to make them less real or less tragic. How could they? How can we? But the Bible and the Christian faith do promise us that we will not have to face these ordeals alone, that no broken heart is beyond repair and no tragedy beyond redemption. Death takes away our loved ones, but it cannot separate us or them from the love of God.

In the 43 Chapter of Isaiah the Word is written:

> "...Fear not, for I have redeemed you; I have called you by name, you are mine. When you pass through the waters, I will be with you, and when you pass through the floods, they shall not overwhelm you; when you walk through the fire...the flame shall not consume you, for I am the Lord your God, the Holy One of Israel, your Savior."
>
> [Isaiah 41:10; 4:1b-3]

Here there is no promise that we will be spared the terrible day, the day of trouble with its floods and fires of heartbreaking anguish and sorrow and suffering. But what we are promised is strength for the journey and companionship along the way - the companionship of one who has been there, who has stood by a grave and wept, who knows personally the pain of a life cut tragically short.

Death intrudes on us all. We walk again today through the valley of its shadow. Its reality cannot be long avoided or denied. Sooner or later, it stalks out our hiding places and calls upon us at the most inopportune times.

No respecter of persons comes to all: to some it comes as a thief in the night; to others it comes as a long-awaited friend, but it comes to all. We never know when it may come to us or to one we love.

It is never fully expected, and we are never completely prepared for it. It always brings sorrow and pain and loss. Its intrusion into our lives dulls life's brightness and casts a shadow of heartbreak on our souls.

But in Christ Jesus that is not the end of the story. While the outward reality is substantially the same, the inner experience is vastly different for those who trust in Jesus Christ. In Christ, death assumes a different face. It is no longer a frightening enemy robbing us of all we hold dear but merely the door into another room in the Father's house. It is no longer the darkness that empties life of its meaning; it is rather the gladness of going home.

> "What then shall we say to this?" the Apostle Paul wrote to the Romans, "If God is for us, who is against us? He who did not spare his own Son, but gave him up for us all, will he not give us all things with him? . . . Who shall separate us from the love of Christ? Shall tribulation, or distress, or persecution, or famine . . . or peril? . . . No, in all these thing we are more than conquerors through him who loved us. For I am sure that neither death, nor life . . . nor things present, nor things to come . . . nor anything else in all creation, will be able to separate us from the love of God in Christ Jesus our Lord." (Rom. 8:31-32, 35, 37-39)

The grave is no barrier to God, and, thus, should be no barrier to us. In God's time, the tomb is no more final than the womb.

"Life is eternal, love is immortal, and death - death is only a horizon. And a horizon is nothing - nothing but the limit of our sight." 1 We cannot see what is beyond that horizon, but we know who is there, and the Resurrected Christ is sufficient to comfort and reassure those who trust in Him.

Let us Pray.   *[I led a closing prayer and a hymn was played.]*

[Benediction and dismissal to place of burial for a committal service.]

NOTES:

Penn, et al., Op. Cit. For more information, see **Appendix A** at the end of this Collection.

JOHN SEVERSON REMARKS/ MEDITATION JUNE 6, 2008

I was asked to help with this service although I barely knew the deceased. I was not asked to do an Obituary/Eulogy, but to participate. Consequently, I did very little in the way of an Obituary and no real Eulogy. Instead, I delivered a Meditation on Hope and Healing.

OPENING

"Blessed be the God and Father of our Lord Jesus Christ! By God's great mercy, we have been born anew to a living hope through the Resurrection of Jesus Christ from the dead."

> *"Praise be to God for we do not grieve as those who have no hope!" Jesus said, "I am the resurrection and the life. Those who believe in me, though they die, yet shall they live."*
> *"Come to me all who are burdened and heavy laden, and I will give you rest."*
> *"Blessed are those who mourn; they shall be comforted."*
> *"Our help is in the name of the Lord who made heaven and earth!"*

We are gathered to pay attention to sorrow, take account of change, and give thanks to God for the life of John Severson.

OBITUARY

[I read the details of the obituary with survivor's list as given to me by the funeral director. I no longer have those details and cannot reproduce them here]

MEDITATION ON HOPE AND HEALING:
WITNESS TO THE RESURRECTION

John loved the outdoors and liked the mountains. Shortly before he died, he was able to take a last trip to the Smokies, an experience by which he was comforted. So the next time you see the mountains rising in the distance or look out upon our local mountains - Bear Den, Hinch, Brady, and Happy Top - let your thoughts of John be happy and your hearts be consoled by these words from the Psalmist.

> *I lift up my eyes to the mountains.*
> *From whence does my help come?*
> *My help comes from the LORD,*
> *who made heaven and earth.*
> *He will not let your foot be moved,*
> *he who keeps you will not slumber.*
> *Behold, he who keeps Israel*
> *will neither slumber nor sleep.*
> *The LORD is your keeper;*
> *the LORD is your shade*
> *on your right hand.*
> *The sun shall not smite you by day,*
> *nor the moon by night.*
> *The LORD will keep you from all evil;*
> *He will keep your life.*
> *The LORD will keep*
> *your going out and your coming in*
> *from this time forth and for evermore.* [Psalms 121]

Events happen to us in this life that cannot be explained or understood. Random and arbitrary events that baffle our minds and disillusion our spirits. Tragedies which make suffering and death and grief everyday companions.

Hurricanes, tornadoes, earthquakes, a stillborn baby, a young husband and father apparently in good health suddenly get sick and die. I do not have an answer to the question, "Why?"

These events are part of the residual chaos and disorder of the universe which yet remains to be brought under the order of God. Tragedies from which there are no exceptions for nice people. We all fall prey to the capriciousness of life in this not yet perfect world and not yet perfect age.

The Bible and the Christian faith do not run from these tragedies. They do not seek to hide from them or to make them less real or less tragic. How could they? How can we? But the Bible and the Christian faith do promise us that we will not have to face these ordeals alone, that no broken heart is beyond repair and no tragedy beyond redemption. Death takes away our loved ones, but it cannot separate us or them from the love of God.

In the 43 Chapter of Isaiah the Word is written:

> ...Fear not, for I have redeemed you; I have called you by name, you are mine. When you pass through the waters, I will be with you, and when you pass through the floods, they shall not overwhelm you; when you walk through the fire...the flame shall not consume you, for I am the Lord your God, the Holy One of Israel, your Savior."
>
> [Isaiah 43: 1b-3a]

Here there is no promise that we will be spared the terrible day, the day of trouble with its floods and fires of heartbreaking anguish and sorrow and suffering. But what we are promised is strength for the journey and companionship along the way - the companionship of one who has been there, who has stood by a grave and wept, who knows the pain of a life cut tragically short.

When Jesus says: "Come to me, all of you who are heavily burdened and I will refresh you," [Matthew 11:28] he speaks as one who knows the weight of a broken heart.

When Jesus returned to his home synagogue in Nazareth after his temptation and was asked to read the scriptures, he turned to a passage from the 61 chapter of Isaiah, where it is written:

"The Spirit of the Lord God is upon me...he has sent me to heal the brokenhearted..." [Luke 4: 18 KJV]. That is not all it says, but that is the part that is relevant to our gathering today. Part of Jesus' purpose is to be the ambassador of God's comfort. He came, in part, to walk with us and help us through just such sadness as is yours today.

I barely knew John Severson. I cannot speak about his standing with his God. But I do know that neither we nor John can venture beyond God's love and care. God's love transcends this life, transcends this death, transcends this tragedy. Tragedies such as that which we confront today are not the will and purpose of God. God's purposes as revealed in the life and teaching of Jesus are health, healing, and wholeness. He is always at work to ease the burden of a broken heart, to bind up the wounds which the world and this imperfect life inflict upon us.

Trust in God helps us to keep sorrow in its proper place. There is a time to be sorrowful. Sorrow is a part of every person's life, and unless kept in its proper place, it can overwhelm us so that we can feel nothing but the bitter pain and awful loss. We are sorrowful because we have experienced loss and feel alone.

But at a deeper level, we cry because we loved and because we are loved. We would know no grief today had we not loved and been loved by John Severson. And however imperfect his love, to the degree that you were loved by him, you know a little of what it is to be loved by God. And to the degree that you loved him, you know a little of what it means to love God.

God can show you much there is that you have to be grateful for even in the midst of loneliness and loss. So beneath the grief of this hour, there may be an abiding gratitude: Gratitude to God for the one you remember today and gratitude for the Resurrection hope we have through Jesus Christ. God can enable you to place your grief in its proper relationship to the rest of life.

Death intrudes on us all. None of us are immune from it. Sooner or later, it tracks down our footsteps and discovers our hiding places. To some, it comes as a long-awaited friend. To others, it comes as a thief in the night. And even though we may know it is coming, we are never fully prepared for it. To those left behind, it always comes as a dreadful surprise and brings with it sorrow, pain, loss, and suffering. Its intrusion into our lives dulls life's brightness and casts a shadow of heartbreak on our souls.

Yet, while the outward reality may appear to be substantially the same for everyone, the inward experience is vastly different for those that are in Christ. In Christ, death assumes a different face. It is no longer a frightening enemy, robbing us of all we hold dear, but merely the door into another room of the Father's house. It is no longer a darkness that empties life of its meaning but rather the gladness of going home.

The grave is no barrier to God, and, thus, should be no barrier to us. In God's time, the tomb is no more final than the womb.

"Life is eternal, love is immortal, and death - death is only a horizon. And a horizon is nothing - nothing but the limit of our sight."1 We cannot know what is beyond that horizon, but we know who is there, and the Resurrected Christ is sufficient to comfort and reassure those who trust in Him.

Let us pray.   *[I led an interim prayer and a hymn was played.]*

[The Rev Pete Ullmann gave a further Meditation and closed the service.]

NOTES:

1.   Penn et al., Op. Cit. For more information, see **Appendix A** at the end of this Collection.

NORA VALLANCE MEMORIAL SERVICE REMARKS SEPTEMBER 3, 2007

Psalm 46: 1-3; 7

> *God is our refuge and strength,*
> *A very present, proven help in trouble.*
> *Therefore, we will not fear*
> *Though the earth should change,*
> *Though the mountains shake*
> *Though its waters roar and foam*
> *In the heart of the sea;*
> *Though the mountains tremble*
> *With its tumult. . .*
> *The Lord of hosts is with us,*
> *The God of Jacob is our refuge.*

How blest you are to grieve today. To live and love is to grieve. Your grief is but the flip side of love. You grieve today because you had the great, rare privilege of loving and being loved by Nora Vallance.

Bill has graciously granted me the privilege of introducing a few comments of my own to this memorial service. I want to share with you three bits of wisdom from my past which I find appropriate for today.

Jim has always found some inspiration in my relationship to my father, who like me, was first and foremost a country preacher. In 1936 my parents lost their first-born son at the age of 10 months. In 1957, they came close to losing their first-born child, my sister, Pat. On Friday, Sept. 13, 1957, (10 days short of 50 years ago), Pat almost died. On Sunday, Sept 15, 1957, in the midst of this crisis, with Pat's life still in danger, my father preached a sermon to the Big Lick congregation entitled, "Reflections in a Day of Trouble."

Part of what he said was, ". . . soon or late a day of trouble, a day of personal and family distress and sorrow comes to all of us. 'Suffering is the common lot of all and all the human devices are unable to make us completely immune from it. Sooner or later, it tracks down our footsteps and discovers our hiding places' . . .

"The Bible and the Christian faith does not run away from the terrible reality of these days of trouble. How could it? How can we? One of the remarkable things about the Bible is its account of how [people] have found their faith raised to the highest level at precisely that point where one expects them to lose it...

"[The promise of God in the day of trouble] finds beautiful expression in [these] words from the prophet Isaiah:

"'Fear not, for I am with you, be not dismayed, for I am your God. I will strengthen you, I will help you, I will uphold you...Fear not, for I have redeemed you; I have called you by name, you are mine. When you pass through the waters, I will be with you, and through the rivers, they shall not overwhelm you. When you walk through fire you shall not be burned, and the flames shall not consume you. For I am the Lord your God, the Holy One of Israel, your Savior.' (Isaiah 41:10; 43:1b-3)

"In these words is no promise that those who trust God will escape the storms and fires of life, no promise of freedom from a day of trouble, no suggestion that the circumstances will be made less terrible. But there is the assurance of God's presence and concern, and therein lies the difference...

Nothing is lost when we make an offering of it.' We can never lose a loved one whom we have committed to God's care... What we really need is the assurance that despite all the perils which surround us, and despite the mystery of death which stands at the end of the road, we belong to a fellowship within which we can find abundant life...this assurance [is] expressed in these word of an [ancient] prayer:

'In those moments when we seem to have reached the end of our own strength, teach us to commit our lives and all that we hold dear to Thy keeping, in the knowledge that Thy wisdom is more certain than all human plans, and Thy mercy is deeper than all human reckoning.'" [1]

Secondly, a story and a poem slightly altered. One of the great, great women in my past was a woman named Anora Kerley, except that the people I grew up among never called her Anora. They thought her name was Nora, but these Scotch-Irish descendants didn't call her that either. They called her "Norie,"- the younger folks called her "Aunt Norie." With that pronunciation as background, and today's memories in the forefront, this slightly altered piece of Robert Burns' poetry:

Highland Mary by the beloved Scottish poet Robert Burns. Slightly altered for this occasion.

[Ms. Vallance was a native of Scotland and her husband a stout Scottish-American.]
[Both revered Burns' poetry.]

> Ye banks, and braes, and streams around
>   The castle o' Montgomery,
> Green be your woods and fair your flowers,
>   Your waters never drumlie!
> There simmer first unfauld her robes,
>   And there the langest tarry;
> For there I took the last fareweel,
>   O' my sweet Highland [Norie]. [2]

Finally, a formulation of my own, inspired in part by a sermon of Bill Coffin's preached at Yale University's Battell Chapel on Easter Sunday, 1966. Nora would have liked Bill Coffin's preaching. Not only was he a skilled and powerful preacher in the Reformed tradition, he agreed with her on many theological, social, and political issues. I have often used this formulation at victory celebrations like the one we observe today.

The final word today is this, "life is eternal, love is immortal, and death is only a horizon, and a horizon is nothing - nothing but the limit of our sight." [3] We cannot know what is beyond that horizon, but we know who is there, and the Resurrected Christ is enough to comfort and reassure those who trust in Him.

[1]"Let not your hearts be troubled; Believe in God, believe also in me. [2]In my Father's house are many rooms; if it were not so, would I have told you that I go to prepare a place for you? [3]And when I go prepare a place for you, I will come again and take you to myself, so that where I am, you may be also."

John 14: 1-3

Let Us Pray: *[I led an interim prayer.]*

[Another minister did the primary part of the service.]

NOTES:
1. I own the rights to the Eugene Smathers material printed here.
2. In the service, I read the whole poem (as altered). I believe the whole poem to be considered in the Public Domain under a ***Creative Common License*** per documentation from the National Library of Scotland, 02/01/2016. However, to be safe, I have printed only the first eight lines of the poem
3. Penn, et al., Op. Cit. For more information, see **Appendix A** at the end of this Collection.

BETTY DEIMLING REMEMBRANCE REMARKS MAY 5, 2009

I was asked to "say a few words" at this funeral. The primary part of the service was conducted by a Roman Catholic priest.

> *"Blessed be the God and Father of our Lord Jesus Christ!"*
> *"By God's great mercy we have been born anew to a living hope through the Resurrection of Jesus Christ from the dead."*
> *"Praise be to God, for we do not grieve as those who have no hope!"*
> *Jesus said, "I am the resurrection and the life. Those who believe in me, though they die, yet shall they live"*
> *"Come to me all who are burdened and heavy laden, and I will give you rest."*
> *"Blessed are those who mourn; they shall be comforted."*
> *"Our help is in the name of the Lord who made heaven and earth!"*

On behalf of Colleen and the rest of the family, I want to thank all those at the nursing home (both staff and residents), and those at Hospice and the hospital who cared so lovingly for Betty during her last months, weeks, and days.

Someone has written (I know not who.):

> *"People come into our lives*
> *And walk with us a mile.*
> *And then because of circumstance*
> *They only stay awhile.*
> *. . .*

God only knows the reason that
We meet and share a smile,
Why people come into our lives
And walk with us a mile."

I know why Betty came into my life and walked with me a mile. I know how we met and why we shared a smile.

It was because our children got married and then bore a child that is our grandson.

I am told that Betty could be obstreperous at times, but with me, she was always gracious, kind, and generous.

She was a caring and loving grandmother - who often took care of her grandson during the first years of his life and was by his testimony, "Way, Way better than a babysitter."

Betty overcame many hardships and struggled with many demons during her life. I don't mean mythical demons, but the real kind that accompany, are brought on by or result from the overuse of certain chemicals. Those hardships and struggles are behind her now. She is at peace. Betty suffered great loneliness after the love of her life, Terry, died a few years ago. She suffers such no more.

Betty slipped quietly and peacefully beyond death's door secure in the knowledge that she was loved in this world and would be loved in the next. She left this world wrapped in your arms and enters the next wrapped in the everlasting arms of God.

Grief is but the flip side of love. We are sad today because we loved and were loved by Betty Deimling. I know that Betty sometimes had unusual ways of showing it, but she loved you, and however imperfect her love, to the degree that you remember that, you know a little bit of the best that it is possible to experience in this life.

Perhaps if she could tell you what she is thinking today, it might be this, in the words of Isla Pascal Richardson:

"To Those I Love"
By Isla Pascal Richardson

"If I should ever leave you whom I love
To go along the Silent Way,
Grieve not,

. . .

Please do not let the thoughts of me be sad,
For I am loving you just as I always have.

. . .

We cannot see Beyond,
But this I know:
I loved you so – t'was heaven here with you." [1]

Death intrudes on us all. It is no respecter of persons. It imposes on great and small alike. Its intrusion into our lives dulls life's brightness and casts a shadow of heartbreak on our souls.

Yet, while the outward reality may appear to be substantially the same for everyone, the inward experience is vastly different for those that are in Christ. In Christ, death assumes a different face. It is no longer a frightening enemy, robbing us of all we hold dear, but merely the door into another room of the Father's house. It is no longer a darkness that empties life of its meaning but rather the gladness of going home.

The grave is no barrier to God and, thus, should be no barrier to us. In God's time, the tomb is no more final than the womb.

"Life is eternal, love is immortal, and death - death is only a horizon. And a horizon is nothing - nothing but the limit of our sight."[2] We cannot know what is beyond that horizon, but we know who is there, and the Resurrected Christ is sufficient to comfort and reassure those who trust in Him.

Let us Pray.   *[I led an interim prayer and the service was completed by the Roman Catholic Priest.]*

NOTES:
1. In the service I read the whole poem, but am restricted to eight lines in print.
2. Penn, et al., Op. Cit. For more, see **Appendix A** at the end of this Collection.

APPENDIX A
QUOTATIONS AND POEMS

"LIFE IS ETERNAL"

By Penn, Raymond, Simon, and Coffin

I have used only one line from this text: *"Life is eternal, love is immortal, and death is only a horizon, and a horizon is nothing but the limit of our sight."*

However, the whole prayer/poem/song is in the Public Domain by virtue of first being published prior to 1923. The first record of this line is in a prayer by William Penn, 1644-1718. This is verified by two sources: The NSW Council of Churches "Selected Christian Prayers PR006L" and also by Father Bede Jarrett, O.P. in his book of prayers where he credits this prayer as "a prayer written by William Penn, 1644-1718." Penn's prayer is as follows:

> *"We seem to give them back to Thee, O God, who gavest them to us. Yet, as thou didst not lose them in giving, so do we not lose them by their return. Not as the world giveth, givest Thou, O Lover of Souls. What Thou givest, Thou takest not away. For what is Thine is ours also if we are Thine. <u>And life is eternal and love is immortal, and death is only an horizon, and an horizon is nothing save the limit of our sight.</u> Lift us up, strong Son of God, that we may see further; cleanse our eyes that we may know ourselves to be nearer to our loved ones who art with Thee. And while Thou dost prepare a place for us, prepare us also for that happy place, that where Thou art we may be also for evermore."* (Emphasis Added)

The second time it was published, without attribution, was also prior to 1923. That was in a poem by Rossiter W. Raymond, 1840-1918. Since Raymond's date-of-death is prior to 1923, the work, if published in his lifetime, had to be published prior to 1923. He took almost all of Penn's prayer for his poem which goes:

> *"We give them back to Thee, dear Lord, who gavest them to us;*
> *Yet as Thou dost not lose them in giving,*
> *So we have not lost them by their return.*
> *Not as the world giveth, givest Thou, O Lover of Souls. What*
> *Thou gavest, Thou takest not away,*
> *For what is Thine is ours always if we are Thine.*
> *<u>And Life is eternal and Love is immortal,</u>*
> *<u>And death is only an horizon,</u>*
> *<u>And an horizon is nothing save the limit of our sight."</u>*
>
> (Emphasis added)

To confuse things more, Carly Simon's song, "Life is Eternal," appeared in her 1990 album, "Have You Seen Me Lately," where she uses the phrase and gives no attribution, claiming the lyrics as her own.

I initially got the phrase from William Slone Coffin, Jr. who used it at Battell Chapel of Yale University on Easter Sunday, 1966. Whether he had the right to or not, he gave me permission to use it. For over forty years, I thought he was the originator of the phrase.

"TO THOSE I LOVE"
By Isla Pascal Richardson

"If I should ever leave you whom I love
To go along the Silent Way,
Grieve not,

. . .

Please do not let the thoughts of me be sad,
For I am loving you just as I always have.

. . .

We cannot see Beyond,
But this I know:
I loved you so — t'was heaven here with you."

[Because of Copyright laws, I have printed here and used herein only as much of this poem as I am permitted to print (eight lines). The full poem is readily

available at many sources including the internet. While this excerpt captures the essence of the poem, I encourage you to look up the entire poem.]

"THIS OLD HOUSE" *(Also "This Ole House")*
By Stuart (or Stewart) Hamblen (October 20, 1908 – March 8, 1989)

. . .
"Ain't goin' need this house no longer;
Ain't goin' need this house no more;
Ain't got time to fix the shingles;
Ain't got time to fix the floor;
Ain't got time to oil no hinges;
Nor mend the broken window panes.
Ain't goin' need this house no longer,
I'm gettin' ready to meet the saints."
. . .

[Because of Copyright laws, I have printed here, and used herein only as much of this song as I am permitted to print. This is the chorus only (eight lines of text). The full song is readily available at many sources including the internet. I encourage you to look up the entire song. It has an interesting history. It was not inspired by a Biblical passage as I sometimes incorrectly asserted in my funeral Remarks, but by a much grizzlier incident, though one still appropriate for a funeral. (Hamblen's father was a minister and he was converted at the very first Billy Graham Crusade in 1949 in Los Angeles, California. So he, too, may have seen a connection between his song and 2 Corinthians 5: 1-5.) As the story is told, Hamblen and John Wayne were hunting during the winter in the back country of the High Sierra mountains when they came upon an old falling-down shack at least twenty miles from the nearest road (according to them). They found a dead body inside. That's why this song is sometimes called "the prospectors epitaph.F I use only the chorus and sometimes one verse of a three-verse song. The other verses are not really suitable for a funeral. This song was 1954 Country Music "Song of the Year.F Rosemary Clooney's pop version hit the top of the charts in both the US and UK in 1954. It topped the charts in the UK a second time in 1981.]

The House by the Side of the Road
By Sam Walter Foss (Born June 19, 1858; died February 26, 1911)

"I see from my house by the side of the road,
By the side of the highway of life:
The men who press with the ardor of hope;

The men who are faint with the strife.
But I turn not away from their smiles nor their tears,
Both part of an infinite plan –
Let me live in a house by the side of the road
And be a friend to man."

. . .

[By Copyright rules I am permitted to reproduce here and use only this eight-line verse of the poem. It is the third of five verses and captures the essence of the whole poem. The Poem was inspired by the following line from the Greek Poet Homer: "He was a friend of man, and he lived in a house by the side of the Road.F The poem was first Copyrighted by Sam Walter Foss in Dreams in Homespun, Lothrop Lee & Shepard, 1897, but was re-Copyrighted by Foss' daughter in 1925. I encourage finding and reading the whole poem.]

SIMPLE GIFTS
A Shaker Hymn
By Elder Joseph Brackett, Jr.

"Tis the gift to be simple, tis the gift to be free
Tis the gift to come down where we ought to be
And when we find ourselves in the place just right
It will be in the valley of love and delight.

When true simplicity is gained
To bow and to bend, we will not be ashamed
To turn and to turn will be our delight
Til by turning, turning we come round right."

[This Shaker dance tune was written by Elder Joseph Brackett, Jr. (death July 4, 1882), and first published in a Shaker Hymnal in 1848. This is documented by David Fisher, Liberty and Freedom: A Visual History of America, Oxford University Press, pp 269-273. The melody was largely unknown outside Shaker circles until used by Aaron Copeland in his 1944 composition "Appalachian Spring.F]

LESS FREQUENTLY USED POEMS AND QUOTATIONS

Excerpt from "Gone"
By John Greenleaf Whittier

1. "There seems a shadow on the day,
Her smile no longer cheers;
A dimness on the stars of night,
Like eyes that look through tears . . .

. . .
3. "Fold her, O Father! In thine arms
And let her henceforth be
A messenger of love between
Our human hearts and Thee."

[No more than this eight-line excerpt of the above listed poem, "Gone,F is used anywhere in this material.)

Excerpt from "The Eternal Goodness"
By John Greenleaf Whittier

1st Verse
"I know not what the future hath
Of marvel or surprise;
Assured alone that life and death
God's mercy underlies . . .
. . .
5th Verse
"I know not where His islands lift
Their fronded palms in air;
I only know I (we) cannot drift
Beyond His love and care."

[No more than this eight-line excerpt of the above listed poem, "The Eternal Goodness,F is used anywhere in this material.)

Excerpt from "Lucy"
By William Wordsworth

[Verse II.2]
"A violet by a mossy stone

Half hidden from the eye!
Fair as a star, when only one
Is shining in the sky.

[Verse II.3]
She lived unknown, and few could know
When Lucy ceased to be;
But she is in her grave, and oh,
The difference to me!"

[No more than this eight-line excerpt of the above listed poem, "Lucy,F is used anywhere in this material.)

A Quote from Homer

"I know not what the future holds,
But I know who holds the future."

[No more than this couplet from Homer's longer work, is used anywhere in this material.)

A Quote from Heraclitus

"No man can step into the same river twice, for he is not the same man, and it is not the same river."

[No more than this single line from Heraclitus' work is used anywhere herein.]

"There is no Death"
- By John Oxenham (November 12, 1852 – January 23, 1941)

"There is no death
To those whose hearts are set
On higher things than this life doth afford;
How shall their passing leave one least regret,
Who go to join their Lord?"

Poem: "Seeds"
- By John Oxenham (November 12, 1852 – January 23, 1941)

[3]*"Yea, we may hope! For we are seeds,*

Dropped into earth for heavenly blossoming.
Perchance, when comes the time of harvesting,
We know not what we shall be--only this-
That we shall be made like Him--as He is."

[I have printed only one verse of each of these poems, to comply with Copyright laws. Although I believe them to be in the Public Domain by virtue of being controlled by a Public Domain Library License or a Creative Common Attribution-ShareAlike License, I am unsure, therefore, the one verse only.

"Now the Laborer's Task is O'r"
By: John Ellerton (December 16, 1826 – June 15, 1893)

Now the laborer's task is o'er;
Now the battle day is past;
Now upon the farther shore
Lands the voyager at last.
Father, in Thy gracious keeping
Leave we now Thy servant sleeping.

This hymn is believed to be in the Public Domain by virtue of being controlled by the Choral Public Domain Library License of Wikipedia and the Free Software Foundation, Boston. It was written in 1870- 75 by John Ellerton, and first published in 1892 in The Hymnal: revised and enlarged as adopted by the General Convention of the Protestant Episcopal Church in the United States of America in the year of our Lord 1892. It is still used today. To be safe, I have used only the first verse in the text of the book.

The Little Boy Blue"
By Eugene Fields

The little toy dog is covered with dust,
But sturdy and stanch he stands;
. . .
Awaiting the touch of a little hand,
. . .
And they wonder, as waiting the long years through
. . .
What has become of our Little Boy Blue,
Since he kissed them and put them there?

[Only these six lines of this poem are printed here and in the text of the book. I do not encourage finding and reading the whole poem. What is here is sufficient.]

APPENDIX B
SCRIPTURE READINGS

I have used the following Scriptures (mixed and matched, and sometimes paraphrased) for the Openings, Closings, and part of the internal texts of Obituaries/Eulogies and Meditations.

Psalm 23

Psalm 27: 1

Psalm 90: 1 or1-2

Psalm 90: 13-17

Psalm 103: 8-13

Psalm 103: 15-18

Psalm 121

Psalm 124: 8

Psalm 130: 1-6

Psalm 139: 7-12

Ecclesiastes 3: 1-11

Isaiah 40: 28-31

Isaiah 41: 10

Isaiah 43: 1b or 1b-3

The Wisdom of Ben Sirach
38:24-32 (Apocrypha)

Matthew 5: 4

Matthew 11: 28

John 3: 17

John 11: 25-26

John 11: 33-36

John 14: 1-3

Romans 6: 3-4

Romans 8: 28

Romans 8: 31-35; 37-39

Romans 14: 7-9

I Corinthians 15: 20-26

I Corinthians 15: 53-57

II Corinthians 4: 7-10

II Corinthians 5: 1 or 1-5

Ephesians 3: 20-21

I Thessalonians 4: 13

II Timothy 4: 7-8

I Peter 1: 3

I Peter 2; 9-10

I Peter 2: 24-25

Revelations 21: 1-4

Below is the Scriptural opening I used more frequently than any other.

> *"Blessed be the God and Father of our Lord Jesus Christ! By God's great mercy we have been born anew to a living hope through the Resurrection of Jesus Christ from the dead."*
> *"Praise be to God, for we do not grieve as those who have no hope!"*
> Jesus said, *"I am the resurrection and the life. Those who believe in me, though they die, yet shall they live"*
> *"Come to me all who are burdened and heavy laden, and I will give you rest."*
> Blessed are those who mourn; they shall be comforted."
> *"Our help is in the name of the Lord who made heaven and earth!"*

APPENDIX C
FRAGMENTS FROM FUNERAL REMARKS BY EUGENE SMATHERS 1932-1968

FUNERAL ADDRESS FOR Mrs. AMY BURGESS
- June 6, 1886 - April 19, 1958
By Eugene Smathers - April 21, 1958

On the evening of April 19, Amy Burgess quietly and peacefully passed through the portal of death to find release from the burden of a mortal body which had been wracked with discomfort and pain for many months.

OBITUARY:

Amy Siever, the daughter of Jacob and Mary Costner Siever, was born in West Virginia, coming to Tennessee with her parents when she was a year old. She was one of nine children. Her early years were spent in the Winesap community, here in Cumberland County. On April 7, 1907, she was married to Vance Burgess, and on that day they came to live in Big Lick, occupying the house which has been her home ever since. From this union six children were born, all of whom survive their mother's passing. Mr. Burgess died on March 9, 1937, so for 21 years Mrs. Burgess has been a widow. Had she lived until June she would have been 72 years of age.

At the age of twelve Amy made a profession of faith and became a member of the Baptist Church, and on September 1, 1929, she became a member of Calvary Presbyterian Church of Big Lick, and through all the years since has been one of its most devout and faithful members. She was a charter member of the Big Lick Ladies Aid Society.

She is survived by the following: *[He read a long list of survivors.]*

Amy Burgess was truly a saint in the Lord - this does not mean that she was perfect, for like all human creatures she had her weaknesses and faults, but she was one who put her trust in Jesus Christ, and was a living witness to the righteousness of God which comes through faith. When the time of her departure had come, she had fought the good fight, had finished the race, had kept the faith, and was ready to meet her Lord and receive from His hands the crown of righteousness which he awards to all who love and faithfully serve Him.

One of the finest tributes we can pay her is to say that she was a Christian wife and mother, one who sought to build her family's whole life upon the solid foundation of the Christian faith. And these words from Scripture are a fitting description of her life as a wife and mother:

[Read Proverbs 31: 10-31.]

Her works do praise her, more than any words can do, for her best and living tribute is her family - the children she nurtured in Christian faith and sent out into life to serve God and their fellowmen. And to you, her children and grandchildren, whose hearts today are sad and lonely because of her departure, I would say: Your highest tribute to her memory, your best expression of gratitude for all which she has meant to you, is not the flowers or the monument in the cemetery, but your own lives, by and through which you seek to carry forward in your own way and in your generation, the work of the Lord who meant so much to her, building the life of your families upon the rock of Christian faith.

Amy Burgess was a Christian neighbor. She opened her hand to the poor and reached out her hands to the needy, and words of kindness were on her tongue. And as she stands before the judgment bar of God, we may be certain that these words of Jesus will apply:

[Read Matthew 25: 31-40]

Mrs. Burgess was a devout and faithful member of the Church, never missing a service except for illness. She was a woman of prayer, carrying her family and her neighbors to the throne of grace. She was willing to bear reproach in her witness to Jesus Christ. The pew which she always occupied is now vacant, but really it is vacant only to physical sight, for her spirit of faith and love and faithfulness will ever hover near, an unseen but deeply experienced inspiration to others who seek to follow her example in living for Christ. She has not left the church, but journeyed, at the call of God, to assume a larger ministry with the multitude who worship and serve the Lord in heaven and on earth.

> *"There is no death*
> *To those whose hearts are set*
> *On higher things than this life doth afford;*
> *How shall their passing leave one least regret,*
> *Who go to join their Lord?"* [1]
> - John Oxenham (November 12, 1852 – January 23, 1941)

This is the season of the year which always meant much to Mrs. Burgess, and she had no peace and allowed none around her to have peace until the garden was planted and farm work was on its way. When the sap began to rise in the trees and the buds and blooms burst forth, she felt the call of growing things and became their companion and friend and fellow-worker. One of the burdens of her illness was here lessened ability to plant and hoe and tend growing things. This spring she knew she could not plant the seeds in her earthly garden, as she was so wont to do. God knowing this, sent the angel of death on an April evening, and called her to labor in the gardens of heaven; and there, I am sure, in a way beyond our present understanding, she will find joy in planting and hoeing and harvesting.

Or to put it another way, she who so loved to plant tiny seeds, which dying rose to newness of life as fruit and flower, has herself become a seed, planted as a frail, pain-ridden body to rise in newness of life. Just as life in nature bursts forth at the calling of the warm spring sun, so beneath the creative sunshine of God's love our beloved will burst forth in a new life, freed from the frailties and hindrances and vexations of life here on earth.

MESSAGE: Poem: "Seeds"
By John Oxenham (November 12, 1852 – January 23, 1941)

3.
Yea, we may hope! For we are seeds,
Dropped into earth for heavenly blossoming.
Perchance, when comes the time of harvesting,

We know not what we shall be--only this-
That we shall be made like Him--as He is." [1]

Beloved, our grief today is not for her, whom we have lost awhile, who has gone through the door, beyond which we cannot see, to abide in the other room of our Father's house. Our grief is for ourselves whose present lives are left empty and lonely. But we need not grieve as those who have no hope, and we may be sure that God's comfort and strength can be ours to sustain and bring peace even in the midst of tears.

This morning it was raining, the clouds hung low and dark, as though even the weather reflected the sadness of the day. Then the clouds began to break, and the sun came through, giving the earth a radiance of light and hope. This too may be symbolic for you whose burden of loss is heavy. The sunshine of God's love and care will break through the clouds of your sorrow and loneliness, enabling you to rejoice and be grateful, as you come to know that your beloved has not been taken away from you, that committed into God's loving care she is forever yours.

Poem: *"He Will Give Them Back"* [Poem currently unavailable.]

Closing Prayer:

Almighty God, our Heavenly Father: We thank Thee for the love that cares for us in life and watches over us in death. May we in faith and hope give back to Thee the life which in love was given us? . . . We believe that in death as in life (she is) in His holy keeping. In our sorrow make us strong to commit ourselves and those we love to Thy never- failing care. In our perplexity, may we trust where we cannot understand, knowing that the eternal God is our Refuge and underneath are the everlasting arms. In our loneliness, make our remembrance grateful, and may we never forget that the God whom fatherhood and motherhood interpret will keep that which we have committed unto Him until the eternal morning breaks; through Jesus Christ our Lord. Amen.

NOTES:
1. I have printed only one verse of each of these poems, to comply with Copyright laws. Although I believe them to be in the Public Domain by virtue of being controlled by a *Public Domain Library License* or a *Creative Common Attribution-ShareAlike License*, I am unsure, therefore, the one verse only.

T. VIRGIL HALE FUNERAL MESSAGE AUGUST 9, 1962

By Eugene Smathers

The sorrow and loss which we experience today should be mingled with the gratitude and joy of victory, for we gather here to pay our tribute of affection and respect to one of God's good men. A man who lived a quiet, simple life close to the soil; a plain, humble man, never accounted "great" or "important" as the world measures these things, but great in those qualities of character which truly endure; never the possessor of a multitude of goods but a man who had a good life, and who was faithful to the place and work to which God had called him.

OBITUARY - T. Virgil Hale 1884-1962

T. Virgil Hale, son of Thomas L. Hale and Sarah Hall Hale, was born May 28, 1884, in the Sequatchie Valley, Cumberland County, and departed this life, after long months of illness on August 7, 1962, having passed by several weeks his 78th birthday.

In 1917, he was united in marriage with Fanny Rector. In 1919, they moved to their present home place, which they have made into one of the better farms of the community, and where they had a good life together.

He is survived by: *[He read a list of survivors.]*

Mrs. Hale would express her abiding appreciation for the kindness and faithfulness of friends during the days of her husband's illness and for the many tokens of affection and respect in evidence here today.

Virgil Hale was a good farmer, a pioneer in many good farm practices which have led to the development of farming on the Plateau. He was one of the first to practice crop rotation; to use lime and phosphate; he was one of the first test demonstration farmers working with the TVA in the use of high analysis fertilizer. He developed one of the finest orchards in the county, managed it correctly and produced quality products which he sold to satisfied customers and on which he won many a first prize at the county fair. Many families were the beneficiaries of the fresh and tasty fruit and vegetables which he tended with such care. He was truly a good and faithful stewards of that portion of the earth which God had entrusted to his keeping.

Something of his feeling, as age and declining health made it impossible for him to continue the tasks which meant so much to him, is expressed in the following poem:

> "Lord, when Thou seest that my work is done,
> Let me not linger on,
> With failing powers,
> Adown the weary hours,
> A workless worker in a world of work.[1]
> - John Oxenham (November 12, 1852 – January 23, 1941)

MESSAGE

Mr. Hale was a good neighbor. To this I can bear personal testimony as one who lived just over the hill from him for over 28 years. He was a kindly man, lover and friend of children. Not blessed with children of his own, nieces and nephews and the children of his neighbors were always given a cordial welcome. One of these he made a member of his family and (this nephew) became to him as a son, and whose children in turn brought great joy to him in the latter years and were to him as grandchildren. To be given the love of little children, which was his in abundant measure, is a mark of inherent goodness and kindness.

He was an informed and responsible citizen. He liked to read and keep abreast of affairs in the county, state, nation, and world, and his opinions and judgments were reliable and true. It has been said that the Christian who would know God's will for our time must read the Bible and the newspaper. This Mr. Hale did.

Also, he was a good churchman, a quality which has meant much to me as his pastor and to the whole life of the church in this place. He accepted

Christ as his Savior and Lord in his early years and became a minister of the Methodist Church. He became a charter member of this church when it was organized in 1921. In 1925 he was elected deacon, and served in this position until he was elected an Elder in 1933. He often represented his church at the meetings of Presbytery. He was faithful in attendance at Sunday school and church as long as health permitted. Since the beginning of Calvary Church Homestead Project, he has served as a Trustee. A man of few words, he did not speak up often, but once he had made up his mind about the truth and rightness of a matter, he had the courage to stand by his convictions, even though unpopular.

A devoted husband, lover of children, helpful neighbor, conscientious citizen, good farmer, and faithful church member - all these and more Virgil Hale was - and those he could not have been without being one of God's good men.

The psalmist asks: *"O Lord, who shall sojourn in thy tent? Who shall dwell on thy holy hill?" And the answer comes: "He who walks blamelessly, and does what is right, and speaks truth from his heat; who does not slander with his tongue, and does no evil to his friend, nor takes up a reproach against his neighbor; Who honors those who fear the Lord; who swears to his own hurt and does not change; . . . who does not take a bribe against the innocent. He who does these things shall never be moved."* (Psalm 15)

It would be difficult to find more fitting words to describe Mr. Hale.

Hidden away among a list of rather meaningless names in the 5th chapter of Genesis we find this meaningful and beautiful sentence: "Enoch walked with God, and he was not, for God took him." (Vs.24) These words written about another of God's good men in a faraway time, apply to him who we remember and respect today.

In remembrance, we ask: "What sort of man was he?" This is what people most want to know. Of Enoch and of our loved one, we may reply, "he walked with God. . ." H was that kind of man.

Once Emerson, now an old man with failing mental powers, stood by the grave of his friend, the poet, Longfellow, and said, "The gentleman who lies here was a beautiful soul, but I do not remember his name." It does not matter what name or title men may give to our dead, if only they may with sincerity speak like that of them. This, I believe, we can do of Mr. Hale.

Again, we ask, "Will there be those who will miss him?" The words used of Enoch, "and he was not . . . "are often used to suggest something strange and unusual about his passing. But what they really mean, put in the simplest form possible is, "the utter sense of loss now that he is gone."

In a lovely poem, William Wordsworth tells of Lucy, a girl "who dwelt among the untrodden ways . . . a violet by a mossy stone, half hidden from the eye."

> "She lived unknown, and few could know
>   When Lucy ceased to be;
>   But she is in her grave, and, oh,
>   The difference to me." [1]

"And, oh, the difference to me!" Here is the real sadness of this experience, not for him who has passed beyond the pain and suffering, the cares and burdens of life here, but for us who remain, when the voice of him whom we loved is no longer heard among us. Always there is an emptiness which cannot be filled by another. Only God can bring the comfort we need - and we have the assurance that He is with us to strengthen and help and to bid us lift or tear-stained eyes to the unseen world which is our eternal home, and in which there is no sadness of parting.

In times like this we also ask, "Is his death the end of him?" Like Job, we cry, "If a man dies, does he live again?" Men's lives are a pointer. The direction is all important. It is tragic when men say of a departed, as they said of Methuselah, "he lived and he died."

But the story of Enoch does not end this way. He was God's good man; he walked with God. Words of despair will not do. Men were sure that he was still with God. Little children sometimes have the most discerning insights into life's puzzling mysteries. A small child once explained these words about Enoch in this way: "Enoch and God used to take long walks together. And one day, they walked further than usual, and God said, 'Enoch, you must be tired. Come into My House and rest.'"

Because of the kind of man Enoch was, his friends believed in a life beyond death. They knew that the direction of his life led not to a grave, but to God, and with God Death has no final power. Many generations after Enoch, it was said of Jesus, "God raised him up, having loosed the pangs of death, because it was not possible for him to be held by it." (Acts 2: 24) Death could not hold Him, for by His Cross and Resurrection, he had brought to believing men the gift of eternal life. Those who are His are bound in a relationship which the grave cannot break. They know His voice. He calleth His own sheep by name. And they go in and out and find pasture. L They walk with Him, here and hereafter. Though their departure brings heart-ache and loneliness, we are sure that in the care and keeping of the Good Shepherd, they are eternally secure.

> *"I know not where His islands lift*
> *Their fronded palms in air;*
> *I only know I cannot drift*
> *Beyond His love and care."* [1]
> - John Greenleaf Whittier (December 17,1802 – September 7, 1892)

In the language of the Church, there is a word much more fitting than "deceased" for such an hour as this. When a Christian moves his membership from one church to another, we use the good word "transferred."

In 1921 Virgil Hale "transferred" his membership to the church here, and now in 1962, it becomes my responsibility and privilege to announce the "transfer" of our beloved brother, with the highest recommendations of his pastor and fellow Elders, from the Church here in Big Lick to the church triumphant and eternal, located in that city "which hath foundations whose builder and maker is God." (Hebrews 11: 10)

Poem: "Seeds"
By John Oxenham

3.
Yea, we may hope!
For we are seeds,
Dropped into earth for heavenly blossoming.
Perchance, when comes the time of harvesting,
We know not what we shall be--only this-
That we shall be made like Him--as He is." [1]

Closing Prayer:

> Almighty God, our Heavenly Father: We thank Thee for the love that cares for us in life and watches over us in death. May we in faith and hope give back to Thee the life which in love was given us? . . . We believe that in death as in life (she is) in His holy keeping. In our sorrow make us strong to commit ourselves and those we love to Thy never-failing care. In our perplexity, may we trust where we

cannot understand, knowing that the eternal God is our Refuge and underneath are the everlasting arms. In our loneliness, make our remembrance grateful, and may we never forget that the God whom fatherhood and motherhood interpret will keep that which we have committed unto Him until the eternal morning breaks; through Jesus Christ our Lord. *Amen*

NOTES:
1. To comply with Copyright laws, I have included only one verse of each of these poems. Although I believe some of them to be in the Public Domain, and suspect that the others may be, I cannot prove it. I have used eight or fewer lines of text from each poem. I encourage the reader to find and read each of the poems in its entirety.

I. L. BURGESS OBITUARY MAY 20, 1959

By Eugene Smathers

Isaac Linville Burgess, better known as I. L. or Ike Burgess, the son of John and Katherine Norris Burgess, was born in the Burgesstown Community, Cumberland County, on May 14th, 1878, and departed this life on May 18th, 1959, having reached the ripe age of 81 years and 4 days.

On January 4, 1902, he was married to Ollie Mae Campbell, and they shared life together, with its ups and downs, for 57 years. To this union, 13 children were born, 3 of whom proceeded their father in death. He is survived by: his wife, Mrs. Ollie Burgess of Big Lick; by 7 daughters:

> Mrs. Bessie Orme, Burke,
> Mrs. Myrtle Nail, Crossville,
> Mrs. Cora Kerley, Crossville,
> Mrs. Amanda Swafford, Big Lick,
> Mrs. Lorene Walker, Elyria, Ohio,
> Mrs. Nellie Houston, Elyria, Ohio,
> Mrs. Fannie Waldron, Elyria, Ohio;

By 3 sons:
> Tommy and Frank Burgess, Big Lick,
> Bill (or Willie) Burgess, Dayton, Ohio;

By:
> 43 grandchildren and 17 great grandchildren, and Numerous relatives and friends.

Mr. And Mrs. Burgess moved from Burgesstown to Big Lick about 53 years ago. In his long residence in this community, Mr. Burgess played a significant part in its development, buying and selling land, helping his children own their own homes, and in various other ways. For many years he served as a member of the County Board of Education, and was in office when the present new school building was planned. He was a charter member of Calvary Church, having united by profession of faith on the day of its organization, October 23, 1921, and was elected one of the first deacons and served some years.

The life and labors and character of Ike Burgess are known to most of you. Now that his book of life on this earth has been written and the pages of 81 years closed, nothing we can say or do today can alter the course of life that has now passed beyond our seeing. But with confidence and good hope we may commit his life beyond into the keeping of a just and merciful Heavenly Father, who "So loved the world that he gave His only begotten Won that whomsoever believeth in Him should not perish but have everlasting life.

Poem: **Now the Laborer's Task is O'r**
By: John Ellerton (December 16, 1826 – June 15, 1893)

Now the laborer's task is o'er;
Now the battle day is past;
Now upon the farther shore
Lands the voyager at last.
Father, in Thy gracious keeping
Leave we now Thy servant sleeping.

NOTES:
1. This hymn is believed to be in the Public Domain by virtue of being controlled by the ***Choral Public Domain Library License.*** It was written in 1870-75 by John Ellerton, and first published in 1892 in The Hymnal: revised and enlarged as adopted by the General Convention of the Protestant Episcopal Church in the United States of America in the year of our Lord 1892. Nevertheless, I have used only the first verse (six lines) here.

OLLIE M. BURGESS OBITUARY EASTER SUNDAY - MARCH 26, 1967

Ollie Mae Burgess, the daughter of Jim F. Campbell and Mary Jane Hall Campbell, was born in the Burgesstown community, Cumberland County, Tennessee, September 4, 1887. She departed this life, following long months of illness, at her home here in Big Lick on Good Friday, March 24, 1967, at the ripe age of nearly four-score years.

She was united in marriage with Isaac Burgess on January 4, 1905, and a few years thereafter, she and her husband moved to Big Lick, where she has made her home since. Mr. Burgess proceeded her in death in 1959, but she remained in the family home with her sons, Tommy and Frank living with her.

She became a member of Calvary Presbyterian Church, on reaffirmation of faith in September, 1929.

She was a devoted mother, grandmother, and great-grandmother - always interested in and concerned for her children and their families. She was a compassionate and helpful neighbor, always ready to assist in any way possible in times of sickness or need. She helped to deliver numerous babies.

She faced hardships and difficulties with determination and courage and as a rural wife and mother, he had her share. She will be missed by all who knew her for she was a unique and loveable person, and the community which was her home for so many years loses one who contributed much to a way of life that is rapidly disappearing. There will never be another Ollie Burgess or "Aunt Ollie" as so many affectionately called her.

She is survived by ten children: [who are named]; by two sisters [who are named]; by 45 grandchildren and 30 great-grandchildren; by other relatives and a host of friends.

One of Mrs. Burgess' greatest joys and satisfactions came from her garden. She loved life and all growing things, and her love gave her a special skill. She was looking forward to Spring, already planning her garden, and just a few days ago was sorting her seeds. But this was not God's plan for her. Instead of the seeds she was looking forward to planting, she herself became a seed, planted on Good Friday, to find, we believe and hope, a new and resurrected life in the springtime of God's Garden. It there are gardens and growing things in the realm beyond our vision, she will be given a task and once again find renewed joy and satisfaction in tending the garden there.

> Poem: **"Seeds"**
> By John Oxenham (November 12, 1852 – January 23, 1941)
>
> 3.
> Yea, we may hope!
> For we are seeds,
> Dropped into earth for heavenly blossoming.
> Perchance, when comes the time of harvesting,
> We know not what we shall be--only this--
> That we shall be made like Him--as He is." [1]

[The full funeral message itself was adapted from one of Eugene Smathers' post-Easter sermons delivered on April 5, 1964, and entitled "A Legacy of Hope from the Upper Room." It is five times as long as this Obituary, and too long to be repeated here.]

NOTES:
1. To comply with Copyright laws, I have included only one verse (no more than eight lines) of this poem. Although I believe it to be in the Public Domain, I cannot prove it. I encourage the reader to find and read the entire poem.

BARBARA JO WRIGHT OBITUARY, OPENING, CORE REMARKS, AND CLOSING PRAYER DECEMBER 28, 1957

(The child died on Christmas day, 1957) By Eugene Smathers

Obituary (very brief):

Barbara Jo Wright, daughter of Homer and Imogene Kerley Wright was born in Crossville, Tennessee, June 30, 1947 and died at her home in Grafton, Ohio, December 25, 1957, at the age of 10 years and 6 months.

She is survived by: *[A short list of survivors was read.]*

Opening Remarks:

As I read of Barbara Jo's early Christmas and saw her picture with a doll beside her on the bed and her other toys in the background, the words of an old poem by Eugene Field, came to mind, and while it refers to a little boy and the toys which he left, I believe they are fitting here.

> *Read:* **"Little Boy Blue."** *[Six-line portion used here]*
> *By Eugene Fields*
>
> *The little toy dog is covered with dust,*
> *   But sturdy and stanch he stands;*
> *. . .*
> *Awaiting the touch of a little hand,*

. . .
And they wonder, as waiting the long years through

. . .
What has become of our Little Boy Blue,
    Since he kissed them and put them there? [1]

"And they wonder . . .
What has become of our Little Boy Blue? . . ."

We do not need to wonder about Barbara. On Christmas morning, she heard the angels sing, and responding to their call, journeyed through the door of death into the realms of glory. She did not go to Bethlehem, rather she when into the brighter room of our Father's house, there to meet Jesus Christ, who Himself was once the Child of Bethlehem and Nazareth, and who is the eternal friend of little children . . .

She has gone to live forever with the Lord . . . Nothing within our power can alter this fact, but what happens to you to whom she was most dear and who will miss her so, depends upon your own attitude toward this fact. You can, if you will, make her your Christmas gift to God. A costly gift to be sure, a gift that brings suffering and sorrow, a gift that only faith and love can give. . . The only way that you can keep Barbara is to give her to God, for nothing is lost when we make an offering of it. Not even death can rob you if you give your beloved child freely and trustfully into God's care. By giving her away, she can be eternally yours. . .

Just a word about this terrible thing which happened to this lovely child. In this terrible and tragic thing, we come face to face with the mystery of evil, with its consequent suffering. In the face of such evil, we must never attribute it to God. This thing was not "the will of God," for the same Jesus who loved little children and revealed God to us said, "It is not the will of my Father who is in Heaven that one of these little ones should perish." (Matthew 18:14) . . . Our chief question should not be "Why?" even though we cannot escape asking it, for we can never find the full and complete answer here; rather our main question should be "How?" How can we find strength and comfort to become victorious over sorrow and loss? How can we allow God to use our suffering as "an angle unawares" to bring us nearer to Him and closer to being what He intends us to be?

David had an experience like yours. During the child's illness, he fasted and hardly slept, just as you have hardly left Barbara for a moment during her illness. But when David's child died, David washed himself and ate. His astounded servants asked him the meaning of his actions, saying, *"You fasted and wept for the child while it was alive, but when the child died, you arose and ate food."* David replied: *"While the child was still alive, I fasted and wept, for I said, 'Who knows whether the Lord will [allow] the child to live?' But now that the child is dead, why should I fast? Can I bring the child back again? I shall go to him, but he will not return to me."* (2 Samuel 12: 15-23)

You did all you could for Barbara. She had the faithful ministry of loving hands and the best that medical skill could provide. Momentarily the battle is lost, and Barbara cannot be brought back to us. But with truth deeper than he knew, David provides the key to ultimate victory, you can go to her. God who sent His Son to lead the way, to be for all who trust Him as the resurrection and the life. Christ is the open door through which your beloved child beckons you.

Read the Poem: **"The Open Door"**
- By Alfred Noyes (September 16, 1880 – June 25, 1958)[2]

Closing Prayer:
> Almighty God, our Heavenly Father: We thank Thee for the love that cares for us in life and watches over us in death. May we in faith and hope give back to Thee the life which in love was given us. We bless Thy name for our Savior's joy in little children and for the assurance that of such is the kingdom of heaven. We believe that in death as in life (she is) in His holy keeping. In our sorrow make us strong to commit ourselves and those we love to Thy never-failing care. In our perplexity, may we trust where we cannot understand, knowing that the eternal God is our Refuge and underneath are the everlasting arms. In our loneliness, make our remembrance grateful, and may we never forget that the God whom fatherhood and motherhood interpret will keep that which we have committed unto Him until the eternal morning breaks; through Jesus Christ our Lord. *Amen*

NOTES:
1. Eugene Smathers used the whole poem, but Copyright law prevents more than eight lines of it from being printed here. it This poem was written by Eugene Fields around 1888. It was first published in 1888 in the literary journal America. It was republished in Eugene Fields, The Little Book of Western Verse by Charles Scribner's Sons

in 1889. It was subsequently Copyrighted by C. Louis Utermeyer, ed., Modern American Poetry, Harcourt, Brace & Howe, 1919. It was then re-printed and re-copyrighted by Bartlebey.com in 1919.

2. No part of the poem is reproduced hear because of Copyright constraints. No small portion of the poem can convey the poems full meaning, and I believe it best to be left out entirely. It appears to be still under Copyright protection.

www.ingramcontent.com/pod-product-compliance
Lightning Source LLC
Chambersburg PA
CBHW020916140626
46545CB00015B/58